*The Heresy of the Free Spirit
in the Later Middle Ages*

Woodcut from *Translation oder tütschungen des hochgeachten Nicolai von Wyle* (Strassburg bei Brise, 1510) illustrating Felix Hemmerlin's *Contra validos mendicantes* (*Das Bůch von den vermügenden bettelern*). The scene depicts Hemmerlin emerging from his dwelling to debate with a beghard who travels with a donkey. In the background someone is bringing bread for the beghard.

THE HERESY

of the FREE SPIRIT

in the Later Middle Ages

ROBERT E. LERNER

University of California Press
Berkeley Los Angeles London

1972

UNIVERSITY OF CALIFORNIA PRESS
Berkeley and Los Angeles, California

UNIVERSITY OF CALIFORNIA PRESS, LTD.
London, England

Copyright © 1972, by
The Regents of the University of California
ISBN: 0-520-01908-3
Library of Congress Catalog Card Number: 78-145790
Printed in the United States of America

DESIGNED BY IKUKO WORKMAN

The woodcut from Hemmerlin's *Contra validos mendicantes* is reproduced in the frontispiece, courtesy of the Newberry Library, Chicago.

For my Mother and Father

ACKNOWLEDGMENTS

The thirteenth-century Dominican moralist, Thomas of Cantimpré, tells of a certain theological master who for a long time was unable to complete his book until he was miraculously rewarded for his perserverance in the faith: all of a sudden he was spirited away to a lonely place where he was able to work in peace, while St. Paul often appeared and attended to his needs. Such has not been quite my luck, but the closest thing to divine intervention has been the intercession of grants from the Germanistic Society of America and the Fulbright-Hays program of the United States' government, which have enabled me to work without interruption on the following book in Europe for the academic years 1962–63 and 1967–68 respectively. Veritable St. Pauls attending to my needs have been subsidiary grants from Princeton and Northwestern Universities.

Of course no research scholar would really want to work in a deserted grotto instead of a good library. The collections that I have relied most heavily are those of the *Bayerische Staatsbibliothek* and the *Monumenta Germaniae historica*, both in Munich. I am particularly grateful to Fräulein Dr. H. E. Lietzmann of the latter, who tolerated numerous interruptions of her own work to help a foreigner in the use of a library that was long buried in the inaccessible caverns of an old *Führerbau*. I would also like to express my thanks for the help of Miss Marjorie Carpenter of Interlibrary Loan at Northwestern and to all the curators of the manuscript collections listed at the back of this book, many of whom provided me with photocopies and answered my queries through the mail.

My search for unpublished manuscripts was aided by generous

tips from Mr. Peter Biller of Oriel College, Oxford, and Dr. Alexander Patschovsky of the *Monumenta*. Professor Dr. Peter Berghaus of the University of Münster helped make this book possible first by cudgelling me into reading German while I was still a graduate student and then by alleviating my initial bewilderment abroad by numerous introductions and kindnesses. The publications of the late Professor Dr. Herbert Grundmann cleared my way with hypotheses and methodological guidelines; that Professor Grundmann personally encouraged my work was for me what being in the company of the seraphim was for my heretics and it was with the profoundest sense of loss that I learned of his death as I was finishing my manuscript. My greatest *Ehrfurcht* is reserved for Professor Joseph R. Strayer who made me into a medievalist and helped this book along in its genesis far more than most would guess (Professor Strayer's reputation has been established in political and institutional history, but his students know him for the polymath that he is). None of these men judged the following in its final stage and none are responsible for the mistakes I must have made. Nor is Professor Howard Kaminsky of the University of Washington who read what I thought was the final draft but by his penetrating comments and suggestions for improvement turned it into the penultimate one. The last statement should by no means be taken to imply that Professor Kaminsky agrees with what I have written about the heresy of the Free Spirit; I doubt that he does and imagine that he might express himself on the subject accordingly. My wife Erdmut has gone over every word of every one of my drafts and has provided me with an aid that would baffle the imagination of a Thomas of Cantimpré.

CONTENTS

ABBREVIATIONS

Abh. bay.   *Abhandlungen der historischen Classe der*
                königlichen Bayerischen Akademie der Wis-
                senschaften
Abh. Berlin   *Abhandlungen der königlichen Akademie*
                der Wissenschaften zu Berlin, Philosophisch-
                historische Classe
AFH   *Archivum Franciscanum historicum*
AfK   *Archiv für Kulturgeschichte*
AFP   *Archivum Fratrum Praedicatorum*
AHDL   *Archives d'histoire doctrinale et littéraire du*
                moyen âge
ALKG   *Archiv für Literatur- und Kirchengeschichte*
                des Mittelalters
Axters   *Geschiedenis van de vroomheid in de Ned-*
                erlanden (Antwerp, 1950–56)
BN   Bibliothèque nationale
CdS   *Chroniken der deutschen Städte*
Cgm   Codex germanicus monacensis
Clm   Codex latinus monacensis
DA   *Deutsches Archiv für Erforschung des*
                Mittelalters
Döllinger   J. J. I. von Döllinger, *Beiträge zur Sekten-*
                geschichte des Mittelalters, vol. II (Munich,
                1890)
Erbstösser   Martin Erbstösser and Ernst Werner, *Ideo-*
                logische Probleme des mittelalterlichen

	Plebejertums. Die freigeistige Häresie und ihre sozialen Wurzeln (Berlin, 1960)
Fredericq	P. Fredericq, *Corpus documentorum inquisitionis haereticae pravitatis Neerlandicae* (Ghent, 1889–1906)
Grundmann, "Ketzerverhöre,"	H. Grundmann, "Ketzerverhöre des Spätmittelalters als quellenkritisches Problem," *DA*, XXI (1965), 519–75
Grundmann RB	H. Grundmann, *Religiöse Bewegungen im Mittelalter* (2nd ed.; Hildesheim, 1961)
Guarnieri	R. Guarnieri, "Il movimento del Libero Spirito," *Archivio Italiano per la storia della pietà*, IV (1965), 351–708
Haupt, "Beiträge,"	H. Haupt, "Beiträge zur Geschichte der Sekte vom freien Geiste und des Beghardentums," *ZfK*, VII (1885), 504–76.
Haupt, "Waldenserthum,"	H. Haupt, "Waldenserthum und Inquisition im südöstlichen Deutschland bis zur Mitte des 14. Jahrhunderts," *Deutsche Zeitschrift für Geschichtswissenschaft*, I (1889), 285–330, III (1890), 337–411
HZ	*Historische Zeitschrift*
Kurze	D. Kurze, "Die festländischen Lollarden," *AfK*, XLVII (1965), 48–76
Lea	H. C. Lea, *A History of the Inquisition in the Middle Ages* (New York, 1888)
Leff	G. Leff, *Heresy in the Later Middle Ages* (Manchester, 1967)
McDonnell	E. W. McDonnell, *The Beguines and Beghards in Medieval Culture* (New Brunswick, 1954)
MGH Constit.	*Monumenta Germaniae historica, Constitutiones*
MGH Epis. Saec. XIII	*Monumenta Germaniae historica, Epistolae saeculi XIII*
MGH SS	*Monumenta Germaniae historica, Scriptores*
Mosheim	J. L. Mosheim, *De Beghardis et Beguinabus*

	commentarius, ed. G. H. Martini (Leipzig, 1790)
PL	J. P. Migne, ed., *Patrologiae latinae cursus completus* (Paris, 1844–64)
RHF	*Recueil des historiens des Gaules et de la France* (Paris, 1738–1876)
RTAM	*Recherches de théologie ancienne et médievale*
Sb. Berlin	*Sitzungsberichte der königlich-preussischen Akademie der Wissenschaften zu Berlin*
Sb. Vienna	*Sitzungsberichte der kaiserlichen Akademie der Wissenschaften*, Philosophisch-historische Klasse
SRG	*Scriptores rerum Germanicarum in usum scholarum*
UB	Urkundenbuch
Wattenbach	W. Wattenbach, "Über die Secte der Brüder vom freien Geiste," Sb. Berlin (1887), 517–44
Wolfenb., Hlmst.	Manuscripts of the Herzog-August-Bibliothek, Wolfenbüttel; Codices Guelf, Helmstedt
ZfK	*Zeitschrift für Kirchengeschichte*

INTRODUCTION

On the last day of May, 1310, a woman named Marguerite Porete was burned at the Place de Grève in what Henry Charles Lea has called "the first formal auto de fé of which we have cognizance at Paris." According to a semi-official chronicler, she wrote a book which taught that "a soul annihilated in the love of the Creator could, and should, grant to nature all that it desires." This sentence implies two heresies: pantheism (or more properly autotheism, a term which will hereafter be used), and antinomianism; that is, not only can a soul become one with God, but in consequence of such a state it can ignore the moral law. This is commonly understood as the essence of the "Free-Spirit" heresy, and since we knew little more about Marguerite's beliefs until very recently, Lea, who loved to issue verdicts, appeared justified in calling her "the first apostle in France of the German sect of Brethren of the Free Spirit."[1]

In the next year, Meister Eckhart, a German Dominican, came to Paris and stayed at St. Jacques. Another inmate of that convent was Berengar of Landora, one of the theologians who had found heresy in Marguerite Porete's book. Perhaps Eckhart learned about her ideas from Berengar or another source, though this is a matter only for conjecture. What we know for certain is that at the end of his life he himself was charged with heresy. Though he defended his case with passion the Pope ended the matter with a bull listing twenty-eight articles taken from Eckhart's works as heretical or suspect. These included the statements that: "I am converted into Him, not as a similar

1. Lea, II, 122–23. The chronicler is the continuator of Nangis, RHF, XX, 601.

being but so that He makes me one with Himself. . . ." and "if a man is rightly disposed he should not regret having committed a thousand mortal sins." Listed so briefly these teachings are more explicitly autotheistic and antinomian than those of Marguerite Porete, yet David Knowles expresses a majority opinion when he says that Eckhart's "radical traditionalism and orthodoxy" is no longer in doubt.[2]

The discrepancy seems strange and appears even stranger when two more facts are introduced. We now know that Marguerite's book survived in numerous monastic copies and translations and that at least one person in the fifteenth century thought that it was written by the great mystic Ruysbroeck. Before it was properly identified as the work of a condemned heretic it was even published in modern English under the auspices of the Downside Benedictines with the nihil obstat and imprimatur.[3] Thus many in the Middle Ages and modern times would have given the book a legitimate place within the tradition of Christian spirituality.

On the other hand, without disputing Eckhart's far more important place within that tradition, it must be pointed out that many in the Middle Ages regarded him as he father of the Free-Spirit heresy. Listen to Jan van Leeuwen, himself a mystic, whose works must have been approved by his spiritual director, Ruysbroeck: "Before Eckhart's time no one knew of these awful free spirits nor of their false teachings which all originate in the stupid doctrine he used to preach that we are God's sons like Christ without distinction."[4] That this was not mere vituperative bombast is reflected in the fact that many who were persecuted by the Church did indeed regard themselves as disciples of Meister Eckart.

These problems concerning the heretic who seemed orthodox and the great theologian who inspired heresy can only be resolved by a careful study of the movement with which they were both associated. The heresy of the Free Spirit is usually understood to have justified

2. "Denifle and Ehrle," *History*, LIV (1969), 4. The articles are 10 and 15 from John XXII's bull, *In agro Dominico*, ed. H. Denifle, "Acten zum Processe Meister Eckeharts," ALKG, II (1886), 638.

3. *The Mirror of Simple Souls*, tr. C. Kirchberger (London and New York, 1927).

4. *Van den tien gheboden*, ed. C. G. N. de Vooys, "Meister Eckart en de nederlandse mystiek," *Nederlandsch archief voor kerkgeschiedenis*, n.s. III (1905), 192.

nihilism and megalomania. Norman Cohn's influential book claims that "these people could be regarded as remote precursors of Bakunin and of Nietzsche—or rather of that bohemian intelligentsia which during the last half-century has been living from ideas once expressed by Bakunin and Nietzsche in their wilder moments."[5] On this model journalists and social psychologists have taken up the Free Spirit in their discussions of student rebellions in the late 1960s. These judgments make the mistake of indiscriminately confusing *tunc* with *nunc*. Neither Marguerite Porete nor Eckhart had much in common with Bakunin. This study examines the Free-Spirit movement as it appeared in its own age and concludes that it was far more typical of the late medieval search for God and godliness than has commonly been supposed. Free Spirits believed that they could attain union with God on earth, but they thought that they could only reach this state by means of bodily austerities and spiritual abnegation and that attainment of the state resulted in detachment from daily concerns rather than in radical engagement in them. Thus their heresy was not a medieval anomaly but was closely related to the orthodox mystical movement of the later Middle Ages and grew out of a concern for a life of spiritual perfection.

Since those who portray the movement as one of megalomania and obscene rites do have sources for quotation at their disposal, it is best here to set forth some methodological postulates. The first is that mere repetition of charges by hostile parties—no matter how seemingly independent they may be—does not establish their validity. In Flaubert's *Bouvard and Pécuchet* the historiographical precept that "appealing to rumor and common opinion is no proof" is presented as a truism so obvious as to be fatuous. Since it is conceded that Jews neither murdered Christian children in medieval England nor in Tsarist Russia, neither poisoned wells in the fourteenth century nor contaminated the water supply in the twentieth, this postulate should now be taken for granted. Yet a recent historian still insists that "even the most patent calumnies can hardly retain their force for over a century . . . without some real ground for doing so."[6]

The reason why scandalous charges were launched, often in-

---

5. Norman Cohn, *The Pursuit of the Millennium*, 3rd ed. (New York, 1970), p. 148.
6. Leff, p. 376.

dependently, against medieval heretics is similar to why they were launched so frequently against Jews. The Church considered Jews, sorcerers, and heretics each in their way as minions of the devil whose threat was age-old. This conviction of timelessness is well illustrated by a fourteenth-century chronicle which saw the fall of Sodom and Gomorrah as a punishment for "heresy."[7] Such a view made a non-polemical description of heretics impossible and as soon as a group or an individual stepped, or was thought to have stepped, beyond the orthodox pale, scandalous charges were sure to ensue. Horace Walpole's dictum that "An historian who shall consult the Gazettes of the times will write as fabulous a romance as Gargantua" has special meaning for the Middle Ages, a golden period of exaggeration and fabrication.

This is just common sense which should be accepted by any trained historian; it is a second presupposition that is based on a special insight of medievalists. Because men of the Middle Ages viewed heresy as something unchanging, they often copied out names or whole passages from patristic catalogues rather than basing their descriptions of sects on actual observation. Just as Thomas Jefferson thought that the mastodon must somewhere be alive since it had once existed, so medieval writers postulated the existence of sects like the *"Tertulliani"* which had been dead for a millennium. In the same fashion names of heresies introduced into blanket condemnations were never deleted. Thus Pope Julius II was still fulminating against the "Arnoldists" in 1511, some three and a half centuries after the death of their supposed founder, Arnold of Brescia, who may have left behind him no sect at all.[8] Similar distortions must be taken into account in writing the history of the Free Spirit.

Far more useful than hostile sources are inquisitorial records. Historians appropriate these with alacrity because of their apparently "objective" nature, but, despite their value, the appearance is deceiving. The distorting influence of torture is obvious and even confessions that were not induced by violence were not necessarily freely given because everyone accused of heresy was aware of the threat of

---

7. Jacob Twinger von Königshofen, *Chronik*, CdS, IX, 904.

8. The *"Tertulliani"* are listed in the Anonymous of Passau as cited by A. Patschovsky, *Der Passauer Anonymus. Ein Sammelwerk des 13. Jahrhunderts gegen Ketzer, Juden, Antichrist* (Stuttgart, 1967), p. 68; Julius II is cited by Kurze, 68, n. 81.

the stake. Not only did confession guarantee mercy from capital punishment, but because inquisitors prized conversions most of all, the more elaborate a confession, the more predisposed the judges would be to grant absolution and mild penance. The cooperation of some suspects may not even have been influenced by threats, for the insights gained from the discussions of the Miranda and Escobedo cases of recent memory make it clear that there is such a thing as a confessing personality, that the mere atmosphere of interrogation or a quirk of the psyche induces some men to confess to crimes that they did not commit.

To make matters even more complicated, medieval protocols were nothing like modern trial records. Most were not taken verbatim but reproduced only the points that the scribe or inquisitor thought most important. Furthermore, they were recorded in Latin, even when, as most often, the interrogations were conducted in the vernacular. The results are best known in the case of Joan of Arc: two men behind a curtain "wrote down and repeated everything that incriminated Joan and nothing that excused her," and a scribe later reported that the judges compelled him to alter the words of the French procès-verbal when translating them into Latin.[9]

Of most importance, procedures were of such a nature that they often produced stereotyped testimony. In the Middle Ages the suspect was not given free rein to say what he believed or what he did on the night of August the fourth; rather, he was confronted with a pre-arranged set of questions that the inquisitor in routine cases did not make up himself but got out of a handbook.[10] For each type of presumed heresy there were forms to be followed and no leeway was allowed for eccentrics. Thus, as will be shown, a favorite text for inquisitions in fourteenth-century Germany was the Clementine decree *Ad nostrum*, which listed autotheist and antinomian errors. Inquisitors presented this to a wide variety of victims who ranged from the orthodox to the insane with the result that they all look at first sight from the protocols like cookies out of a mold. With such evidence scholars had no hesitation in putting all these specimens into the jar of the "Free Spirit" and then arguing that there was a wide-

9. E. F. Jacob, *The Fifteenth Century* (Oxford, 1961), p. 251.
10. The standard work on this subject is A. Dondaine, "Le manuel de l'inquisiteur (1230–1330)," AFP, XVII (1947), 85–194.

spread, tightly organized sect of that name. These methodological problems do not rule out the use of inquisitorial records. On the contrary, because individual answers to standardized questions do sometimes differ, discrepancies from the stereotype help to illuminate the beliefs of some victims of the Inquisition. But for these reasons the study of protocols must be scrupulous and closely related to texts written by the presumed heretics themselves.

It may come as a shock to the reader that any Free-Spirit writings have survived. The later Middle Ages was not a time of tolerance and it might be thought that inquisitors would have been efficient enough to consign all the writings of allegedly dangerous heretics to the flames. But in fact it was never simple to determine who was a Free Spirit. The charge was easy enough to bandy about, but one could never be sure that it might not boomerang. The northern mystics were hurt most this way: all of them were adept at accusing their enemies of "Free-Spirit" deviancy, but none immune to suffering from such allegations himself.

Because it was so hard to distinguish between these mystics and Free Spirits, works of the latter survived under the protective mantle of the former. The name of Meister Eckhart on a title page, even when he clearly could not have been the author, preserved the work of mystics less orthodox than he, and we have seen that Marguerite Porete's book passed under the name of Ruysbroeck. Thus sufficient texts have been preserved and show by their mere survival, and even more by their contents, that one must look twice before classifying bona fide Free-Spirit thought as medieval anathema. The twofold nature of the sources accounts for the organization of this book. It looks at the heresy as closely as possible through the medium of hostile sources and inquisitorial records and when these are exhausted it lets the Free Spirits speak for themselves.

Though the heresy has come into vogue as a means for approaching contemporary problems, no one has yet tried to denude the manuscript repositories and published source collections for a full account. An essay published in 1960 by two scholars from the East German University of Leipzig was not an attempt at an ordered synthesis nor a study based on new materials, but aimed "to set forth the ideology of the Free-Spirit heresy as the expression of certain social relationships and to investigate the effect of the sect and its teachings on the class struggle of the thirteenth and fourteenth centuries."[11] As this quotation implies, the authors assumed the Free-Spirit heresy comprised a sect with a social ideology and tried to prove that it was limited to one class. In my opinion neither view is correct and the work has little to offer beyond occasional sociological insights, especially since it does not even try to assemble all the evidence.

The last deficiency is by no means the failing of Romana Guarnieri's "Il movimento del Libero Spirito," an exhaustive work on folio pages published, oddly, as a journal article.[12] Students of the Free Spirit bear an enormous debt to Guarnieri for having identified the original Old French version of Marguerite Porete's *Mirror of Simple Souls*, the text of which comprises half of her "article." The first half is a vast prolegomenon which attempts to place the *Mirror* in context by listing "cases" of the Free-Spirit heresy year by year in the manner of a chronicle. When a career, such as that of Eckhart, stretches over several decades and the author insists on presenting a separate entry even for natal year, one not only has to flip back and forth through folio pages to get ahead with the story, but on doing so finds that no integral story is ever told. Rather, on ending what Guarnieri herself calls the "*peregrinatio*", one has gone through a heap of cases which, when not repetitive, seem contradictory because the author largely abdicates the historian's function of explaining, connecting, and illuminating.[13] In addition, she all too often recapitulates unreliable earlier work that has no just claim to being so embalmed and treasured up. When she presents fresh material, which she seldom does for northern Europe, she usually excels, but otherwise her work is a compendium that must be used with considerable care.

Guarnieri's most original thesis is that the heresy of the Free Spirit proliferated to the south as well as to the north of the Alps, but the former is an area that the following study will avoid. The reasons for this are twofold: practical and theoretical. Were one to analyze all the expressions of extreme mysticism in late medieval Spain, southern France, and Italy, one would issue forth a book so sprawling and dis-

---

11. Erbstösser, p. 13.

12. *Archivio Italiano per la storia della pietà*, IV (1965), 351–708.

13. Guarnieri, 499, forthrightly admits these drawbacks. See also the review of H. Grundmann, DA, XXII (1966), 318–19, which points out that despite her claims to all-inclusiveness Guarnieri omits some of the most important cases.

jointed as to lose most qualities of readability. This would be especially true if the author, as in the present case, has no new materials or insights to present on the southern European cases. But there are also theoretical objections to subsuming Cisalpine areas into a history of northern Free Spirits. Beyond occasional similarities of doctrine, Guarnieri's strongest evidence of a unified movement lies in the Italian career of *The Mirror of Simple Souls* and certain assertions of the Spanish Franciscan Alvarus Pelagius, but so far as can be told *The Mirror* travelled in orthodox monastic circles and Alvarus is an unacceptable witness because he never in his life was in Germany.[14]

A third recent study of the Free Spirit is found in Gordon Leff's *Heresy in the Later Middle Ages*, "an attempt at synthesis" that makes no pretense to completeness or originality of research. This being so it is unfortunate that its hundred pages on the Free Spirit abound with errors and cannot be recommended for the purpose of reference. Reviewers have also shown how Leff's picture is distorted by uncritical reliance on hostile sources and inquisitorial records rather than careful attention to the body of authentic Free-Spirit literature that is now available.[15] In terms of interpretation, I agree with Leff that the heresy was a "state of mind" rather than an organized sect, but disagree that "its incidence was inseparable from the Beguines and Beghards," and, most importantly, take sharp opposition to his thesis that the heresy was a medieval anomaly characterized by "lechery, hypocrisy and megalomania."[16] Leff sees Free Spirits as sui generis whereas I maintain that they cannot possibly be understood unless one places them within the context of the religious movements of their day. In showing that Free Spirits were motivated by pious desires for a truly apostolic life and communion with divinity this study reinterprets old materials and introduces others that have not been examined before.

I must admit that my initial interest was based on some of Leff's assumptions. As a young radical at the University of Chicago I was captivated on its first appearance by Norman Cohn's *Pursuit of the Millennium*. Harboring none of Cohn's conservative reservations I

14. Guarnieri, 416, 435, 450.
15. M. D. Lambert, *History*, LV (1970), 75–79; H. S. Offler, *English Historical Review*, LXXXIV (1969), 572–76; and H. Grundmann, DA, XXIV (1968), 284–86. I have tried to avoid peppering my text with contentious footnotes, but I do point out, where relevant, Leff's more serious factual errors.
16. My quotations are from Leff, pp. 400, 404, 330.

was fascinated with his description of "an elite of amoral supermen" and resolved to delve further into a study which Cohn explained had barely begun. The preliminary result was my Princeton doctoral dissertation entitled "The Heresy of the Free Spirit in the Thirteenth Century." It is customary in scholarly circles to look askance at books that have recapitulated dissertations, but in this respect my conscience is clear: the following study is so far removed both in content and especially in conclusions from my dissertation that it is a source of embarrassment to me that the latter is still available on microfilm. Perhaps this is because I am no longer so young or radical, but I like to think that the real reason lies in a more careful examination of the sources. I had already felt distinctly uneasy when working on the thirteenth century, but when I examined the fourteenth-century evidence (by all accounts the most important) my search for an organized sect comprised of lower-class Bakunins seemed like a continual shearing away at a shaggy dog that turned out to be nothing but shag. Faced with such diminishing returns I had no choice but to abandon my previous assumptions and develop a new interpretation which I now believe fully justified by the sources and which I will defend with the conviction of a convert.

Chapter One

HERESY AND FORNICATION

Anyone who has heard of the medieval heretics of the Free Spirit will expect a book about them to be full of shocking stories, and indeed there are enough to tell. Modern historians who maintain that Free Spirits were lechers and megalomaniacs only repeat what was most often said about them in the later Middle Ages. In this chapter we will begin to develop a critical position on this subject by examining some representative cases.

1. THREE RACY STORIES

The narrative writers were most sensational. Here are three instances. The fourteenth-century Franciscan chronicler John of Winterthur told of three heretical "beghards"—a word often used, as we will see, to denote heretics of the Free Spirit—who were seized in Constance in 1339 and examined before the entire populace of the town on a raised platform in front of the Cathedral.[1] According to John, they confessed to more than thirty errors so vile that they made their audience sick, but he limited himself to repeating four points. One was that there was as much divinity or divine goodness in a louse as in man or any other creature, another that communion bread should be served to pigs. They also supposedly maintained that if a man and a woman had sexual

---

1. Johannes Vitoduranus, *Chronica*, ed. F. Baethgen, MGH SS, new series, III, 148–50.

intercourse on an altar at the same time as the consecration of the host both acts would have the same worth. Finally, though this was not an error so much as an anecdote, when one of the heretics was asked by three women to teach them about the Trinity, he had them take off all of their clothes and lie on their backs. Then, after binding each by the leg to the other, he violated them all sexually "in the most scandalous manner," and, "casting his lecherous eye on their exposed shame," he said "here is the Holy Trinity." Afterwards he had intercourse with each of them separately.

A character in a fourteenth-century German dialogue called *The Book of the Two Men* told of his own encounter with a hermit who had a popular reputation for godliness but who turned out to be a similar sort of pervert.[2] The narrator pledged obedience to this hermit in the hope of following him in a life of piety but was astonished that his teacher first insisted that he should regale himself on the best foods and wines with the explanation that this would purge his spirit of all impediments. After two weeks of such preparation, the hermit brought in two humbly dressed "beguines"—a term for lay women who imitated the life of nuns and who were widely suspected of being heretics of the Free Spirit—and discoursed with them in rarified language about "high and divine things." The beguines repeated his teaching that only those who grant to themselves all that they please without remorse of conscience can become one with God and then departed, only to return in the most worldly and expensive clothing, their bare heads revealing beautiful golden braids. The hermit retired with one of them, leaving his guest alone to be ardently embraced by the other, who said that they should be mutually obedient. But the dismayed narrator fled.

One could cite other similar stories from the fourteenth century, but we may take our last example from the fifteenth when they became rarer. According to the Dominican John Nider, who wrote in 1435, a certain "beghard" who sometimes wore worldly clothes and other times dressed himself in a habit wrote German books in a subtle but very dangerous style.[3] Under the mantle of piety he gained en-

---

2. *Das Zweimannenbuch*, ed. C. Schmidt, *Nicolaus von Basel* (Vienna, 1866), pp. 224–33 (also ed. F. Lauchert, *Rulmann Merswins Buch von den zwei Mannen* [Bonn, 1896]).

3. *Formicarius*, ed. G. Colvener (Douai, 1602), Lib. III, cap. 6, pp. 221–23.

trance into a house of pious women where he spoke of "perfection" and the "steps of contemplation." After he had gained a favorable hearing, he went further and criticized fasts and prayers as acts of imperfection, advising that one must seek only rest of the body and contemplation. He chose special disciples whom he instructed in private and then he completed his work of seduction by telling them that chastity was unnecessary for perfection so that they joined him in complete sexual abandon.

These accounts clearly have much in common. In each of them the featured character is a trickster who seduces submissive women with religious doctrines that are merely pretenses for fornication. In the last two stories the villians speak the rarified language of mysticism, but this makes them no holier; the most appropriate term for them is "Tartuffes." This name reminds us that the religious trickster was a famous literary type whose career can be traced from Faussemblant in the *Romance of the Rose* through Ben Jonson's Alchemist to Elmer Gantry. In the waning Middle Ages when the three stories we have recounted were told as fact, frank inventions about pious hypocrites seem to have proliferated the most; stories of Boccaccio and Chaucer or manuscript marginalia depicting wily foxes dressed up as friars preaching to silly geese are only the most famous examples.

How can we tell whether our three reports about hypocritical lecherous heretics were fact or fiction? Unfortunately there are no incontrovertible criteria, but no modern-day historian would accept the three stories uncritically without worrying about his reputation. All fail the basic test of corroboration. In no case is there a second independent witness to substantiate the accuracy of the report; if we do not believe the narrator we have no court of second resort. Nor are there reasons to be trusting. John of Winterthur was not present at Constance to hear the heretics he described confess their scandalous errors and crimes and he did not even indicate the source of his information. *The Book of the Two Men* was not a history at all but was one of a number of complete fictions written by the banker and mystic of Strassburg Rulman Merswin under the name of an invented character he called "the Friend of God"—the hero of a sort of fourteenth-century *Pilgrim's Progress*.[4] The incident of the fictional narrator's

4. This conclusion reached by the great nineteenth-century scholar Denifle has never been refuted although it has often been ignored. Many studies in

close call with heresy and lust is so patently contrived that the detail of the temptresses with the golden braids could well have been taken out of an Arthurian *roman*. With Nider, finally, we return to a story told at secondhand with little attempt at substantiation. Nider did say that he learned about the lecherous "beghard" from the virgins the latter had deflowered, but he gave neither his name nor locality and neglected to say if he was ever apprehended or punished. This vagueness is particularly suspect in view of the fact that Nider, as we will see, told other stories about heretics with many more circumstantial details. As one might guess, these are much less spicy.

Other narratives that describe antinomian heretics can be called into question along the same lines and no doubt would have been put aside by critical historians long ago if it were not for the fact that their descriptions seem to be confirmed by documents. We may take as our examples the two earliest.

2. THE HERESY IN THE SWABIAN RIES

Historians used to consider the thirteenth-century heresies of Amaury of Bène, Ortlieb of Strassburg, and William Cornelius of Antwerp as early manifestations of the Free-Spirit heresy, but there is now a growing consensus, to be found in the work of Herbert Grundmann, Romana Guarnieri, and Gordon Leff, that these were isolated cases that had no integral relationship to what came later. This view is somewhat arbitrary because the earlier heresies did have doctrinal similarities to that of the Free Spirit; but they also had significant differences and it is impossible to prove any direct connections between these heresies, all of which dated from the first half of the thirteenth century, and the heresy of the Free Spirit (the present author speaks from experience since he once diligently tried to find such connections). On the other hand, scholars usually count a heresy discovered in the later thirteenth century in Swabia as an early case of the Free-Spirit heresy, and with good reason. Not only was it closer in time to later cases, but some copies of the documents that describe it call it the "heresy of the

English continue to refer to Merswin's "Friend of God" as if he were a real person and Guarnieri, 455, tells the story of the devious hermit without recognizing that it is a fiction. An excellent summary of Denifle's findings is the article on Rulman Merswin by P. Strauch in the *Algemeine deutsche Biographie* (Leipzig, 1875–1912), XXI, 459–68.

New Spirit," a variant of the term Free Spirit. In addition, the surviving descriptions resemble many later accounts of the Free-Spirit heresy so much that they may be regarded as typical. It is true that even the heretics of Swabia may not have directly influenced others who came later, but they do seem to have spoken the same language.

Two independent documents describe their beliefs. The first, and probably more reliable, is helpfully headed in an early copy: "this is the determination of Master Albert, formerly Bishop of Regensburg, Order of Preachers, concerning the articles of the heresy found in the Ries, in the diocese of Augsburg."[5] This heading not only tells us that the author of the text was the great scholastic theologian Albertus Magnus and that the heretics came from that part of Swabia known as the Ries, but it also allows us to date Albert's work to between 1262, when he retired as Bishop of Regensburg, and 1280, when he died. This date is supported by the evidence of a south German chronicle which reports that in 1273 a controversy between the Dominicans and Franciscans about a heresy in the Ries near Augsburg was settled.[6] Most likely Albert was drawn into this dispute and wrote his "determination" at that time. If this is true, then he probably wrote at secondhand because he was then stationed at Cologne.

Such an assumption is strengthened by the form of his document which is meant not so much to describe as to classify and refute. Albert introduces ninety-seven tenets, compares most of them to heresies of the ancient world, and then rejects them, usually on the basis of Scripture or works of the Fathers. Here is an example:

> To say that a sin is not a sin is an error of the Pelagians and a
> lie according to truthful doctrine. 1. John, 1, 8: "If we will

5. From a MS of Mainz described by Haupt, "Beiträge," 556–59. A convenient collation of Haupt's readings with the original edition of the *determinatio* published by W. Preger, *Geschichte der deutschen Mystik im Mittelalter* (Leipzig, 1874–93), I, 461–69, is ed. J. de Guibert, *Documenta ecclesiastica christianae perfectionis studium spectantia* (Rome, 1931), pp. 116–25. A. Patschovsky, *Der Passauer Anonymus* (Stuttgart, 1967), p. 39, n. 57, notes two more MSS not known by Preger or Haupt, but neither have the authority of the Mainz MS used by the latter.

6. *Annales colmarienses,* MGH SS, XVII, 195. (The *Monumenta* edition refers to this section of the *Annals* as *Annales basileenses.*) I follow on this point and the entire matter of dating Grundmann RB, pp. 407–408. That the heresy described in Albert's determination actually flourished in the Ries is confirmed by the internal evidence of tenet 88: "Dicere in Recia esse veritatem. . . ."

say that we have no sin, we will be seduced and truth is not in us." (proposition 55)

This is the sort of pigeon-holing that a learned man like Albert could have done in the comfort of his study on the basis of statements sent to him from afar. How the tenets were obtained we do not know. Since there are frequent repetitions and contradictions which Albert did not attempt to expunge, one must infer that they were taken from many persons, some of whom did not necessarily agree with others. There might also have been an admixture of hearsay. Whatever the case, we should not let the prestige of Albertus Magnus blind us to the fact that we have here not an inquisitorial protocol but a scholastic exercise.

A second list of errors, similar in content to those in Albert's determination, is headed in one late fifteenth- or early sixteenth-century copy: "here is the heresy recently found in Mordlingen."[7] There is no place called Mordlingen, but there is a town called Nördlingen right in the heart of the Swabian Ries and that is one reason for assuming that the list—to be called here the Nördlingen list—pertains to the same heresy refuted by Albertus Magnus. Another reason is that several copies of the Nördlingen list refer to the heresy as that of the "New Spirit,"[8] a name which corresponds to the heading of some versions of Albert's work as *Conpilatio de novo spiritu*. Unfortunately we know neither the identity of the author nor the circumstances of composition. It is impossible to tell whether the list was written during the time of the original investigation or perhaps a generation later because the earliest copies date from the fourteenth century, and even if it was contemporaneous, its author, like Albertus, probably wrote it at secondhand because it appears to be a condensation meant for inclusion in inquisitorial handbooks.

7. First described by H. Haupt, "Ein deutscher Traktat über die österreichischen Waldenser des 13. Jahrhunderts," ZfK, XXIII (1902), 188, n. 2. The MS is Vienna 3271, on which see Patschovsky, p. 17.

8. Viz. MS Clm, 14959, ed. Döllinger, 391–93; MS Clm 4386, ed. Wattenbach, 522; MS Strassburg B174 (destroyed in 1870), ed. C. Schmidt, "Actenstücke besonders zur Geschichte der Waldenser," *Zeitschrift für die historische Theologie*, XXII (1852), 248–50. To these I can now add a fifteenth-century copy in MS Vat. Pal. 600, fol. 226r. The variants of the Nördlingen list that do not contain the term "new spirit" are described by Patschovsky, pp. 18–19.

Bearing in mind the uncertainties concerning the reliability of our documents, we can examine them together for their major themes. Both lists agree in attributing to the heretics of the Ries three groups of errors later associated with the heresy of the Free Spirit: the beliefs that they could become one with God, that they could dispense with the ministrations of the Church, and that they could violate without sin the moral law. Foremost was their claim that it is possible for man to become deified: "man is able to become God;" "the soul is able to be deified" (A14, 26, 28, etc.).[9] Some of the heretical tenets were outrightly pantheistic in stating that everything created is God or is full of God (A76; N8), but it is doubtful that the heretics took this abstract metaphysical doctrine too seriously. Rather than believing that everything or even all men were ipso facto God, they believed for practical purposes that men became God *by attaining a certain state*, a state, as they said, in which God works everything in these men (A15, 56).

There is a submerged current of pantheism in Christianity. Henry Adams has pointed out, for example, that Gregory the Great's characterization of God "as one and the same and wholly everywhere" is "likely to be mistaken for frank pantheism by the large majority of religious minds who must try to understand it without a theological course in a Jesuit college."[10] Putting aside such problems of metaphysical terminology, expressed properly the belief that the human soul can in some way become united with God is not heretical but is the basis of orthodox mysticism.[11] Whether this is arrived at by God's grace or by nature, however, is a crucial distinction which the examiners of the Swabian heretics pressed several times with differing results. Those that compiled Albert's list once obtained the bold answer that man becomes God according to his own will (A36) and Albert was able to label this without any difficulty as the heresy of the Pelagians. But another answer maintained cryptically that "the good man is able truly to say that he has and does not have grace" (A2)—a state-

---

9. In the following, A stands for Albert's determination and N for the Nördlingen list in the version of Strassburg B147 as edited by Schmidt.

10. *Mont-St.-Michel and Chartres* (Boston and New York, 1933), p. 283.

11. On deification and unification see, for example, Dom Cuthbert Butler, *Western Mysticism*, 3rd ed. (London, 1967), pp. 108–14. My entire discussion of the heresy in the Ries in terms of comparison with orthodox mysticism is heavily endebted to Grundmann RB, pp. 402–31.

ment that even the great scholastic could not classify. To complicate matters, two tenets from the Nördlingen list indicate that the heretics thought that they had grace (N21, 25). Most likely the heretics gave or were willing to give longer answers that would have made their positions more intelligible, but all we have are short sentences for refutation or inclusion in handbooks which are contradictory or incomprehensible.

Another distinction between orthodox and heretical mysticism is the question of its relationship to the ministry of the Church. So far as can be told from our lists, it was here that the heretics of the Ries became really extreme. For them identification between God and the soul was so immediate and complete that there was no need for any mediation on the part of the clergy or any need to seek counsel from learned men (A16, 17). They saw no reason to worship the saints and rejected prayers, fasting, and confession as useless and unnecessary for the deified (A22, 41, 44). Indeed, some of their most extreme tenets maintained that prayers, fasts, confessions, vigils, and other good works actually stand in the way of the good man (A50, 79; N15).

What then was the proper model of conduct? Both of our reports portray the heretics of the Ries as apologists for lawlessness. Supposedly they said that the deified man could no longer sin: for him sin was not sin and he could commit a mortal sin without sinning (A94, 6, 55). Since he was possessed by the Holy Spirit he could exceed the traditional bounds of charity and arrive at a state beyond good and evil (A33, 12). Both lists abound with practical examples. A man unified with God could rob from others, could lie or perjure himself without sin, and, if a servant, could give away the property of his master without license (A43, 69, 92; N18). More than that, the perfect could eat in secret as much and whatever they wished and could avoid work to see how delightful God is in their leisure (N19, 16).

The lists record a similar antinomianism in sexual matters, though there is a vast difference in degree among the various statements reported. Of four tenets that deal explicitly with the subject in Albert's determination, one states pardoxically that a mother of five boys can still be a virgin, another allows sexual relations for the unmarried, a third limits this only to kissing, and a fourth says that a child born out of wedlock is without stain (i.e. original sin) (A97, 53, 81, 54). In addition, Albert's determination includes the statement that whatever is done by the good "under the belt" is not sinful (A63). Much more extreme than these tenets is the statement in the Nördlingen list that whoever is unified with God can satisfy the desires of his flesh in every way (N12).

From all this it sounds like the heretics of the Ries were scandalous libertines, but there are some indications to the contrary. Albert's determination reports one tenet which calls for the imitation of Christ, who was no lecher, and another says that man should abstain from all exterior things, a view that Albert compares to the ascetic Ortliebian heresy. (A23, 78). There are several ways of explaining these inconsistencies. Most obviously it would seem that the lists report the views of many different people who expressed themselves in different ways and might not have agreed with each other. Second, one must wonder, as one must for many later records of Free-Spirit heresy, if the extremism reflected in some statements resulted from the way the questions were posed. Third, if no propositions were suggested outright by the examiners, it is likely that those who intensely believed in the possibility of deification were prepared to give diverse examples of their freedom without necessarily taking them literally. One is led toward such a conclusion when there is no supporting evidence whatsoever that the heretics practiced what they allegedly preached.

Since we do not know how the tenets from the Ries were gathered and compiled, the previous speculations cannot be proved, but they do seem to be confirmed by our knowledge of contemporary mystical thought similar to that of the Swabian heretics, particularly that of the orthodox German beguine Mechthild of Magdeburg. In the ecstatic, often erotic strophes of her *Flowing Light of the Godhead*, which she wrote at about the same time that heretics of the "New Spirit" were examined in the Ries, Mechthild exulted in the wonder and thrill of knowing God. For her, this knowledge was like the union between bride and bridegroom: "thou art in Me and I in thee."[12] Many of the heretics of the Ries were also females[13] and at least one expressed herself in the same erotic way, saying that Christ had known her carnally (N28).

12. Cited by Lucy Menzies, *The Revelations of Mechthild of Magdeburg* (London, 1953), p. xxxi.
13. The evidence for this is presented by Grundmann RB, pp. 411–12.

Mechthild of Magdeburg was fully cognizant of the doctrine of grace, but she still stressed the role of nature in the mystical union. Thus at one point she had the Lord say to the soul: "thou art so natured (*genaturt*) in me that absolutely nothing can stand between thee and me."[14] Later on in her book Mechthild admitted that the reader might have misunderstood her when she said that "the Godhead is my father by nature" because such a statement seems to conflict with the orthodox doctrine that "all that God has done with us is by grace and not by nature." To this she answered provocatively: "you are right and I am also right," but then went on to explain herself by means of a parable which put her down on the right side of orthodoxy.[15] Unlike Mechthild, the heretics in the Ries were not allowed to explain themselves and their cryptic remark that "the good man is able truly to say that he has and does not have grace" might have been equivalent to Mechthild's "you are right and I am also right" without the explanatory parable.

Mechthild's *Flowing Light* contains none of the blasphemous attacks on the Church found in the lists from Swabia, but she did think that she was different from others in being able to reach God in an extrasacramental way.[16] Similarly, she never provided shocking examples of how the unified soul could violate the moral law, but she did say that such a soul becomes free of sin: "when the soul begins to rise, the dust of sin falls away and the soul becomes a god with God, because what God wills the soul wills, otherwise the two could not be united in perfect union" or "the uncleanliness of sin disappears before His divine eyes."[17] Perhaps the heretics of the Ries would not have gone much further than Mechthild of Magdeburg had they not been goaded to give shocking examples of their freedom by the suggestive questioning of inquisitors. Even if, as is likely, they were far more radical than Mechthild, the similarity of many of their tenets with positions she took in her *Flowing Light* suggests that heretical and orthodox mystics were close relatives.

---

14. *Offenbarungen der Schwester Mechthild von Magdeburg oder das fliessende Licht der Gottheit*, ed. G. Morell (Regensburg, 1869), p. 22 (I, 44).

15. *Ibid.*, p. 205 (VI, 31).

16. On this see Menzies, p. xxxi.

17. *Offenbarungen*, pp. 174–76 (VI, 1).

3. HERESY AND FORNICATION: A *TOPOS* OF THE THIRTEENTH CENTURY

Our discussion of the heresy found in the Ries has been based on the assumption that the heretics actually uttered all the tenets that were attributed to them, but several pieces of evidence provided by Albertus Magnus show that that is by no means certain. To begin with, it will be recalled that among the antinomian tenets in Albert's determination is one which states that whatever is done by the good "under the belt" is not sinful. But the same tenet appears so often in other medieval descriptions of completely disparate heresies that it is hard to believe that it was really a dogma of any one of them. Two different thirteenth-century writers ascribed it, almost certainly without foundation, to the ascetic French and Italian Cathars, and two late medieval writers, probably following an earlier source, ascribed it to heretics burned in Strassburg in 1211 who were either ascetic Waldensians or ascetic Ortliebians.[18] In the fourteenth century, as we will see, the tenet also reappeared in the confession of the Moravian Free Spirit Albert of Brünn. Certainly heretics from southern France, Italy, different parts of Germany, and Moravia, scattered over two centuries and otherwise professing widely different beliefs did not spontaneously utter the same formula about there being no sin under the belt. Rather, the men who described these heresies must have read the same sources or each other. Albertus Magnus wrote that the statement was a heresy of the Heliotiste (or Elyoriste, depending on which manuscript reading one prefers), whose founder was a disciple of the fifth-century Bishop Julian the Pelagian. If it were possible to find the original patristic description of this heresy (a task to which I have devoted many hours in vain), it might prove to be the common antecedent for the various later reports.

One must also wonder about the veracity of the call to fornication found in both Albert's determination and the Nördlingen list. Albertus Magnus referred to heretics of the "New Spirit" once in his other

18. Pierre des Vaux-de-Cernay, *Hystoria albigensis*, tr. P. Guébin and H. Maisonneuve (Paris, 1951), I, 17; Anselmus de Alexandria, *Tractatus de haereticis*, ed. A. Dondaine, "La hiérarchie cathare en Italie, II," AFP, XX (1950), 310; Jacob Twinger von Königshofen, *Chronik*, CdS, IX, 649; Johannes Nauclerus, *Chronica. . . ad annum 1500* (Cologne, 1544), p. 807.

works–in his late *Summa theologiae*–but there he ascribed to them only the belief that unclean touching, kisses, and embraces were no sins rather than an unlimited call to fornication.[19] This *Summa* was written after 1274, presumably after Albert refuted the heresy from the Ries. Such an argument ex silentio would not be convincing in itself, but since it is coupled with the discrepancies in Albert's long refutation and the uncertain authorship, date, and purpose of the Nördlingen list it would seem wisest to leave the sexual ethic of the German heretics as an open question.

In the same section of his *Summa theologiae*, Albert did write of men who said that fornication was not mortally sinful, but instead of mentioning the heretics of the New Spirit or of the Ries, he ascribed the tenet to the Greeks, who he said were forced to retract it at the Second Council of Lyons (1274). Albert did not invent this allegation but found it in a report of Jerome of Ascoli–a papal legate in Constantinople during the preparations for the Second Council of Lyons. The Greek-speaking Jerome (later to become Pope Nicholas IV) had stayed in the Byzantine capital over a year, during which time he had taken the opportunity to study Greek theology and conduct discussions with a former Patriarch. Nonetheless, he maintained in a dispatch to the pope that the Greeks did not believe "simple fornication" to be a mortal sin.[20] Certainly the Latins at this time were negotiating with the Greeks in good faith, but that did not prevent the best informed men from believing falsely that the schismatics were apologists for fornication.

Even earlier, in 1249, a full generation before Jerome's report and well before the discovery of the heresy in the Ries, Albertus Magnus had written, purely in the abstract, about the heresy of believing fornication not to be mortally sinful.[21] A decade later, his

19. Ed. A. Borgnet, *Opera omnia* (Paris, 1890–99), XXX, 396–99.

20. On Jerome's legation and report see B. Roberg, *Die Union zwischen der griechischen und der lateinischen Kirche auf dem II. Konzil von Lyon* (Bonn, 1964), pp. 102–103, 129–34, and text 229–31 (230: "Item simplicem fornicationem non credunt esse mortale peccatum.") Roberg, p. 133, admits: "es lässt sich nachweisen, dass Hieronymus teilweise recht unpräzise Angaben machte." That this report was the source of Albert's statement is suggested by A. Franchi, *Il Concilio II di Lione* (Rome, 1965), pp. 171–72.

21. *In IV Sentent.*, ed. Borgnet, XXIX, Dist. XVII, art. 33, 705: ". . . videtur, quod duplex est haeresis, scilicet aperta, et implicita. Aperta haeresis, quae expresse contrarium praedicat, vel quod antecedit articulum, vel sequitur illum:

student, St. Thomas, also wrote in the same vein: trying to decide what sort of propositions were to be considered heretical, the Saint unhesitatingly included those which offended morality such as the doctrine that "fornication is not a sin."[22] That Thomas had any direct contact with heretics who taught this is greatly to be doubted,[23] and that Albert was more likely to believe that the Greeks and Swabian heretics taught it after he had written about the doctrine in theory is most probable.

Examination in fact shows that heretics of all stripes were simply assumed to be immoralists throughout the thirteenth century. This is shown by the sermon literature of the age. Philip, the Chancellor of the University of Paris, a representative preacher of the first part of the century, peppered his sermons with references to the heretic as a type. For example, he claims in one of his homilies on the Psalms that heretics, along with hypocrites, false brothers, and bad Christians, are "smiths of the devil who fashion utensils of death out of Holy Scripture." "Their furnace is the fire of concupiscence, for the cause of all heresy is either lechery (*luxuria*), cupidity, or pride."[24] In his most extensive sermon on heresy Philip states in a similar fashion that three "occasions" of heresy are lechery, gluttony, and avarice. If heretics by nature were moral degenerates it followed that they would try to justify immorality and Philip refers explicitly in the same passage to

---

ut quod Deus non sit trinus et unus, est haeresis contra articulum; quod fornicatio non sit mortale peccatum, est haeresis contra consequens articulum. . . ." The dating of this work to 1249 is by F. Pelster, *Kritische Studien zum Leben und zu den Schriften Alberts des Grossen* (Freiburg, 1920), p. 114.

22. *In Epistolam ad Titum, Opera omnia* (Parma, 1862–70), XIII, cap. 3, lect. 2, 659. This is dated to between 1259 and 1265 by P. Glorieux, "Essai sur les commentaires scripturaires de Saint Thomas et leur chronologie," RTAM, XVII (1950), 258.

23. Thomas' fourteenth-century biographer wrote that the Saint combatted the error he called "de novo spiritu libertatis" (de Tocco, *Vita S. Thomae Aquinatis*, ed. P. Prümmer, *Revue Thomiste*, XXI–XXII [1913–14], *Supplément*, 93–94), but there is no contemporary report to that effect and no evidence for it at all in Thomas' writings.

24. Philip the Chancellor (mistakenly called de Grève), *In psalterium davidicum CCXXX sermones* (Paris, 1523), II, fol. 186v–87r: "Hypocrite, heretici et falsi fratres et mali Christiani sunt fabri diaboli, qui de sacra scriptura fabricant vasa mortis. . . . Fornax horum est ignis concupiscentia: quia causa omnia heresis est vel luxuria, vel cupiditas vel superbia. . . ."

those who preached that "work of the flesh" is not sinful.[25] Elsewhere he talks of those who say that lechery and usury are no sins.[26]

If any heretics of Philip's day did justify usury it was the Albigensians, but they certainly did not apologize for lechery.[27] In fact he probably had them in mind when he wrote of heretics who praised virginity and attacked marriage. But again the gap between the actual and the type becomes apparent when he goes on to say in the same sermon that although heretics seem to lead austere lives, in secret they are more voluptuous than others.[28] Philip's assumption was that all heretics were morally depraved and all appearances to the contrary could not make him change his mind.

These sermons were typical of a genre and were so well designed that they were used as a model by the Dominican William Perrault (Peyraut). This influential writer did not copy Philip verbatim, but did include his assertion that the errors of heretics have their origin in vice, again giving the example of lechery as in the case of those who said that the work of the flesh is not sinful. Perrault also repeated Philip's reference to heretics who praised virginity and slandered marriage, but he added a new contradiction by saying that a basic doctrine of all heretics is that they preach pleasure (or things pleasant to hear).[29] These words in turn were plagiarized in the next century by

25. *Sermones super evangelia*, MS Clm 3740, fol. 249ra: "tria enim sunt vicia que dederunt occasionem diversis heresibus: luxuria et gula et avaricia. Et ex hoc est quod quidam predicaverunt non esse peccatum opus carnis." (This MS of Munich seems to have a better reading than the older one cited below, n. 28, because it avoids an awkward jump and is corroborated in this by MS Cambridge, Peterhouse, 1. 3. 9, fol. 139va. For permission to use the latter I am grateful to Mr. E. J. Kenney and the Master and Fellows of Peterhouse, Cambridge.)

26. *Sermones festivales*, MS BN 3280, fol. 120rb: "concedunt quod usura et luxuria non sunt peccatum."

27. Asceticism was the outstanding feature of the Albigensian ethic. Despite the allegations noted above (n. 18), there is only one unreliable shred of documentary evidence which suggests immorality. (See Arno Borst, *Die Katharer* [Stuttgart, 1953], 182.)

28. *Sermones super evangelia*, MS BN 3281, fol. 247ra: ". . . virginitatem laudant ut matrimonio detrahant. . . ."; fol. 247rb: "Hii sunt in exteriori vita rigidi, in occultis plus ceteris voluptuosi."

29. MS BN 12422, fol. 89va: "Et sciendum quod errores hereticorum ex aliquo vicio habuerunt originem ut ex vicio luxurie error illorum qui dixerunt opus carnis non esse peccatum. . . . heretici possunt cognosci ex doctrina et ex vita. Ex doctrina: . . . secundo quia placentia predicant. . . tercio quia illa commendant

the Augustinian Jordan of Quedlinburg, whose collection of sermons came to rank among the most popular of the later Middle Ages.[30] A study of the homiletic literature of the thirteenth century—the bulk of which is still unpublished—would doubtless show the continued repetition of these stereotypes. Certainly if negotiaters with the Greeks were prepared to believe that they were immoralists, how much easier was it to make such charges against all heretics—the enemy within.

This is what happened in the last case we will look at: that of the so-called Averroists of Paris. Among the errors of the philosophers condemned by the Bishop of Paris in 1277 were the claims that happiness comes in this life, not the next (176), that continence is not "essentially" a virtue (168), that perfect abstinence from sexual acts corrupts virtue (169), and that delight in acts of the flesh does not impede the intellect (172).[31] In addition, one stating that "simple fornication among two unmarried people is not sinful" (183) was a repetition of the tenet raised in theory by Albertus Magnus and St. Thomas and then ascribed to the Swabian heretics and the Greeks before returning as a supposed belief of Parisian theologians in 1277.[32]

What people, if any, uttered these propositions we do not know, though it would definitely seem that the Bishop's list was not "the faithful reproduction of an entire corpus of heretical thought,"[33] but rather a scattershot volley against all sorts of propositions that a suspicious and conservative divine thought might be in the air. Even Andrew the Chaplain's *De amore* mentioned in the preface to the condemnation does not contend that fornication is not sinful or explicitly

---

que propinqua sunt erroribus eorum, unde virginitatem multum laudant ut matrimonio detrahunt." (The published version in Guilelmus Alvernus, *Opera omnia* [Orléans, 1674] is so corrupt that it is necessary to quote from MS.)

30. *Opus postillarum et sermonum de tempore* (Strassburg, 1483), fol. 335v. The same passage is in Lucas de Bitonto, *Sermones viae et veritatis* (n. p., 1483), *sermo* 88 (no pag.), but could not have been written by the thirteenth-century Franciscan of that name because it is not found in the two oldest Parisian MSS (BN 15958 and BN *nouv. acq.* 410).

31. *Chartularium Universitatis Parisiensis*, ed. H. Denifle and E. Chatelain (Paris, 1889–97), I, 553, #473.

32. *Ibid.*: "Quod simplex fornicatio, utpote soluti cum soluta, non est peccatum."

33. F. Heer, *The Intellectual History of Europe* (Anchor Books ed., Garden City, N. Y., 1968), I, 213.

state any of the other outrageous tenets,[34] and it is certainly doubtful that Siger of Brabant, who was deeply influenced by Albertus Magnus and St. Thomas, and immortalized in Dante's *Paradiso*, taught such things.

4. ADAMITES AND LUCIFERANS IN THE FOURTEENTH CENTURY

If most orthodox spokesmen maintained in the thirteenth century—an age relatively free from hysteria—that heretics were apologists for fornication, it is not surprising that in the turbulent fourteenth century it was widely reported that heretics actually practiced shocking nude rites and worshiped the devil. Though the fourteenth-century reports differed little, except in their greater number, from similar ones issued spasmodically since the eleventh century, and though the chroniclers who issued them preferred to call the promiscuous nudists Adamites and the devil-worshipers Luciferans (when they used any names at all), modern historians who think that Free-Spirit heretics were practicing antinomians often cite these fourteenth-century reports as illustrations of Free-Spirit rites. That presents us with two problems to conclude our initial survey: were the heretics charged with such practices really Free Spirits? and did the reports of sexual license and blasphemies have any substance?

To take one example from the many lurid stories, the Swabian chronicler John of Winterthur, who described the antics of heretics from Constance recounted at the beginning of this chapter, told in an entry for 1338 of heretics in Austria who met in cellars.[35] Supposedly their ceremony was as follows: their leader sat on a raised chair and asked aspiring novices whether a thorn pricks. If the newcomers were innocent they answered yes, but if they were suitable for membership in the heretical organization they answered no. Then, after the leader

---

34. This is conceded by A. J. Denomy, "The *De Amore* of Andreas Capellanus and the Condemnation of 1277," *Mediaeval Studies*, VIII (1946), 107–49, who otherwise argues that Andrew's work was the basis of this part of the Parisian condemnation. John V. Fleming, *The Roman de la Rose: A Study in Allegory and Iconography* (Princeton, 1969), pp. 214–18, shows that there was no relation between the condemnation and ideas propounded in the *Romance of the Rose* and presents evidence that the question "whether simple fornication is a mortal sin?" had previously been aired in Paris just as a scholastic exercise.

35. *Chronica* (as above, n. 1), 144–45.

delivered a sermon in which he preached the sect's errors with dazzling eloquence, four disciples entered with burning torches and were followed by a monarch wearing a sparkling diadem carrying a glowing scepter and surrounded by a handsome bodyguard. He maintained that he was the king of heaven and confirmed the teachings of the sect's leader. Then a grasshopper jumped on the mouths of all present, transmitting to them such ecstacy that they could no longer control themselves. The lights went out and everyone then seized a partner for an orgiastic celebration.

The latest judgment of John's description is that "most of this can be classified as arrant nonsense"[36] and the only emendation one would want to make in this verdict would be to change the word "most" to "all." That is because the heretics who were accused of practicing such rites must have been ascetic Waldensians. Of all the high medieval sects, only the Waldensians took root in Austria and it was they who were still the greatest concern of the Inquisition in the later Middle Ages.[37] Along with John of Winterthur, the Austrian Abbot John of Viktring reported for the year 1327 that there were heretics in Austria who celebrated orgies in underground caves, but a fifteenth-century monk from the vicinity who recopied John's passage simply assumed that they were Waldensians.[38]

That the story is the same for Bohemia can be shown from a case that excellently reflects the hatred and hysteria that motivated later medieval heresy hunts. On April 1, 1318, Pope John XXII ordered the Bishop of Prague, John of Dražic, to defend himself at Avignon against charges that he had protected heretics in his diocese.[39] Accord-

36. P. P. Bernard, "Heresy in Fourteenth Century Austria," *Mediaevalia et Humanistica,* X (1956), 56.

37. On Waldensians in Austria in the thirteenth century, Haupt, "Waldenserthum," I, 327–28 and M. Nickson, "The 'Pseudo-Reinerius' treatise, the final stage of a thirteenth-century work on heresy from the diocese of Passau," AHDL, XLII (1967), 288–91. On the campaigns against Waldensians there in the late fourteenth and early fifteenth centuries, below pp. 145–46.

38. Johannes Victoriensis, *Liber certarum historiarum,* ed. F. Schneider, SRG, XXXVI, 2, 130–31. MS Clm 17541, copied in the Augustinian cloister of Schlehdorf in Upper Bavaria, heads John of Viktring's description of the heretics in Austria as "Waldenses heretici" (fol. 50ra).

39. Ed. J. Emler, *Regesta diplomatica nec non epistolaria Bohemiae et Moraviae* (Prague, 1855–1954), III, 173–76. The best secondary accounts are F. Palacky, *Über die Beziehungen und das Verhältniss der Waldenser zu den ehemaligen*

ing to the Pope, these heretics not only rejected oaths, administered penances, allowed rebaptism, and denied the resurrection of the dead and the doctrine of the Trinity, but they also expected Lucifer to reign and indulged in disgraceful secret orgies. Most of these tenets, except the last, were characteristic of the Waldensians, who it is hard to imagine had become Luciferans and libertines, but the Pope's letter explains the origins of his charges. A personal enemy of the Bishop of Prague reported to the Pope that the local Inquisition, at the urging of the King of Bohemia, condemned fourteen heretics and wished to hand them over to the secular arm for the death penalty. But the Bishop, an enemy of the mendicant orders that directed the Inquisition, freed all the condemned by force of arms. It was this hostile informer who told the Pope of the scandalous heretical errors and it stands to reason that he wished to make these appear as heinous as possible.[40] Certainly no bishop, whatever his motives, would forcibly intercede for devil-worshipers, yet John XXII typically took the hostile account at face value and imprisoned John of Prague at Avignon for eleven years.[41]

The most compelling evidence that most alleged fourteenth-century antinomian heretics were really Waldensians concerns cases in Brandenburg. According to John of Winterthur, a "rector of boys" in an unnamed city of Brandenburg offered to show the Holy Trinity to a Franciscan friar in 1338.[42] The latter agreed but prudently brought along a concealed consecrated host to the appointed meeting place. There the rector showed him an impressive looking man with royal clothes next to an elegant youth and a beautiful child who he said represented the Father, Son, and Holy Ghost. But when the friar took out his host and asked "and what is this?" the apparition disappeared with a terrible smell. By this means a group of heretics were discovered who were then burned because they refused to recant.

John's date of 1338 for these events coincides with an indepen-

---

Secten in Böhmen (Prague, 1869), pp. 11–18, and S. H. Thomson, "Pre-Hussite Heresy in Bohemia," *English Historical Review*, XLVIII (1933), 30–32.

40. The fact that the Pope's informant, Henry of Schönburg, was an enemy of the Bishop who had abused him for being a bastard is reported by Petra Žitauského, *Kronika Zbraslavská* (*Chronicon Aulae Regiae*), ed. J. Emler, *Fontes rerum Bohemicarum* (Prague, 1873–1932), IV, 248.

41. On later heresy in Czech regions, see below Chapter V.

42. *Chronicon* (as above, n. 1), 151.

dent report in *The Deeds of the Archbishops of Magdeburg* that around 1336 Jordan of Quedlinburg, then lector of the Augustinians at Magdeburg, was sent as Inquisitor to examine suspected "Luciferans" in the town of Angermünde in Brandenburg.[43] Of the many persons examined, fourteen, of both sexes, could not clear themselves canonically and were burned at the stake by the secular arm. This would be all that was known about the case if it were not for the fact that it transpired in Angermünde, a town where later Inquisitors turned up heretics in 1392–94 and again in 1458, and which thus became popularly known as "Ketter-Angermunde." By 1458 the heretics had been absorbed into the Hussite movement, but the evidence of the trials of 1392–94 is that they were then ascetic Waldensians who knew nothing about worshiping Lucifer. Their heterodoxy consisted primarily in their refusal to take vows and they were deemed so harmless that the local clergy saw little need to bother them. There can be no doubt that these heretics were direct descendants of the "Luciferans" of ca. 1336 because one woman who was over ninety years old at the time of the second persecution said that she had been born into the sect and another admitted that she had held her beliefs for fifty years. The husband of the latter had been burned at Angermünde during the first persecution and she herself only avoided the same fate because she was then pregnant. Here then were "Luciferans," but they were as much worshipers of devils as Jews were poisoners of wells.[44]

Among the entire mass of material concerning obscene fourteenth-century devil-worshipers, there are only two shreds of evidence that any of them might have been Free Spirits. In the Austrian town of Krems on the Danube an examination of heretics in 1315 supposedly uncovered devil-worshiping orgiasts.[45] The Inquisitors

43. *Gesta archiepiscoporum Magdeburgensium*, MGH SS, XIV, 434–35.

44. I had reached these conclusions before the article of D. Kurze, "Zur Ketzergeschichte der Mark Brandenburg und Pommerns vornehmlich im 14. Jahrhundert: Luziferianer, Putzkeller und Waldenser," *Jahrbuch für die Geschichte Mittel-und Ostdeutschlands*, XVI/XVII (1968), 50–94, came to my attention. Kurze's discovery of new manuscript material confirms our common conclusion—already suggested in the nineteenth-century articles of Wattenbach cited by Kurze, 55, n. 2—that the "Luciferans" were actually Waldensians.

45. The sources concerning this event are described and edited (in some cases re-edited) by Nickson (as above, n. 37), 303–314. Unfortunately the most recent account in English in the article of Bernard (as above, n. 36), 50–51, is

there in the course of their examinations reportedly asked a condemned young girl named Gisla (who, a later chronicler, perhaps using his imagination, said had "a most beautiful body"[46]) if she was a virgin. To which she replied, "above the earth I am a virgin, within it, honestly, no."[47] This frank but cryptic answer could be interpreted as an assertion that conventional morality has no bearing for the spiritually free, but since there is no further elaboration it is hard to know exactly what to make of it, especially since most of the heretics of Krems too were probably Waldensians.

Historians of the Free Spirit have concentrated more on reports of obscene rites in Cologne because that city was known as a center of heretical mysticism and because the alleged orgiasts there were in one source called "beghards" and "lollards"—terms often used in the fourteenth century as synonyms for heretics of the Free Spirit. The reports in question were reverberations of an inquisition of 1326 ordered by Archbishop Henry of Virneburg.[48] This prelate was most famous for his prosecution of Meister Eckhart and his inquisition of 1326 might have had something to do with that, possibly having been meant to show that Eckhart was an accomplice or teacher of real heretics. Whatever the case, a commission composed of Dominicans, Franciscans, and other "*viri litterati*" discovered a number of suspects, some of whom confessed and repented while others perservered in

---

based on only half of the sources. The date of 1312 that Bernard gives for the inquisition in Krems is found in only one of the four sources while the others all agree on 1315.

46. J. Trithemius, *Annales Hirsaugienses* (St. Gall, 1690), II, 140.

47. Nickson, 313.

48. *Chronica regia Coloniensis*, ed. G. Waitz, SRG, XVIII, 369, and *Notae Colonienses*, MGH SS, XXIV, 365, the two sources written nearest in time and place to the events, give the date 1326 and William of Egmont (Guilelmus Procurator), *Chronicon*, ed. A. Matthaeus, *Veteris aevi analecta*, 2nd ed. (The Hague, 1738), II, 643, gives 1325. The *Annales Agrippinenses*, MGH SS, XVI, 737, give 1336, which might well be the result of some editorial error in one digit. The *Gesta Trevirorum*, ed. J. H. Wyttenbach and M. F. J. Müller (Trier, 1836–39), II, 244, has 1324 and John of Viktring (as above, n. 38), 129, and John of Winterthur (as above, n. 1), 126, date the events to roughly 1327 and 1328 respectively. Lea, II, 373, Leff, p. 335, and McDonnell, p. 519, make the mistake of following the sixteenth-century chronicle of Tritheim in referring to a trial in 1322, but this date appears in no known contemporary source. Because of the disparate years given by the chroniclers, Lea and McDonnell assume that there were several different heresy trials in Cologne, but it is clear that the sources refer to the same incident.

their errors. One of the latter was a priest named Walter who was defrocked by the Archbishop and burned at the stake; the others—another priest, a layman, and six women—were imprisoned for life. A single report that heretics were drowned in the Rhine is almost certainly false.[49]

The beliefs of Walter and his followers are enveloped in mists of legend. John of Winterthur, whose talents as a story-teller we have already several times observed, reported that a certain citizen of Cologne suspected his wife of attending heretical conclaves.[50] One day, when she announced that she was going to Church, he followed her and was led instead to an underground assembly. When an orgy began he grabbed her and slipped a ring off of her finger without her recognizing him because it was dark and he had disguised himself. At home afterwards she denied all his accusations but could say nothing when he presented her with the ring and beat her to the ground. Then he exposed the heretics to the city authorities and although some fled, most (according to John, fifty) were burned.

Complementing this story is John of Viktring's description of the heretical rites.[51] According to him, men and women of various classes assembled at midnight in an underground hideaway which they named a temple. There Walter, "a priest of the devil," said mass and delivered a sermon. Then the assembly put out the lights, chose partners, and feasted, danced, and fornicated. This, they said, was the state of paradise in which Adam and Eve lived before the fall. Their leader Walter called himself Christ and claimed that though condemned to be executed he would rise on the third day. He presented a beautiful young virgin as Mary, but taught that Christ was not born

49. I have taken the details of the trial from the *Chron. reg. Colon.*, which seems to be the most immediate and sober of the sources and which is confirmed in the statement that only one man (a defrocked priest) was burned by the *Gesta Trevirorum*. Only William of Egmont, 644, reports the drowning of heretics in the Rhine, which Lea, II, 373, rightly considers "a novel punishment for heresy."

50. *Chronica*, 126.

51. *Liber certarum historiarum*, 129–30. Leff, p. 335, n. 5, cites two MSS of Munich on Walter as unpublished, but these are verbatim extracts from John of Viktring, whose account of the heretics of Cologne found its way into encyclopedic lists of heresies and was frequently copied in that form in the fifteenth century.

of a virgin, that God was neither born nor suffered, and that fasting was unnecessary.

William of Egmont (Holland) also presented the essentials of the stories told by the two German chroniclers.[52] A man followed his wife on Good Friday to a nocturnal bacchanal and later apprehended her by means of her ring.[53] At this meeting in an underground place which the heretics called "paradise" were two people who called themselves Jesus and his mother Mary.[54] After the leader gave a sermon in the nude in which he exhorted his listeners to discard their clothing came the inevitable lights-out celebrations, which the chronicler compared to the "manner of pigs." William of Egmont's most important remarks, which appear in his chronicle alone, were that the heretics were "beghards" and that the suspicious husband dressed himself up as a "lollard" to escape notice. On the basis of these words, historians have judged that the victims of the inquisition in Cologne were heretics of the Free Spirit and have gone on from there to conclude that the heresy entailed the practice of nocturnal orgies. But in the Low Countries, where William lived, the words "beghard" and "lollard" were often used without relation to the heresy of the Free Spirit as terms of abuse for scoundrels or presumed hypocrites.[55] The use of these two ambiguous words in one source does not prove that the condemned heretics of Cologne were Free Spirits, and even if they were, we should not rely on the legends of distant chroniclers to conclude that they were orgiasts.

If most of the heretics discussed in this section were austere Waldensians, why do charges of "Adamite" sexuality and "Luciferan"

52. William of Egmont, 643–44. I limit myself to the contemporary sources and purposely avoid use of the confused stories in the late chronicle of Tritheim.

53. Wherever this story may have originated, it became a popular one. As noticed by Lea, III, 97, two early sixteenth-century Italian chroniclers, Jacobus Philippus Bergomensis and Bernardinus Corio, told it in connection with Italian events of the years 1298 and 1300 respectively.

54. I doubt the suggestion of J. Asen, "Die Begarden und die Sackbrüder in Köln," *Annalen des historischen Vereins für den Niederrhein*, CXV (1929), 169, that the heretic who called himself Jesus was identical with the "Gerardus dictus Jhesus" mentioned in a document as residing in a house of beghards in Cologne in 1310 because it seems idle to try to winnow out grains of truth from the chaff of such fables.

55. For examples see below, pp. 40–41.

blasphemy occur against them with such persistent frequency?[56] The most helpful clue is provided by John of Viktring when he says that the heretics of Cologne were "Adamites" who were best described by Isidore of Seville and thereupon cites the appropriate passage from Isidore's Encyclopedia. Just as the belief in the existence of unicorns and harpies was transmitted to the Middle Ages by the *Physiologus*, so belief in the existence of heretics known as Adamites was transmitted through the catalogues of St. Augustine and Isidore of Seville, the latter of which circulated in the *Decretum* of Gratian. According to both patristic authorities, the Adamites were heretics who were so called because they imitated the nakedness of Adam. They called their church paradise and there they heard readings, prayed, and celebrated their sacraments together with women in the nude.[57] Since most men in the Middle Ages had little sense of historical perspective this description had an active life for over one thousand years and even reappeared in a catalogue of heresies written by the independent thinker Sebastian Franck in the sixteenth century.[58] Thus it is not surprising that John of Viktring believed that the heretics of Cologne were the same as the Adamites described by the fathers hundreds of years earlier and much of his account can be seen as an imaginative set of variations on a patristic theme.

The transmission of a belief in Luciferans is a bit more complicated. St. Augustine and Isidore both mentioned heretics of that name but described them as followers of a fourth-century Bishop named Lucifer rather than as devil-worshipers.[59] But it was a medieval commonplace that all heretics were instruments of the devil. For example, John of Winterthur, after describing the heretics of Austria, ex-

---

56. For much of what follows I am indebted to the brilliant article of H. Grundmann, "Der Typus des Ketzers in mittelalterlicher Anschauung," *Kultur- und Universalgeschichte, Festschrift für Walter Goetz* (Leipzig and Berlin, 1927), pp. 91–107.

57. St. Augustine, *De haeresibus*, ed. and tr. Liguori G. Müller (Washington, D. C., 1956), pp. 76–77 (see also pp. 150–51, where the editor notes that even in ancient times this sect probably never existed); Isidore of Seville, *Etymologiarum sive originum*, ed. W. M. Lindsay (Oxford, 1911), Lib. VIII, cap. 5, 14.

58. *Ketzerchronik*, in *Chronica, zeÿtbuch und geschÿchtbibel. . .* (Strassburg, 1531), fol. 343.

59. Augustine, ed. Müller, pp. 114–17; Isidore, ed. Lindsay, Lib. VIII, cap. 5, 55. On the subject of "Luciferans," see further the excellent article of E. Amann, *Dictionnaire de théologie catholique*, IX, 1, 1044–56.

claimed that "heretics are special sons of Satan because they carry out and imitate his words and works."[60] With such a belief widely ingrained and the term Luciferan already at hand, the concept of heretics as devil-worshipers emerged with ease in the high Middle Ages.

In fact descriptions of rites in honor of Satan were current hundreds of years before there were any Waldensians or Free Spirits. As early as 1022 heretics discovered in Orléans were charged with obscene devil-worship.[61] Supposedly they assembled together at night singing the names of the devil with candles in their hand until Satan himself appeared in the form of a beast. Then the lights went out and a general debauch ensued. Later a child born of the orgiastic union would be sacrificed in flames and its ashes reverentially preserved because they contained a diabolical power so potent that whoever tasted the smallest part of them could never leave the heresy or return to the path of the truth. Similar tales reappeared in the twelfth century and became an obsession in the thirteenth during the campaigns of the Inquisitor Conrad of Marburg.[62]

Fourteenth-century chroniclers had a special reason for relating such stories. Friedrich Baethgen has shown that one purpose of compiling historical narratives in the later Middle Ages was to provide material for preachers. This was a major aim, as he notes, of John of Winterthur and John of Viktring.[63] Since one of the favorite subjects of late medieval sermons was the danger of heresy, the chronicles contained numerous stories that could be used to illustrate this point. For such purposes the two Johns, and obviously other chroniclers, used

60. *Chronica* (as above, n. 1), 145.

61. *Gesta synodi Aurelianensis*, RHF, X, 538; Adhémar of Chabannes, *Chronicon*, RHF, X, 154; and Raoul Glaber, *Historiae*, PL, 142, 659–64. For earlier mention of devil-worship in Regino of Prüm and Burchard of Worms, see J. Hansen, *Quellen und Untersuchungen zur Geschichte des Hexenwahns und der Hexenverfolgung im Mittelalter* (Bonn, 1901), pp. 38–44.

62. Guibert of Nogent, *Histoire de sa vie*, ed. G. Bourgin (Paris, 1907), pp. 212–215; Radulphus Coggeshall, *Chronicon anglicanum*, RHF, XVIII, 93; Aubry of Trois-Fontaines, *Chronicon ab orbe condito*, MGH SS, XXIII, 931; Gregory IX, *Vox in rama*, MGH Epis. Saec. XIII, I, 433, #537. As noticed by John F. Benton, *Self and Society in Medieval France: The Memoirs of Abbot Guibert of Nogent* (New York, 1970), p. 213, n. 2, Guibert of Nogent's account was probably based on that in the *Gesta synodi Aurelianensis*.

63. "Franziskanische Studien," HZ, CXXXI (1925), 435–47 (reprinted in Baethgen's *Mediaevalia: Aufsätze, Nachrufe, Besprechungen* [Stuttgart, 1960], pp. 331–41).

suitable words and passages from Augustine and Isidore as excellent points of departure for the most sensational stories that they could find or invent.

It does not require any great amount of scientific criticism to recognize that the recurrence of such stories is no proof of their veracity. Just as fearful children imagine the most lurid shapes in the dark, so can grown men believe in patent fables concerning movements that they fear and do not understand. Further comments along these lines may be left to the psychologist, but the historian may recall the charges of ritual murder, sexual promiscuity, and adoration of obscene divinities launched against the early Christians as well as against other minority groups throughout the ages.[64]

64. For example, W. Schulze, "Der Vorwurf des Ritualmordes gegen die Christen im Altertum und in der Neuzeit," ZfK, LXV (1953/54), 304–306. In the *Octavius* of Minucius Felix, Christians were charged with worshiping the heads of donkeys and the genital organs of their priests.

Chapter Two

BEGHARDS AND BEGUINES

The noted thirteenth-century Archbishop of Rouen, Eudes Rigaud, earned a reputation in his day for quick wit. A collection of *exempla* from Tours includes several instances which display his gift for repartee. One runs as follows: the Archbishop once asked a certain beghard[1] whether he was anything other than an honest man. When the answer came that "a beghard is an honest man and something else more," the prelate returned: "if that's the case, I'll keep the honest man and give you all the rest."[2] It is not likely that this rejoinder will earn Eudes a rank among the wits of the ages; the story is told here

---

1. The original uses the word *beguinus* which was most prevalent in France. It is replaced here and whenever it appears for males with *beghard* because that is the standard English form which avoids confusion with the early fourteenth-century *beguins* of southern France. On the latter, who were lay followers of Franciscan zealots, see Raoul Manselli, *Spirituali e beghini in Provenza* (Rome, 1959).

2. P. Andrieu-Guitrancourt, *L'Archêveque Eudes Rigaud et la vie de l'église au XIIIe siècle* (Paris, 1938), p. 34, citing MS Tours 468, fol. 71. On this MS, L. Delisle, "Notes sur quelques manuscrits de la Bibliothèque de Tours," *Bibliothèque de l'Ecole des Chartes*, 6 ser., IV (1868), 598–604, and J. T. Welter, *L'exemplum dans la littérature religieuse et didactique du Moyen Age* (Paris and Toulouse, 1927), pp. 236–44. Both authorities agree that though the MS was written in the fifteenth century, the original compilation of *exempla* was made between 1267 and 1297 in the Touraine-Maine-Anjou region, most likely by a Dominican.

because it is typical of medieval suspicions of beghards and their female counterparts known as beguines. The term beghard was often used in the later Middle Ages as a synonym for heretic of the Free Spirit and we will see in subsequent chapters that some beghards and beguines were indeed radical mystics or Free Spirits. But most were not. The purpose of this chapter is to investigate why Eudes Rigaud and his like were so wary of beghards and beguines and how their mistrust led to hostilities and unwarranted persecutions.

1. ORIGINS AND SOURCES OF HOSTILITY

Men and women known as beghards and beguines were lay representatives of the religious movement of the high Middle Ages that sought the *vita apostolica*—the "apostolic life" of poverty, mendicancy, and preaching. When this ideal was voiced and practiced in the twelfth century by unlicensed itinerant preachers who were dissatisfied with the laxities they found in the hierarchical Church it seemed heterodox. In the thirteenth century it became respectable as a result of papal support for the Franciscans and Dominicans, but about the same time that the friars received their license to preach, the Fourth Lateran Council decreed in 1215 that no new orders were to be established. This prohibition accounts for the success of the beghards and beguines, some of whom had existed a few years before 1215. The recognized orders could not possibly absorb all who strove for the religious life and compromises had to be made.

Beghards and beguines organized themselves in a half-secular, half-religious fashion.[3] They belonged to no approved order and followed no common rule, yet they did try to lead the apostolic life, short, in most earlier cases, of preaching. The women called beguines vowed themselves to chastity and most lived in convents known as beguinages, earning their livelihood by manual labor or taking alms. Though females unquestionably predominated in the movement, it is a mistake to underestimate the role of males.[4] Some of them also lived in convents, primarily in the Low Countries, but more frequently the men were wandering beggars; indeed the thirteenth-century *An-*

3. The basic work on this subject in English is McDonnell.
4. This is done by McDonnell, who devotes only one chapter out of forty to the beghards.

nals of Colmar defined beghards as "brothers without domicile."[5] Because there was no universal order the only common factor which characterized the movement was the attempt to satisfy the religious urge without worrying too much about formalities. Most early beghards and beguines would probably have entered orders if they could have done so, but the fact that they could not allowed them a considerable amount of independence and contact with the secular world.

From the start both beguines and beghards encountered hostilities. Because official opposition to the *vita apostolica* movement had become engrained in the later twelfth century, especially after the condemnation of the Waldensians, even the first followers of St. Francis who arrived in northern Europe were taken for heretics.[6] Beguines were faced with the same problem; indeed, it has been argued convincingly that the very word beguine was first a nickname for heretics, originating from an abbreviation for "al-*bigen*-sis" and only later taking on a special meaning to denote semi-regulars pursuing the apostolic life.[7] Further evidence that beguines were marked in the eyes of some by an heretical taint comes from the writings of Philip the Chancellor. In a sermon written most likely in the early 1230s he explained that one can know heretics "by their fruits" such as works of the flesh and what issues from works of the flesh, namely fruits of the belly. For example, he said, beguines, though supposedly chaste, find themselves pregnant after consorting with heretics.[8] Similarly, in his homilies on the Psalter, Philip criticized the conduct of beghards who

5. MGH SS, XVII, 227.

6. On the early resistance to the mendicant orders, Grundmann RB, pp. 153–56, and K. Esser, "Ordo fratrum minorum. Über seine Anfänge und ursprünglichen Zielsetzungen," *Franziskanische Studien*, XLIII (1961), 176–77.

7. J. van Mierlo, "Ophelderingen bij de vroegste geschiedenis van het woord begijn," *Verslagen en mededeelingen der koninklijke vlaamse academie voor taal-en letterkunde* (1931), 983–1006. That there was no real doctrinal relationship between the beguines and the Cathars is proved by L. J. M. Philippen, "Les béguines et l'hérésie albigeoise," *Annales de l'académie royale d'archéologie de Belgique*, LXXIII, ser. 7, vol. 3 (1925), 233–52.

8. *Sermones super evangelia*, ms BN 3281, fol. 245va: "Secundo modo dicitur fructus eorum carnalia opera et quod sequitur ex carnalibus operibus, scilicet fructus ventris, quando post contubernium eorum mulieres inveniuntur pregnantes ut contigit in boguinis que credebantur virgines." For the dating of Philip's sermon, see my article, "Weltklerus und religiöse Bewegung im 13. Jahrhundert: das Beispiel Philipps des Kanzlers," AfK, LI (1969), 101–103.

came together with "little women" in conventicles and compared them to the false prophets who seduce women laden with sin mentioned by St. Paul in his Second Epistle to Timothy, a passage that was a medieval *locus classicus* for attacks on heretics.[9]

As sharp as they were, neither of these passages explicitly accused beguines and beghards of heresy and even innuendoes of this sort became less frequent for a while after the papacy, notably in the person of Gregory IX, began to defend them. During the thirteenth century, when the mendicant movement was enjoying popularity, churchmen who had a real sympathy for the *vita apostolica* praised the beguines as models of piety. Robert Grosseteste referred to the beguinal way of life as most perfect and holy, a Parisian Dominican insisted that even without a rule beghards and beguines were the most devout Christians of their age, and Robert of Sorbon declared that beguines would fare better on judgment day than many theologians.[10]

Yet even with such eloquent supporters beguines and beghards were always subject to abuse. One complaint against them was that they were, of all things, too pious. Writing in the mid-thirteenth century, Stephen of Bourbon showed how the term "beghard" could be used as a boyish insult. According to him, three boys were once together in bed during a thunderstorm; when one began praying the others laughed and called him a beghard, but thereupon a bolt of lightening came down and killed the laughing boys on the spot, leaving the pious one untouched in the middle. Examples of similar usage appear in the writings of Caesarius of Heisterbach and Robert of Sorbon who showed respectively how beguines were thought to be fanatics and

9. MS BN 14594, fol. 100ra: "Unde periculosa est quorundam religio qui in conclavi cum mulierculis conveniunt et colloquuntur sicut dicuntur facere Beghuini, de quibus Apostolus ii Thimo. iii: *Habentes speciem quidem pietatis* etc." I cite from MS because the printed text of 1523 adds after "Beghuini" the words "et bagarbi"—a corruption which is found in none of the numerous thirteenth-century MSS I have examined.

10. Grosseteste and Robert of Sorbon cited by Grundmann RB, pp. 322–23; the Dominican, who wrote in the 1240s, cited by C.-V. Langlois, "Sermons Parisiens de la première moitié du XIIIe siècle, contenus dans le manuscrit 691 de la Bibliothèque d'Arras," *Journal des savants* (1916), 553: "Inter homines qui in seculo sunt non sunt aliqui ita devoti et frequentes in oracionibus, laboribus et elemosinis sicut illi quos vocamus beginos et beginas. Et tamen aliqui nostrorum clericorum dicunt: 'Domine! non habent regulam et proptera periculum est eas sic esse.' "

how "beghard" was employed as a term of derision for someone doing penance.[11]

This mocking for excessive piety was closely related to the most persistent complaint—that of hypocrisy. Excess, real or presumed, becomes easily resented and thus throughout the thirteenth century beguines and beghards were accused of having base motives and of leading immoral lives under the mantle of piety. The earliest example comes from the poems of Gautier de Coincy, who, sometime between 1222 and 1224, interpolated into his miracle poem, *De Sainte Léocade*, an extended diatribe against beghards and beguines for being arrant hypocrites who appeared pious but actually led scandalous lives.[12] One choice sally was his claim that many were homosexuals who joined *hic* with *hic* like grammar when nature joins *hic* with *haec*. Comically, in light of modern quarrels about the etymology of the word beguine, Gautier derided the idea that the word came from *benignitas* and suggested instead, in his finest barnyard style, that it came from *begun* (which meant a mixture of animal urine, manure, and rainwater).[13]

Similarly, the chronicler William of Nangis told later in the century of a beguine who was consulted by King Philip III of France to ascertain whether his queen was guilty of poisoning and conspiracy. Even though the beguine found the queen innocent to the apparent satisfaction of the court, Nangis gratuitously called her a pseudo-prophetess who lived without an approved rule and lied to God. To this he added that she and her ilk had an outward appearance of austerity but this was only deception and their presumed spirit of prophecy was really a spirit of lies.[14] Also in the thirteenth century, satirical poems written in Arras referred to "*beghinage*" as a cover for sin and luxury, the German preacher Berthold of Regensburg placed "*Pi-*

11. Stephen of Bourbon, *Tractatus de diversis materiis predicabilius,* ed. A. Lecoy de la Marche, *Anecdotes historiques. . . d'Etienne de Bourbon* (Paris, 1877), p. 62; Caesarius of Heisterbach, *Dialogus miraculorum,* ed. J. Strange (Cologne, 1851), I, 89; Robert of Sorbon cited by Grundmann RB, p. 385.

12. The significance of this poem for the history of the beguines was first noted by Grundmann RB, pp. 378–84.

13. Ed. E. Vilamo-Pentti (Helsinki, 1950), pp. 169, 171–74, 183–84, 233. A good summary of this section is in Erhard Lommatzsch, *Gautier de Coincy als Satiriker* (Halle, 1913), pp. 26–31.

14. *Gesta Philippi Tertii Francorum Regis,* RHF, XX, 502. The complicated story is told in detail by R. Kay, "Martin IV and the Fugitive Bishop of Bayeux," *Speculum,* XL (1965), 466–73.

kardi" (i.e. beghards) among those mendacious scoundrels who are loved neither by God nor men, and a poem, *The Life of Countess Jolande of Viande*, made "*begardie*" equivalent to "*truandie*," or wandering and shiftless life.[15]

The earliest illustrations of the word "lollard," an exact synonym for beghard, also provide an excellent example of the view that such people were pseudo-religious scoundrels. According to the chronicle of Hocsemius, certain "wandering hypocrites" known as lollards deceived noblewomen in Hainaut and Brabant in 1309 under the pretense that they were lords who had survived the battle of Courtrai.[16] This report is clarified in a bizarre story told by an eye-witness, Gilles Li Muisis, Abbot of St. Martin's at Tournai.[17] John of Vierzon, lord of Mortagne and castellan of Tournai, fell at Courtrai in 1302 and his wife Marie, the sole heiress to his lands, continued to mourn for him until men posing in religious garb visited her and other noble ladies, assuring them that they would soon have news of their supposedly dead husbands. Marie believed this, for, as the Abbot smugly maintained, it is in the nature of women to be deceived, and sure enough in 1308 a man who claimed to be her husband entered Tournai in the company of Louis of Evreux. The latter was the cousin germane of the dead John of Vierzon and vouched for the imposter's claims, but he also was the brother of the King of France, Philip the Fair, and an instrument in a fantastic plot to obtain Mortagne for the French crown. Marie, hard though it is to believe, supposedly accepted the imposter as her husband and lived with him for some time before he was finally exposed and buried alive. Li Muisis says that the pseudo-

15. *Chansons et dits artésiens du XIIIᵉ siècle*, ed. A. Jeanroy and H. Guy (Bordeaux, 1898), p. 56, see also p. 51; A. E. Schönbach, "Studien zur Geschichte der altdeutschen Predigt. 3: das Wirken Bertholds von Regensburg gegen die Ketzer," Sb. Vienna, CXLVII, 5 (1904), 81-82, 107 (see also the remarks of Caesarius of Heisterbach edited by Schönbach, Sb. Vienna, CLIX [1907], 27, and commentary 42-47); Bruder Hermann, *Leben der Gräfin Iolande von Vianden*, ed. J. Meier (Breslau, 1889), p. 57.

16. Ed. G. Kurth (Brussels, 1927), p. 127. (The extract is also in Fredericq, I, 154, #162.) The continuation of William of Nangis, RHF, XX, 597-98, reports the same incidents for the year 1308.

17. Ed. J. J. de Smet, *Corpus chronicorum Flandriae* (Brussels, 1841), II, 160-62. The affair is put into perspective by A. d'Herbomez, "Un Episode du règne de Philippe le Bel: l'annexion de Mortagne à la France en 1314," *Revue des questions historiques*, LIII (1893), 27-55; see also F. Kern, *Die Anfänge der französischen Ausdehnungspolitik bis zum Jahr 1308* (Tübingen, 1910), p. 249.

prophets were *"loesdieu"* and Hocsemius says that they were called *"lollardi sive Deum laudantes,"* both expressions which indicate that they went around shouting "praise God."[18]

By the later Middle Ages the beghard or lollard had become the prototypic sanctimonious swindler for many poets. To cite just a few examples, in the fourteenth-century Netherlandish dramatic fragment *De Truwanten*, the lollard Broeder Everaet is excoriated as a scoundrel who, under the mantle of piety, seduces a silly woman into taking up a rootless life of self-indulgence, and in *De Buskenblaser*, a more ribald play from the same collection, an old farmer, who makes a fool of himself trying to regain his potency for the sake of his young wife, accuses her of having had an amorous liaison with a "brother lollard."[19] A similar mid-fifteenth-century example tells of the knavish lollard who inveigled a precious cloth out of a peasant's wife with the promise that his prayers would bring her to heaven.[20] When her husband found this out and angrily demanded his property back, the scoundrel prophesied God's wrath and secretly set fire to the cloth which burned the peasant on his way home. This supposed miracle convinced the simpleton of the lollard's powers and prompted him to renewed generosity. At the end of the century, Sebastian Brant's Latin version of the *Ship of Fools* still included lollards whose mask of piety served their bellies and beguines who led lives of scandal.[21] The view of beguines as hypocrites was so persistent in Strassburg that until relatively recent times a sumptuous meal was called there a "beguine's penance."[22]

While modern audiences are amused by Tartuffes, religious hypocrisy in the Middle Ages was no laughing matter. As the Dominican

18. Best on the lollards is the study of Kurze. From the foregoing it can be seen that there is no justification for the statement of Leff, p. 319, that the activity of the lollards of 1308–1309 was "of an heretical nature."

19. On the former piece, see my article, "Vagabonds and Little Women: The Medieval Netherlandish Dramatic Fragment *De Truwanten*," *Modern Philology*, LXV (1968), 301–306. *De Bukenblaser* is ed. P. Leendertz, *Middelnederlandsche dramatische poezie* (Leiden, 1907), pp. 70–76.

20. Recounted by Kurze, 73, from Matthew of Kemnat.

21. *Das Narrenschiff*, ed. F. Zarncke (Leipzig, 1854), pp. 119–21. Further examples are in Kurze, 70–73.

22. M. Goldberg, "Das Armen-und Krankenwesen des mittelalterlichen Strassburg," *Jahrbuch für Geschichte, Sprache und Literatur Elsass-Lothringens*, XXV (1909), 301.

William Perrault put it in his widely circulated *Summa of the Virtues and Vices*: "the reason why the Lord persecutes hypocrites is because they are traitors who pretend to be on the side of God but are actually on the side of the devil. They seem to be friends but are actually enemies and are able to do much harm to the Church. Whence heretics deceive men through hypocrisy and Antichrist, who will be the head of evil, will deceive men through hypocrisy."[23] This view stemmed from a prevalent interpretation of the Book of Revelation which interpreted the four horses as periods of Church history. The black horse was the time of heresy until the end of the great councils and the pale horse the time of "false brothers" which extended into the present; in other words, hypocrisy was a clearer and more present threat to the Church than even heresy.[24] This explains why Jean de Meung, in the *Romance of the Rose*, dressed the character Astenance Contrainte (Constrained Abstinence) as a beguine and then described her face as being as pale as the fourth horse of the Apocalypse because of her hypocrisy.[25]

The mention of Jean de Meung introduces a final reason for hostility to beghards: their similarity to the mendicant orders. This was entirely an elective affinity on the part of the former. Not only did beghards wear gray habits, but their begging cry "Brot durch Gott,"

23. Guilelmus Peraldus, *Summa virtutum ac vitiorum* (Cologne, 1629), II, 277. Hypocrisy was also sometimes personified as the second daughter of the devil: see, for example, "Le mariage des neuf filles du diable," ed. P. Meyer, "Notices du MS Rawlinson Poetry 241," *Romania*, XXIX (1900), 63, and *The Exempla of Jacques de Vitry*, ed. T. F. Crane (London, 1890), p. 102, #254.

24. The view is found in the *Glossa ordinaria* and was elaborated by twelfth-century historical theorists such as Anselm of Havelberg and Gerhoh of Reichersberg, see W. Kamlah, *Apokalypse und Geschichtstheologie* (Berlin, 1935), pp. 27–30, 64–70, and E. Meuthen, "Der Geschichtssymbolismus Gerhohs von Reichersberg," in *Geschichtsdenken und Geschichtsbild im Mittelalter*, ed. W. Lammers (Darmstadt, 1965), pp. 200–46. That it lasted into the thirteenth century is shown by a passage from a sermon of William Perrault in Guilelmus Alvernus, *Opera omnia* (Orléans, 1674), II, 308: "Cum sint quatuor impedimenta Ecclesiae in via praesentis vitae, scilicet aperta persecutio tyrannorum, deceptio haereticorum, simulatio falsorum fratrum et fallacia Antichristi et suorum. . . ." The judgment that the sermons in this edition are those of Perrault and were mistakenly attributed to William of Auvergne has stood since the investigation of J. Quétif and J. Echard, *Scriptores ordinis praedicatorum* (Paris, 1719–21), I, 131–36.

25. Ed. E. Langlois (Paris, 1914–24), III, 226–27.

appears to have originated with the friars.[26] They also tried to bask in the same sun: at a chapter meeting of Dominicans in Basel in 1302 eighty beghards appeared in a procession begging for food and the next year three hundred of them came in processions begging for alms at a meeting of Franciscans at Colmar.[27] So outwardly similar were beghards to licensed mendicants that they were called *religiosi, conversi,* and sometimes even *fratres* by thirteenth-century sources.[28]

But the mendicant orders had many enemies who were quick to attack the beghards as easier game. Gautier de Coincy, who was no friend of the Franciscans, poured out most of his bile on the beghards and beguines.[29] Later, in the 1250s, William of St. Amour defended himself for what was patently a frontal attack on the mendicant orders by cleverly explaining that he only had in mind a criticism of men like beghards. Similarly, poets like Rutebeuf and Jean de Meung became famous for their verses against both friars and beguines.[30]

To make matters worse, the friars themselves were often opposed to the beghards. We have already noted the hostility to them on the part of the Franciscans Eudes Rigaud and Berthold of Regensburg; another example is that the beghards who tried to associate with the Franciscans at Colmar were rebuffed by the chapter there which published an edict in 1303 prohibiting its members from having contacts

26. Rutebeuf, *L'etat du monde,* ed. E. Faral and J. Bastin, *Oeuvres complètes de Rutebeuf* (Paris, 1959–60), I, 384: "Après si sont li mendiant/ Qui par la vile vont criant:/ 'Donez, por Dieu, du pain aus Frères!'" See further, McDonnell, p. 509, n. 31.

27. *Annales colmarienses maiores,* MGH SS, XVII, 227–28.

28. Since the German word for *conversus* is *Bekehrte,* some scholars have seen in this the origin of the name beghard. Thus F. Merzbacher, *Die Hexenprozesse in Franken* (Munich, 1957), p. 14: "Begharden, was soviel wie Bekehrte (conversi) bedeutet." One difficulty with this theory is that the earliest known use of the word *begart* is by the *Frenchman* Gautier de Coincy (ed. Vilamo-Pentti, as above, n. 13, p. 184, vv. 1532–35).

29. It is noteworthy that Gautier also compared beghards to Renard the Fox (ed. Vilamo-Pentti, p. 179), an image that would later be used to great effect against the friars, see C. Dahlberg, "Chaucer's Cock and Fox," *Journal of English and Germanic Philology,* LIII (1954), 277–90.

30. William of St. Amour, ed. E. Faral, "Les 'Responsiones' de Guillaume de Saint-Amour," AHDL, XXV/XXVI (1950–51), 342–43, and commentary 380–81 (William used the term *bonus valetus* instead of beghard); Rutebeuf (as above, n. 26), esp. I, 330–35; Jean de Meung's attack is described along with that of Rutebeuf in McDonnell, pp. 456–73.

with the semi-regulars.[31] But all that was just verbal. Wasting no words, the Dominican Robert the Bougre was the first to execute a beguine and in 1290 the lector of the Friars Minor at Colmar arrested beguines and beghards for heresy.[32] Once outright persecutions began in the fourteenth century, friars became leading persecutors (outside of a few notable exceptions in areas where they supervised beguinages), for the mendicant orders were generally most hostile to those groups outside the pale. This is a familiar historical phenomenon: those who feel insecure in their acceptance by society often become the most pious and vigorous opponents of those on the other side of the narrow fence.

So far as can be told, beghards and beguines were probably less hypocritical than some members of approved orders. Since becoming a beghard or beguine entailed the risk first of opprobrium and later of persecution, it is doubtful that many did so out of cynicism or shiftlessness. No doubt there were cases of beguinal laxity, but we will see later that beghards and beguines were often obliged by their own superiors to undergo appallingly ascetic regimens and suffer bodily torture. Surely most were motivated by piety and for that reason they always had their defenders despite the steady rain of abuse and intermittent papal anathemas. For example, a long south-German didactic poem of the fifteenth century referred on the one hand to lollards as companions of shameless nuns, but on the other praised the pure life of beghards and beguines as being holier than that of the clergy because they not only suffered hunger, thirst, and poverty, but also endured constant abuse for the sake of God.[33]

2. THE HERESY OF LAY PIETY

Charges of hypocrisy did not hamper the growth of the beguinal movement for most of the thirteenth century. This period was the

---

31. *Annales colmarienses maiores*, MGH SS, XVII, 217.

32. See below, pp. 64 and 62.

33. *Des Teufels Netz. Satirisch-Didaktisches Gedicht aus der ersten Hälfte des fünfzehnten Jahrhunderts*, ed. K. A. Barack (Stuttgart, 1863), on lollards p. 192, on beguines pp. 188–91, and on beghards pp. 193–99, e.g. lines 6091–6100: "Wan si lidend durch got/ Smachait und grossen spott/ Von der boesen welte,/ Anherren und och schelten./ Hunger, durst und armout/ Nemends als für guot,/ Das kain gaistlicher mer tuot./ Darumb fürends den hoechsten grad/ Den die hailig cristenhait hat,/ Und volgends cristo nach mit flisz...."

heroic age of the mendicant orders and beghards and beguines who imitated the friars in pursuing the *vita apostolica*, though derided by some, found official approbation. But toward the end of the thirteenth century a reaction began to set in. To a large degree beghards and beguines seem to have been victims of shifting sentiment concerning the friars. By the later thirteenth century the latter were losing much of their pristine zeal though enjoying many ecclesiastical privileges and their enemies began to take advantage of public disenchantment by pressing for restrictive legislation. The total effect of this was a far less favorable climate for experiments in apostolic living and beguines and beghards began to suffer accordingly. Not only did the secular clergy attempt to restrict their activities, but the friars, far from seeking a popular front, tried to protect themselves by attacking their left flank (if such anachronistic expressions be pardoned). Those beghards and beguines who were not intimidated reacted by pursuing their ideal of the apostolic life with more urgency than ever. The result was that they were charged with heresy not for laxity or religious indifference but for insubordinate zeal.

The first important milestone was the Second Council of Lyons of 1274. Three tracts written in advance to propose actions for the Council were all hostile to the beguinal movement for similar reasons.[34] One written by the secular cleric, Bishop Bruno of Olmütz, complained that men and women who belonged to no papally approved order still dressed and behaved themselves like friars, refused obedience to their parish clergy, and wandered about without discipline through the cities. Discipline, indeed, was Bruno's only concern, for he explicitly denied that any heresy existed among these people. A second report by the Dominican Humbert of Romans proposed that "poor religious women" should not be tolerated unless they had the wherewithal to support themselves without begging or wandering, a complaint which shows that this friar was fundamentally hostile to lay pursuit of the mendicant life. Most detailed and illuminating of the three tracts was one written by the Franciscan Gilbert of Tournai who claimed that certain beguines had translated the Bible

---

34. The best evaluation of these reports is by Grundmann RB, pp. 333–40, which, however, incorrectly attributes the last one to Simon of Tournai, a theologian who died in 1202. See also the translation of the pertinent passage in the last report by McDonnell, pp. 366–67.

into the Gallic idiom, that they were reading their vernacular commentaries not only in conventicles, but openly in public squares, and that he himself had seen one of their Bibles which Church officials had exhibited in Paris in order to display the many heresies and errors contained therein. Gilbert did not say what any of these heresies were, no doubt because he thought that the beguines' greatest crime was simply daring to translate and discuss the Bible even though they were mere laypeople. Here then we see that the basic criticism of beguines and beghards was for their intense, unlicensed lay piety and that their sharpest critics were the friars who themselves were to be on the defensive at Lyons.

Such attitudes made ecclesiastical action inevitable. The Second Council of Lyons repeated the ban of the Fourth Lateran on the creation of new orders, adding a corollary that all orders that had arisen after 1215 without papal confirmation were to be dissolved.[35] Although this did not mention beghards and beguines by name it no doubt was meant to apply to them as well as to other unlicensed religious associations. The ban of the Council of Lyons was followed by more specific German synodal legislation. Earlier German decrees had already inveighed against beguines for alleged indolence and licentiousness, but a synod of Trier in 1277 was the first to legislate against beghards who preached in streets and alleys because they supposedly spread heresies among the populace.[36] Likewise, a synod at Eichstätt in the 1280s, without explicitly mentioning beghards, warned against ignorant laymen who were delivering unauthorized sermons in secret and leading simple souls into error.[37]

The climax of attacks on the beguinal movement for unauthorized and excessive pursuit of the apostolic life came at the following ecumenical council which met in Vienne from 1311 to 1312. In the

35. J. D. Mansi, *Sacrorum conciliorum nova et amplissima collectio* (Florence and Venice, 1759–98), XXIV, 96.

36. Fredericq, I, 141–42, #147. There is some doubt about the dating of this synod, but the authoritative investigation of F. Arens, "Zur Datierung einer Trierischen Synode des 13. Jahrhunderts," ZfK, XXXIII (1912), 84–105, followed by J. Heydenreich, "Zu den Trierer Synodalstatuten des 13. Jh.," *Zeitschrift der Savigny Stiftung für Rechtsgeschichte, Kanonische Abteilung,* XXV (1936), 478–85, places it in 1277.

37. *Pastoralblatt des Bistums Eichstätt,* XXXII (1885), 74.

next chapter we will discuss in detail the actions of this council insofar as they were related to the composition of *Ad nostrum*, a decree which defined the heresy of the Free Spirit and maintained that it was to be found among beghards and beguines. Here we will limit ourselves to the decree *Cum de quibusdam mulieribus* which was equally fateful for the future of the beguinal movement. This decree spoke only of women "commonly known as beguines" who were not regulars because they neither took vows of obedience, nor gave up private ownership, nor followed an approved rule. Nonetheless, it complained, they wore a special habit and some "as if insane" discoursed on the Trinity and the divine essence. They spread opinions contrary to the articles of the faith and sacraments of the Church, leading simple people into error under the pretense of sanctity. For these reasons, the decree (issued by the Pope with the approval of the council) forbade women to follow the beguinal way of life. But after stating this prohibition, it concluded with a concession that truly pious women might be allowed to live penitently, with or without vows of chastity, in communal houses.[38] This escape clause contradicted the whole purport of the decree and was the product either of a later revision or disagreement within the council or uncertainty about how to distinguish between "good" and "bad" beguines.

The decrees of Vienne, to be known as the "Clementines," after Pope Clement V who presided at Vienne, were not immediately put into effect. The council had not put most into finished form at the time it was abruptly terminated in May 1312 and Pope Clement wanted to polish them and send them to the Universities but was stopped by his death in 1314. A long vacancy preceded the election of John XXII who made his own revisions of the Clementines and finally published them in October of 1317.[39] As soon as the terms of *Cum de quibusdam* were known, authorities began to harass and dissolve orthodox beguinages all over northern Europe. A synod of the diocese

38. Fredericq, I, 167–68, #171, which falsely dates all the statutes of Vienne to 1311 instead of 1312. The text is also in E. Friedberg, *Corpus iuris canonici* (Leipzig, 1879–81), II, 1169, and many other collections. An English translation which omits the escape clause is in McDonnell, p. 524.

39. Some of the Clementines might not even have been discussed at Vienne at all, but *Cum de quibusdam* must have been since it refers to being a conciliar action in its text.

of Mainz, for example, in 1318 invoked the newly published constitutions to excommunicate all who could be considered beguines by status, habit, name, or any other means.[40]

To complicate matters John XXII's bull *Sancta Romana*, published on December 30, 1317, gave the impression that Franciscan tertiaries, often difficult to distinguish from beguines, were to be persecuted as well.[41] Thus the contemporary chronicle of the Franciscan Province of Strassburg noted with horror that in 1318 many German prelates forced devout women to discard their penitential dress, give up their vows of chastity, and return to the world: worse, they even ordered the same for members of the Franciscan third order "and in this way tried to involve the Friars Minor as patrons of condemned persons in the sentence of excommunication."[42] Thirty years later the memory of this persecution was so vivid that the Franciscan John of Winterthur wrote a more detailed account, full of exclamations of shock and sorrow, punctuated with a lamentation from Jeremiah, and terminating with an *exemplum* which showed the orthodox beguines and tertiaries triumphant.[43] John did not question the justice of condemning beguines who followed no approved rule, but he believed that *Cum de quibusdam* clearly exempted pious women who lived in houses and served the Lord in a spirit of humility, as in fact it did.

In response to this situation John XXII, on August 13, 1318, issued the bull *Racio recta* which ordered the clergy to protect all beguines who led stable lives and refrained from disputing about the Trinity, divine essence, or sacraments of the Church.[44] But he was careful to add that these concessions did not imply that the beguines

---

40. Mansi, XXV, 627–28.
41. Friedberg, II, 1213–14. On the interpretation of *Sancta Romana*, McDonnell, p. 536, and Leff, p. 332.
42. *Chronica Provinciae Argentinensis*, ed. L. Lemmens, AFH, IV (1911), 682–83.
43. Johannes Vitoduranus, *Chronicon*, ed. F. Baethgen, MGH SS, new series, III, 73–75. Part of John's account is translated by McDonnell, pp. 530–31, but this omits the story of the bet of a hateful priest who was certain that the condemned beguines would never be rehabilitated as well as John's attempt to distinguish between "good" and "bad" beguines.
44. Fredericq, II, 72–74, #44. John XXII addressed himself to the problem of the Franciscan tertiaries in the bulls *Etsi apostolicae* and *Dilectos filios* of 1319. Best on this subject is M. Bihl, "De Tertio Ordine S. Francisci in provincia Germaniae superioris sive Argentinensi syntagma," AFH, XIV (1921), 168–82.

were to be recognized as an approved order and he continued to approve the search for heretics among them. *Racio recta* in fact afforded orthodox beguines a time of peace, but it turned out to be only a temporary lull: since *Cum de quibusdam* and *Ad nostrum* remained in the corpus of canon law and since even *Racio recta* authorized the search for heretics in beguinages, orthodox beguines and beghards were to become game for inquisitors intermittently throughout the next hundred years.

By that time the term "beghard" was often used as a synonym for heretic of the Free Spirit and this confusion has led many historians to believe that every late medieval persecution of beguines or beghards reflected an incidence of Free-Spirit heresy. But such was demonstrably not the case. For example, during the lull between the issuance of *Racio recta* and organized campaigns of the Papal Inquisition against the beguinal movement in the second half of the fourteenth century there was an examination of beghards in Metz in 1334 ordered by the Bishop of that city and directed by an episcopal inquisitor named Garin.[45] The accused called themselves "brothers of the highest poverty" (*"fratres de altissima paupertate"*). They explicitly claimed to be following the example of Christ and the apostles in having property only in common, saying that they preferred to obey the Gospels rather than the pope or any prelates. They owned nothing—not even their habits—and considered God alone to be master of all their goods. Though they lived in houses they begged for their living and handed over the proceeds to their head, who redistributed them as he saw fit. For these reasons they said, probably with justice, that the religious orders did not imitate Christ nor follow the precepts of evangelical poverty as much as they did.

Their hostile rivalry with the established orders led the beghards of Metz to form an organization of their own. The head of each house was called on apostolic principles neither prelate, master, doctor, nor rector, but simply servant. Every year the inmates of all houses would

45. The record of this examination is ed. Döllinger, 403–406. A similar document that need not be analyzed here at length because it is less detailed is an anonymous and undated (probably fourteenth-century) inquisitorial report that describes *fratres de paupere vita*, ed. Wattenbach, 523–26. These brothers, like those of Metz, thought that they could reach "the highest state of perfection in Christian and evangelical life" and practiced great asceticism. The report says nothing about radical mysticism.

hold large congregations which they attended on the pretext of going on pilgrimages. At these meetings about ten of them who were judged to be the most "prudent" would make decisions concerning the supply of food and other material matters, while another twenty would decide on organizational matters which they then only revealed to the most trustworthy. The master who presided over these congregations would say that they were called together by the Holy Spirit rather than by the Roman Church.[46] But it was the persecution of the Church that forced them into heresy. The beghards refused to acknowledge that they could be excommunicated and said that it was mortally sinful for ecclesiastical or secular judges to make use of information that had been disclosed in confession—both practices that they had probably suffered from themselves. Likewise, they refused to take oaths because, as the inquisitor noted, they did not want to incriminate others when they were examined.[47] They also were opposed to the taking of life, even, as they said, "for justice against robbers, murderers, or heretics," which shows that they did not consider themselves to have been heretics at all.

There is no mention in the record of the examination at Metz of radical mysticism. The most dominant characteristics of the accused seem Waldensian, and since Waldensians had existed in Metz it has been argued that the beghards of 1334 were their descendants.[48] But

46. I cannot agree with the view of Erbstösser, p. 64, that each house had two functionaries, a "servant" and a "master." The latter term was mentioned only in connection with the large congregations and it is clear that the official termed "servant" was in fact only the head of an individual house. On the basis of the reference to secret decisions, Erbstösser also sees a sharp distinction between "esoteric" and "exoteric" circles which he then uses to explain the fact that the document contains no explicit mention of antinomian mysticism. According to this theory, the beghards examined were only novices who knew nothing about the esoteric speculations of the others, but the only secrets the document refers to are of an organizational, not doctrinal, nature, and it is furthermore inconceivable that a mass arrest of beghards would include only novices and not the most important functionaries.

47. Leff, p. 361, incorrectly paraphrases "ipsi exponunt verba evangelii de juramento contra glossas ordinarias et expositiones sanctorum doctorum" as "they did not accept the official interpretation of the bible by the doctors and *sancti*." The point at issue was only the matter of oaths not the entire Catholic exegetical tradition.

48. Henri J. Delacroix, *Essai sur le mysticisme speculatif en Allemagne au 14ᵉ siècle* (Paris, 1900), pp. 114–17.

this does not account for their semi-monastic organization and the many practices that were typical of contemporary beghards. For example, there is an impressive similarity between the description of how the beghards of Metz received a novice and an account later to be examined of how one John of Brünn was received into a house of beghards in Cologne.[49] Thus it is incorrect to say that "this description has no real bearing upon the Beguines and Beghards."[50] Far from having no bearing on the subject, Garin's inquisitorial document shows that beghards could be persecuted for their unlicensed apostolic conduct and organization without their having subscribed to the heresy of the Free Spirit.

Two years later beguines were examined for heresy in Magdeburg. Unfortunately, the only report we have of this comes from an unreliable chronicle which says that the women blasphemed against Christ and the saints in articles so detestable that the chronicler did not wish to repeat them, but after their examination they repented and were immediately released without penalties.[51] This seems like lenient treatment unless we concede that their heresy was not so shocking as the report made out. In fact the chronicler gives us a different sort of clue about the beliefs of the beguines of Magdeburg when he says that they called themselves "of the high spirit." The Augustinian lector in Magdeburg at that time was Jordan of Quedlinburg who mentioned the term "high spirit" in one of his sermons written without question after 1336 when he must have heard about or possibly even examined the Magdeburg beguines (he is known to have been an inquisitor in two other cases).[52] Jordan says in this passage that

49. Cf. Metz (Döllinger, 404): ". . .modus eorum talis est, quod iste, qui vult assumere habitum venit ad praesentiam aliorum et genu flexo petit admitti ad societatem ipsorum, dicens quod desideret esse pauper. . ." with John of Brünn (ed. Wattenbach, 529): ". . . intravi domum pauperum . . . et cum in predicta domum essem, genua flexi. . . petens me ex caritate recipi. . . procurator eorum quesivit a me, quid ego apud pauperes et contemptibiles facerem, utrum paupertatem voluntariam (observare) et ab omnibus contempni vellem. Cui ego humiliter respondi: 'Vere, frater etc.'" More similarities follow. On the confession of John of Brünn, see below pp. 108–12.

50. Leff, p. 362.

51. *Gesta archiepiscoporum Magdeburgensium*, MGH SS, XIV, 434.

52. *Opus postillarum et sermonum de tempore* (Strassburg, 1483), fol. 183vb. R. Arbesman and W. Hümpfner (eds.), *Jordan of Saxony, liber vitasfratrum* (New York, 1943), p. xix, indicate that Jordan was still working on the sermons

certain people scorn to hear the word of God preached in church because they consider themselves to be of the "high spirit" and think that they are worthy of hearing only the highest things. It is hardly necessary to add that there is a great difference between scorning preachers for not being "high" or holy enough (many medieval sermons were deliberately delivered in a "low" style) and blaspheming against Christ and the saints.[53]

In France a generation later two unlicensed mendicants actually met their deaths because of persecution. In 1365 Pope Urban V ordered French Inquisitors and the Bishop of Paris to be on the lookout for "sons of Belial of both sexes commonly known as *begardi* or *beguini*."[54] There were no known results and probably nothing further would have developed had it not been for the favor shown to the Inquisition by King Charles V, who, on February 2, 1373, paid ten pounds *parisis* to the Dominican Inquisitor of the province of France, Jacques de Morey, to defray the expenses of the latter in proceeding against the "*turlupins*" and "*turlupines*." A month later Pope Gregory XI commended Charles for the zeal he had shown in aiding the work of the Inquisition against "the sect of beghards who are otherwise called *turlupins*."[55]

The last quotation shows that the word *turlupin* was a French synonym for beghard.[56] All we know about the nature of the case

---

in this collection in 1365, but A. Zumkeller, *Manuskripte von Werken der Autoren des Augustiner-Eremitenordens in mitteleuropäischen Bibliotheken* (Würzburg, 1966), pp. 301–302, refers to sermons on the *Pater noster* from the same collection that were copied in MS Clm 8151 dated 1348. Cases in which Jordan acted as an inquisitor and as reported by the *Gesta archiepiscoporum Magdeburgensium* are discussed above p. 28 and below pp. 128–30.

53. The only other use of the term "high spirit" that I know of comes from a sermon of Tauler, which indicates that he was called this himself. (See below p. 189) Thus the beguines of Magdeburg were perhaps as orthodox as he.

54. J.-M. Vidal, *Bullaire de l'inquisition française au xive siècle* (Paris, 1913), pp. 375–77, #257–58. The first bull is also in Fredericq, I, 205–206, #208.

55. The King's payment in Ducange, *Glossarium mediae et infimae latinitatis*, under word *turlupini*; Gregory's bull in Vidal, pp. 396–97, #276.

56. The earliest known use of the word reflects its range of meanings. This comes from the *Lamentations de Matheolus*, ed. A. G. van Hamel (Paris, 1892), a free translation of a late thirteenth-century work executed by Jehan le Fèvre in 1371–72. The original Latin had a long attack on beguines which runs in the French translation: "Au jour d'hui soubs turlupinage/ Trouveroit on en tapin-

against those persecuted by Jacques de Morey comes from chronicle sources which relate that he and the Bishop of Angers, then acting as a vicar for the Bishop of Paris, proceeded in the first week of July 1372 against the "sect, habit, and books of the *turlupins*."[57] (It should be noted that the Bishop of Angers was Milo de Dormans, a leading adviser of Charles V, who, despite his episcopal office, lived at court and was president of the *Chambre des Comptes*.) On a Sunday they burned the vestments and the books of the heretics at the Place de Grève and on the following day they burned at the pig market a young woman called Jeanne or Péronne Daubenton along with the body of a male confederate who had died in the episcopal prison during his trial two weeks earlier (his corpse had been preserved in lime for the grisly ceremony). The sources add only that the *turlupins* preferred to be known as the "association of the poor." Since nothing is said about mystical or antinomian beliefs one must conclude that, like many German beguines, Jeanne Daubenton and her associates were seekers of the *vita apostolica* whose greatest crime consisted in being unlicensed and bereft of influential support.[58]

Meanwhile Inquisitors in Germany were persecuting beghards and beguines with papal encouragement until influential parties began to complain. In a bull of April 1374 addressed to all prelates in Germany, Brabant, and Flanders, Pope Gregory XI answered an unidentified plea for the protection of "poor people" of both sexes who lived humbly and honestly in poverty and chastity, visited church regularly, and involved themselves in no errors by admitting that he was not well informed about the problem and by ordering his prelates to report all that they knew about it.[59] Though he used neither the

---

age/ Envie, dol, ipocrisie,/ Pensee par fraude brisie,/ Especialment es beguines." (van Hamel, p. 90). L. Spitzer, "Turlupin," *Modern Language Notes*, LXI (1946), 104–108, attempts to provide an etymology based on an obscene connotation which is not found in the sources.

57. Passages from *Les Grandes Chroniques de France* and the *Croniques de France* of Robert Gaguin in P. Beuzart, *Les hérésies pendant le Moyen Age et la Réforme dans la région de Douai, d'Arras et au pays de l'Alleu* (Le Puy, 1912), pp. 52–53.

58. In February 1373 Gregory XI ordered the French Inquisitor to absolve all those *beguins* (a name he equated with *turlupins* and lollards) who desired to return to the bosom of the Church, provided that their repentance was sincere and that they undertook suitable penance (Vidal, pp. 393–94, #274).

59. Fredericq, I, 228–31, #220, from Mosheim, pp. 394–98. Another copy is

term "beghard" nor "beguine," obviously to avoid an appearance of inconsistency after he had already attacked both in no uncertain terms in earlier bulls of 1372 or 1373,[60] there could have been no doubt about the subject of his order.

Even then the persecutions did not stop. The Bishop of Strassburg ordered a campaign against beguines in August of 1374, as we will see later, and beghards and beguines were still being harassed by an Inquisitor in Cologne. In February or March of 1375, the magistrates there complained to the Pope that a Dominican Inquisitor was examining "poor men and women who begged according to evangelic counsels," and was posing such difficult questions that even a gifted theologian could hardly answer them without great deliberation and perusal of books.[61] The magistrates went on to explain that the Inquisitor was acting counter to a decision of secular clerics who had already ruled that the people in question (obviously beghards and beguines) had never deviated from the faith, but were good Christians who served God. Moved no doubt by such appeals, Gregory XI finally intervened in favor of orthodox beghards and beguines in the bull *Ad audientiam nostram* of December 1377.[62] Again avoiding the terms beghard and beguine, he wrote of "poor people of both sexes" who had been molested by episcopal officers and papal Inquisitors even though their faith was pure, and he ordered that this should stop. As long as the *"pauperes"* remained orthodox they were to be protected, and if any had been excommunicated they were to be returned to the arms of the Church. Thus Gregory restored the distinction between "good" and "bad" beguines arrived at by John XXII more than half a century before, but, as we will see, *Ad audientiam nostram* just initiated another lull rather than a real end to persecutions.

---

ed. G. Schmidt, *UB der Stadt Halberstadt,* I (*Geschichtsquellen der Provinz Sachsen,* VII) (Halle, 1878), 463–64, #574.

60. Ed. P. Kehr and G. Schmidt, *Päbstliche Urkunden und Regesten aus den Jahren 1353–1378.* . . . (*Geschichtsquellen der Provinz Sachsen,* XXII) (Halle, 1889), 295, #1081–84.

61. L. Ennen and G. Eckertz, *Quellen zur Geschichte der Stadt Köln* (Cologne, 1860–79), V, 88–90, #82.

62. Fredericq, I, 237–38, from Mosheim, pp. 401–402. Another, better, copy is edited in *UB Halberstadt,* I, 476–78, #589.

3. CONRAD OF MEGENBERG AND JOHN WASMOD OF HOMBURG

Final evidence that many fourteenth-century beghards and beguines were called heretics merely because they sought the apostolic life comes from the two most detailed fourteenth-century German polemics against them.

The prolific canon of Regensburg, Conrad of Megenberg, attacked beghards and beguines as a device for agitating against the friars. Part of his polemic, published in the seventeenth and eighteenth centuries as *De erroribus begehardorum*,[63] has frequently been used by historians on the assumption that it was a separate tract, but in fact it was the first chapter of a larger work, written in Regensburg about 1364–65 entitled *Lacrima ecclesiae*. Fortunately there are two manuscripts of the entire work that allow us to examine Conrad's attack in its proper context.[64] The *Lacrima ecclesiae* was actually a polemic against the mendicant orders, an intent shown best by Conrad's later title of it as *Tractatus contra mendicantes*. It begins by attacking the beghards and adds an additional chapter against the beguines (not contained in the fragment *De erroribus begehardorum*), but these were just preliminaries. The bulk of the tract was aimed at the friars and shows that Conrad was less concerned with the alleged heretics as such than with using them as a wedge to drive against his real enemies.

This, of course, did not make his opening polemics any milder. He complained that despite the decrees of Vienne the menace of beghards was growing because no prelates took action against them. (He made no mention of the Inquisition, then at a peak of activity, probably because it was directed by friars.) According to Conrad, most beghards were able-bodied "rustics" or "mechanics" who had

63. Most accessible in J. Gretser, *Opera omnia* (Regensburg, 1734–41), XII, part 2, 98–99.
64. The discovery and identification of *Lacrima ecclesiae* was made by H. Meyer, "*Lacrima ecclesiae*, neue Forschungen zu den Schriften Konrads von Megenberg," *Neues Archiv der Gesellschaft für ältere deutsche Geschichtskunde*, XXXIX (1914), 469–503. The two MSS, both of the fifteenth century, are Wolfenb., Helmst., 876, fol. 73v–94v, and Trier, Priesterseminar 81, fol. 121v–144v. I use the former.

no knowledge of letters and preferred a life of rootless begging to hard work. He maintained that they deceived beguines and good women in secret conventicles with their false teachings, but we must remember that the deception of women was a figure from Paul's Second Epistle to Timothy without which no medieval polemic against hypocritical mendicants could be complete.

Conrad claimed to have met two beghards himself. The first was a Swabian who was arrested in Regensburg for teaching that man can become the equal of Christ by means of good works and affirming all eight articles of *Ad nostrum* (i.e. the heresy of the Free Spirit) and who supposedly died blaspheming the sacraments in an episcopal dungeon. The second was one John of Mechlin (Brabant?) who, acting like a priest, preached throughout upper Germany and attracted large crowds not only of the simple, but also of clerics and nobles. All called him "master," but Conrad thought that he was entirely ignorant of Scripture. John preached obscure Christological errors and tried to perform miracles similar to modern carnival tricks. He also allegedly tried to seduce innocent women by secretly whispering to them in their sleep that he was an angel or the Holy Spirit come to impregnate them with a child who would become the equal of John the Baptist. To this Conrad added, like many a teller of tales, "God knows that I do not lie." Conrad must have called John of Mechlin a beghard only because he was a wandering religious charlatan. This probability is confirmed by Conrad's statement that heretics like "poets," "poor men of Lyons," and others go about in the guise of beghards, which shows that his definition of beghard was so lose as to include wandering scholars and Waldensians.[65]

Conrad's description of beguines or "*sorores*" in the next chapter relies heavily on the decrees *Cum de quibusdam* and *Racio recta*.[66] He insists that beguines have not desisted from the evil practices attributed to them in those documents and therefore should be disbanded. It is in this chapter that his hostility to the mendicant orders first comes to the surface. He describes the close relations between beguines and friars in defiance of obligations to the parish clergy and sharply attacks the friars for their support of the proscribed women.

---

65. MS Wolfenb., *Helmst.*, 876, fol. 75v, differs from Gretser's edition, 99H, in the addition of the term "*poete.*"

66. MS *cit.*, fol. 75v–78v.

(In fact only friars in certain areas supported beguines, but Conrad might also have been thinking of Franciscan tertiaries.) He also added some details concerning nomenclature, saying that beguines in some parts wished to be called "good daughters" (*"bone filie"*), just as beghards in Alsace had changed their name to lollards and those in Bavaria to "little brothers" (*"fraterculi"*) in order to avoid the stigma attached to the name beghard.[67] These terms were probably accurate, but Conrad's remark cannot explain the origin of the word "lollard" because this was first used in the Low Countries, not Alsace, decades earlier. Conrad came closest to charging beguines with doctrinal heresy in a bit of characteristically polemical logic. After criticizing them for their way of life, he went on to say that they were to be suspected of upholding the errors of *Ad nostrum* because they seldom confessed to parish priests or took the Eucharist from them![68] But he could refer to no specific examples of heretical women.

When it came to proposing remedies in the second part of *Lacrima ecclesiae* for the problems listed in the first, Conrad had the mild suggestion that both beghards and beguines should be denounced in public sermons and the men forced to work, another indication that it was mendicant conduct that most upset him.[69] Unless he knew much more than he wrote, it may be assumed that he had direct knowledge of only one Free Spirit and one religious eccentric; and since his tract was devoted primarily to castigating the friars it may be concluded that the latter were his major concern.

Unlike Conrad of Megenberg's polemic, John Wasmod of Homburg's *Tractatus contra hereticos, beckardos, lulhardos, et swestriones* has been discounted by historians as a useful source even though it was the work of an Inquisitor. John was a leading theologian from the secular clergy who became rector of the University of Heidelberg in 1399 and before then was an Inquisitor in the province of Mainz. It is true that his tract, written in the form of a sermon sometime shortly after 1396, is a farrago of citations from texts mixed with reports

---

67. *Ibid.*, fol. 77v: "Et sic beghardi nomen sui status in aliquibus locis propter constitutionem Viennensium concilium mutaverunt quia in Alsatia lullehardi et in Bavaria fraterculi nominantur, sic begine huius bone filie volunt nuncupari in plerisque locis. . . ."

68. *Ibid.*, fol. 77v–78r.

69. *Ibid.*, fol. 87v–88v.

of contemporaries, but it also includes observations from his own inquisitorial experience.[70] It used to be argued that he ignorantly confused beghards and beguines with Waldensians,[71] but beguines were in fact similar to Waldensians in their pursuit of apostolic piety and Wasmod of Homburg's testimony just confirms this.

Much of John's polemic was conventional and no doubt copied from other sources. For example, his criticism of beghards for shouting "bread for God's sake" in busy streets even on feast days instead of staying in their homes was probably taken from earlier legislation from the province of Mainz that John must certainly have had among his inquisitorial records.[72] He also reiterated the familiar charges of immorality: allegedly beghards gorged themselves on rich foods and guzzled fine wines in the houses of the rich; worse, they indulged their unnatural urges in disgraceful homosexual acts. But scholars have already pointed out that these charges are inconsistent with many other passages that describe apostolic conduct and austerities.[73]

According to John—and here he seems to have been on his own—the beghards of the Rhineland called themselves "followers of Christ and the Apostles," "poor good youths," and, like the friars, "*fratres.*" They thought of their way of life as being superior to that of the Church and therefore rejected the sacramental system without caring about excommunication. In keeping with this they developed a special liturgical terminology that emphasized their humility: they said "I am a poor boy" instead of "I am a poor man" and, impersonally, "it is said to you" instead of "I say to you." They also preferred simplicity

70. Ed. A. Schmidt, *Archiv für mittelrheinische Kirchengeschichte*, XIV (1962), 336–86. See 340: ". . . ex relacione fide dignorum plurium et ex propria eorum confessione. . . scribam."

71. This was the view of Haupt, "Beiträge," 547–56, which influenced the statement of Leff, p. 363, that "as an insight into either the heresy of the Free Spirit or the Beguines and Beghards. . . the treatise is valueless," and the similar contention of Eva G. Neumann, *Rheinisches Beginen-und Begardenwesen* (Meisenheim/Glan, 1960), p. 158. The tract does mention Waldensian heretics condemned in 1392 at Bingen, but this appears in a prefatory section before John begins his attack on beghards and beguines *per se.*

72. On this legislation see below, pp. 67–68.

73. E.g. G. Ritter, *Die Heidelberger Universität, I. Das Mittelalter* (Heidelberg, 1936), p. 351: "[er] berichtet in einem Atem über sexuelle Orgien, lasterhafte Verkommenheit und überspannten asketischen Eifer, so dass man unwillkürlich misstrauisch wird."

of expression and did not invoke the names of the virgin and all the saints, but said "listen to my guilt for God's sake."

John was particularly annoyed with patricians of the Rhenish cities who made it difficult for authorities to execute papal bulls against beghards and beguines by their determined support of the latter. This was no doubt a reference to his own experience and shows that influential parties were still trying to protect orthodox beghards and beguines in the 1390s as they had in the 1370s. The pro-beguinal party said correctly that the Roman Church had issued many constitutions in favor of "such simple people," but John was able to cite the uncompromisingly hostile *Ad perpetuam rei* promulgated against beghards and beguines by Pope Boniface IX in 1396.[74] When the papal legislation was enforced, the victims insisted that they were not beghards or beguines and proclaimed that they did not believe in the errors ascribed to them.[75] Insofar as these had to do with gross immorality their protestations must have been just since it may be taken as certain that the Rhenish magnates who so aroused John's ire were not sheltering homosexuals or arrant hedonists. On the other hand, John's description of apostolic beliefs has the ring of truth in its detail. Certainly it was not heresy but the mendicant way of life that he objected to when he concluded his work with a call for beghards to return to honest work so that they might have a life of grace and future glory.

Throughout the fourteenth century, then, beghards and beguines were persecuted for heresy when very often it was only their simple piety and the issue of discipline that was at stake. We can see how they sought the apostolic ideal by taking such names as "brothers of the highest poverty," "the association of the poor," "good daughters," "little brothers," "followers of Christ and the Apostles," "poor good youths," and simply "brothers" and "sisters," but the friars, who also called themselves "brothers," often resented them as rivals and the secular clergy resented their imitation of the friars and their frequent unwillingness to obey parish priests. Worse, their uncompromising pursuit of the *vita apostolica* must have embarrassed more worldly

---

74. See below, p. 148.

75. Ed. Schmidt, 354: ". . . agitati per Romanas et apostolicas constituciones et excommunicaciones se beckardos vel beginas non esse affirmant nec aliquibus erroribus implicati. . . ."

members of both regular and secular clergy while their houses were tempting fruits for confiscation. The popes who ordered procedures against them thought that they would earn reputations as reformers (which they sorely needed) by becoming hammers of heresy and found unprotected beguines obvious targets. But despite all this it is doubtful that there would have been so many persecutions had it not been for the existence among the Clementine decrees of legislation which explicitly associated the beghards and beguines with antinomian heresy. It is to the origins of that legislation that we must now turn.

Chapter Three

THE CONDEMNATION

As if their history had been plotted by the Red Queen, heretics of the Free Spirit were condemned before very many of them can be proved to have existed. In the first chapter we saw that there was a great fear of antinomian heresy in the later Middle Ages that was often unjustified by actual circumstances, and in the second we saw that beghards and beguines were subjected to abuse and persecution for many reasons that had nothing to do with the upholding of doctrinal error. What are we to make, then, of the fact that in 1312 the Council of Vienne in the decree *Ad nostrum* charged beghards and beguines with upholding a radically mystical and antinomian heresy? Was this a figment of the fathers' imagination or, if not, how much of the charge rested on reliable information?

1. THE THIRTEENTH CENTURY

What we must look for is evidence of extreme mysticism among beghards and beguines before the meeting of the Council of Vienne. We have seen that a mystical heresy did exist in the Swabian Ries in the later thirteenth century and that beghards and beguines were charged with being sowers of heresy at about the same time. But the Swabian heretics were not called beghards and beguines and the beghards and beguines we have seen charged with heresy were not accused of upholding radical mysticism. There are other examples of beghards and beguines being disciplined in the thirteenth century, but most are inconclusive. In 1286 the beghards of Malines were expelled from their convent "because of their excesses or other reasons;" in 1290 two beguines and two beghards were taken into custody at Colmar on suspicion of heresy and others were arrested in Basel on the same charge; and much farther down the Rhine the Augustinians of Mainz severed a contract with a beguine named Katherina in 1296 because she was undependable in her wandering life and was allegedly spreading errors.[1] But in none of these cases do we have a statement of how the accused erred and it is quite possible that they were being harassed merely because of their pursuit of the *vita apostolica*.

In fact the only known source that explicitly connects mystical antinomianism with thirteenth-century beghards or beguines is the *Annales suevici* of Martin Crusius. This reports for the year 1261 that beghards entered cloisters in Swabia and persuaded many of the inhabitants that it was better to live without a rule and serve God through "liberty of the spirit."[2] But we can hardly rely on this since Crusius wrote in the late sixteenth century and the only evidence he cites is a lost history of Felix Fabri, a Dominican of Ulm who wrote in the late fifteenth century at a time when beghard was often understood as a synonym for Free-Spirit heretic.

Perhaps, however, it is wrong in elucidating the origins of *Ad nostrum* to look for mystical *heretics* among beghards and beguines instead of looking for mystical beghards and beguines who were *orthodox*. Many who took the *vita apostolica* most seriously believed that it was a mystical path. For them the imitation of Christ was not just a means for becoming *like* Christ, but more a means of becoming *one with* Christ or having immediate knowledge of Him. In particular this became a goal in the thirteenth century of cloistered nuns and beguines. Most famous among the former were the German "saints of

1. J. Vannérus, "Documents concernant les Bogards de Malines," *Bulletin de la commission royale d'histoire de Belgique*, LXXX (1911), 237–38 (also cited by Grundmann RB, p. 354); *Annales colmarienses maiores*, MGH SS, XVII, 217 (text cited by Grundmann RB, p. 433); Eva G. Neumann, *Rheinisches Beginen- und Begardenwesen* (Meisenheim/Glan, 1960), pp. 145–46. citing MS Staatsarchiv Darmstadt 86.

2. (Frankfurt, 1595–96), II, 99: "Hi persuadebant multis coenobiis, ut sine regula viverent, melius sic deo serviri posse per libertatem spiritus." This text was first noted by Mosheim, p. 199.

Helfta"—the two Gertrudes and Mechthild of Hackeborn—and the Flemish Beatrice of Nazareth, and among the latter the German Mechthild of Magdeburg and the Flemish beguine Hadewich. Actually our distinction between nuns and beguines is artificial since relationships between the two groups were very close: Beatrice of Nazareth was trained as a young girl by beguines, Hadewich probably knew Beatrice's work, and Mechthild of Magdeburg ended her life as a nun among the saints of Helfta.

One colorful example of the fervor among beguines for union with God is a story told by the mid-thirteenth-century Dominican, Thomas of Cantimpré. A certain canon regular preaching on the first day of May in the beguinage of Cantimpré near Cambrai said that the human soul can become so inseparably one with God that its union is like the inseparable mixture of water with wine (an image borrowed from the *De diligendo Deo* of St. Bernard). This analogy worked up the preacher's springtime audience to such a pitch that, according to Thomas, who was probably there himself, one woman "bubbled over like new wine in an air-tight container, burst a blood vessel, and died on the spot.[3] Better evidence still is the ecstatic mystical poetry of the beguines Hadewich and Mechthild of Magdeburg. This is not the place to discuss these works in detail since they have been well treated elsewhere.[4] Suffice it to say that they expressed a *Minnemystik* or "bride-mysticism" which daringly, often erotically, compared the union of the soul and Christ to that of bride and bridegroom. No scholar today doubts that such mysticism was orthodox and many regard the strophes of Hadewich and Mechthild as worthy precursors of the works of Eckhart and Ruysbroeck.

Only recently has some question been raised regarding the case of Hadewich. Unfortunately we are very poorly informed about the career of this Flemish beguine and do not even know for certain when she lived, although it seems most probable that she flourished in the first half of the thirteenth century. The leading modern authorities,

3. Thomas of Cantimpré, *Bonum universale de apibus*, ed. G. Colvener (Douai, 1627), II, 49, 2, p. 442. A. Combes, *Essai sur la critique de Ruysbroeck par Gerson* (Paris, 1945–59), I, 673–74, edits the same passage.

4. Axters, I, 335–82; J. van Mierlo, "Hadewijch, une mystique flamande du treizième siècle, *Revue d'ascétique et de mystique*, V (1924), 269–89, 380–404; Jean-Baptiste Porion, *Hadewijch d'Anvers* (Paris, 1954); J. Ancelet-Hustache, *Mechtilde de Magdebourg* (Paris, 1926).

including the Jesuit van Mierlo and the Dominican Axters, believe that Hadewich's mystical poems are not only orthodox, but of outstanding literary quality—indeed, "some of the best pieces of medieval Christian lyricism."[5] But it has now been argued from the difficult and elliptical language of one of her poems that she herself thought that she had once fallen into errors which she later regretted.[6] Possibly, though the evidence is not conclusive, she even had to justify herself before an inquisitor. If this is so, the investigator in question must have been the notorious Robert the Bougre, a former heretic who had joined the Dominican order and who conducted extensive heresy hunts in northern France and the Low Countries during the 1230s and early 1240s. Whatever Hadewich's own case, she tells us in her "List of the Perfect" that Robert actually had a certain beguine executed "because of her righteous *Minne*."[7] Hadewich's assumption that this woman was an innocent martyr is confirmed by sufficient evidence that Robert was at best overzealous in his proceedings.[8] And her own willingness to renounce any errors she might have made shows that despite her mystical zeal she was most anxious to stay on the right side of orthodoxy.

There is no evidence that mystical beguines became more radical in the course of the thirteenth century and it is certainly noteworthy that there were no further persecutions. Of course many clerics always feared with some reason that mysticism, even if orthodox, tended to pose a dangerous alternative to concentration on the sacraments. Mechthild of Magdeburg was the target of criticism that probably

---

5. See above note. My quotation is from L. Génicot, *La spiritualité médiévale* (Paris, 1958), p. 88.

6. A. Brounts, "Hadewijch en de ketterij naar het vijfde Visioen," *Handelingen XXII der Koninklijke Zuidnederlandse Maatschappij voor Taal-en Letterkunde en Geschiedenis* (1968), 15–78.

7. *Visionen*, ed. J. van Mierlo, cited by Grundmann RB, p. 185, n. 32: "die meester Robbaert doedde om hare gherechte minne."

8. On Robert's career, C. H. Haskins, "Robert le Bougre and the Beginnings of the Inquisition in Northern France," in Haskins' *Studies in Medieval Culture* (Oxford, 1929). A good indication of Robert's lack of care to discriminate among the "heretics" he arrested is the remark of Matthew Paris, *Chronica majora*, MGH SS, XXVIII, 146: "Ipsos autem nomine vulgare Bugaros appellavit, sive essent Paterini sive Joviniani vel Albigenses vel aliis haeresibus maculati." For Lea, II, 116, Robert was "little better than a madman."

influenced her decision to leave Magdeburg for the nunnery of Helfta and Albertus Magnus warned Augustinian nuns in a sermon delivered in Cologne that they should not aim for visions and miraculous things.[9] Another recently identified sermon of Albert's, delivered in German in the Dominican Church in Cologne, is thought to contain an attack against heretics of an antinomian complexion and the fifteenth-century Dominican, John Nider, remarked that he had seen Albert's "handbook" which contained Albert's refutation of the heresy in the Swabian Ries along with a note that the same heresy existed in Cologne.[10] Perhaps, then, there were progenitors of the Free-Spirit heresy in Albert's time in Cologne, but without any more evidence we cannot tell if they were mystics similar to Hadewich and Mechthild of Magdeburg.

2. THE GERMAN DECREES

Albertus Magnus never said that antinomian heresy was propagated by beghards and beguines. The first time such a claim was made was in legislation issued in 1307 in Cologne. This might have had some influence on decisions later made at Vienne, but what the objective basis for it was is impossible to tell. The only mention of heresy in Cologne between the death of Albertus in 1270 and the decree of 1307 is the vague and uncorroborated statement in a late fifteenth-century source that a Cistercian theologian named Alanus had engaged in a dispute with heretics in 1294.[11] Though synods elsewhere had legislated against beghards and beguines, none had done so in Cologne even though that city had the largest concentration of such semi-regulars

9. J. B. Schneyer, "Predigten Alberts des Grossen in der Hs. Leipzig, Univ. Bibl. 683," AFP, XXXIV (1964), 58.

10. On Albert's sermon, *ibid*. Dr. Schneyer is planning an edition of this collection of sermons but has informed me in the meantime that the passage in question has no exact historical information. Nider's remark is in his *Formicarius*, ed. G. Colvener (Douai, 1602), Lib. III, cap. 5, p. 215.

11. *Chronicon monasterii Campensis*, ed. G. Eckertz, *Fontes adhuc inediti rerum rhenarum* (Cologne, 1864–70), II, 365. One might also adduce the case of John of Brünn who confessed sometime between 1335 and 1350 to having entered a house of antinomian beghards in Cologne some twenty-eight years earlier, but this is evidence from the mid-fourteenth century about conditions *after* 1307 and John's testimony was colored by his motives for confessing, about which see Chapter V, Section 1 below.

outside of the Netherlands[12] and even though it was probably already a center of mysticism.

The decree of 1307 was the work of Archbishop Henry of Virneburg, the prelate who led a campaign against heresy twenty years later and who directed the questionable prosecution of Meister Eckhart.[13] Henry was always concerned with discipline at any price and for such a man unregulated beghards were an obvious annoyance. Therefore, a year after his consecration in 1306, he included a decree directed against beghards of both sexes in a series of synodal decisions aimed at reforming the state of his diocese.[14] The document contained many of the complaints we have already heard about the beghards' unlicensed pursuit of the *vita apostolica*. It referred to them as *"Apostoli"* who practiced a new form of life under the guise of poverty, wearing habits, preaching their doctrine publicly, and begging for alms instead of working, all in violation of the Church's ban on new orders. To make matters worse, the beghards, despite their illiteracy and lay status, interrupted sermons of Dominicans and Franciscans and engaged the friars in public dispute, another indication of the intense rivalry between licensed and unlicensed mendicants that was so detrimental to the latter.

So much is familiar, but significantly new was the part of Henry's decree that accused the beghards of heresy. Allegedly they said that whoever did not follow in their path could not be saved and that all those moved by the Spirit of God were not under the law (*Gal.* V, 18) because the law was not made for the just (I *Tim.* I, 9). In this class they counted themselves and added that they were without sin. Perhaps some beghards did say things to this effect, but one becomes suspicious when the decree further attributes to them the belief that "simple fornication is not a sin" because this sentence was a stereotype in descriptions of heresy.[15] Moreover, the text also reports that the

12. J. Asen, "Die Beginen in Köln," *Annalen des historischen Vereins für den Niederrhein*, CXI (1927), 81.

13. On Henry, G. Schwamborn, *Heinrich II., Erzbischof von Cöln (1306–1332)* (Neuss, 1904). On the subsequent campaign against heresy, above pp. 29–31.

14. Ed. J. Hartzheim, *Concilia Germaniae* (Cologne, 1759–90), IV, 100–102, reprinted in Fredericq, I, 150–54, #161.

15. Cf. Chapter I, notes 20 and 21 above with Fredericq, I, 153: "Item dicunt fallaciter mentientes, simplicem fornicationem non esse peccatum."

beghards believed that a woman who lost her virginity in marriage should deplore the fact and a man could legitimately send away his lawful wife in order to follow God, indications that they favored asceticism rather than fornication.[16]

The decree threatened the accused with excommunication and secular justice unless they discarded their habits and returned to honest work, but it is not possible to determine if any were actually apprehended or punished. There is a tradition that the great theologian Duns Scotus was called to confute the heretics, but aside from the incontrovertible fact that he did die in Cologne in 1308 there is no proof of this story, let alone the pendant to it that he expired from over-exhaustion pursuant to a debate with a stubborn beghard.[17] The greatest noticeable result of the decree was only that it called forth others. In 1308 a second synod at Cologne reiterated it and in 1310 Bishop Guy of Utrecht issued a statute ordering a search for heretics in his diocese.[18] Guy did this after returning from a provincial council in Cologne, but his statute neither specified any particular heretical doctrine nor mentioned beghards or beguines. Thus he probably acted at the bidding of Henry of Virneburg but had no immediate concern about antinomian heresy.

Legislation issued in 1310 in provincial councils of Trier and Mainz did refer specifically to beghards but made no mention of the antinomian tenets reported at Cologne. Again, as in the thirteenth century, the primary complaint was about unregulated mendicancy. One statute of Trier threatened the excommunication of anyone who received or gave alms to beghards who called themselves "Apostles" (the same term mentioned at Cologne) and another charged beghards in the city, diocese, and province of Trier with holding conventicles where they explained the Scriptures to simple people. These beghards refused to work and, although they were laymen, wore a special habit

16. The sentence "blasphemant deum fore in quadam perditione" is as incomprehensible to me, despite the attempt of Schwamborn, p. 66, to make sense out of it, as it was to Grundmann RB, p. 435, n. 188.

17. Lea, II, 268, and Schwamborn, p. 67. A good summary of the problem with a citation of further literature is in McDonnell, pp. 518–19.

18. Fredericq, I, 161, #167, is a misdated, inferior edition of the Bishop's statute. The best text is ed. J. G. C. Joosting and S. Muller, *Bronnen voor de geschiedenis der kerkelijke rechtspraak in het bisdom Utrecht, 4–5: provinciale en synodale statuten* (The Hague, 1914), 97–98.

denoted by tabards, long tunics, and long hoods.[19] Similarly, the Mainz legislation said nothing about heresy but inveighed against all beghards and beguines who wandered through towns and villages crying "Brod durch Gott."[20]

3. MARGUERITE PORETE

Despite all the lamentations and threats of the German synods and councils, if any trials were held they are unknown to us and it is impossible to find a single nameable Free-Spirit heretic in Germany until after the Council of Vienne. In France, on the other hand, the first years of the fourteenth century were, as Michelet long ago noted, nothing but a long trial. The first beguine known to have been executed since the time of Robert the Bougre met her end in the Paris of Philip the Fair and we are fortunate in having an impressive amount of evidence concerning her case. But before we investigate it it will be helpful to lay out some background.

A favorite charge of Philip the Fair's lawyers was moral turpitude. Bernard Saisset, the fractious southern Bishop, was accused of saying that fornication was not a sin for the clergy; Boniface VIII was called a horrible sodomite and was supposed to have maintained that fornication was no more sinful than rubbing the hands; and the heinous nocturnal practices ascribed to the Templars are too well known to bear repeating.[21] Though there will always be historians who will believe these charges it is not likely that many of them were well founded for we have seen how they had already become a *topos*

19. In Hartzheim, IV, 139 and Fredericq, I, 154–55, #163. The statute says that the papacy had already banned the "Apostles," no doubt a reference to a bull of Honorius IV of March 11, 1286 (ed. M. Prou, *Les registres d'Honorius IV* [Paris, 1888], I, 236, #310), renewed by Nicholas IV in 1290, against the Italian followers of Gerard Segarelli. But there is no reason to believe that use of the term "Apostles" in Cologne and Trier indicates that the heresy of Segarelli and Fra Dolcino had spread to Germany. Rather, German prelates who were aware of Honorius' legislation simply cited it to cope with their own problems. Leff, p. 318, is mistaken in saying that the statute referred to "false Beguines" or made mention of "false doctrines."

20. Ed. Hartzheim, IV, 200–10. Another text in MS Wolfenb., Helmst., 311, fol. 108rb–va, is almost identical to that in Hartzheim, but is undated: on the problems of dating connected with this council, see H. Finke, *Konzilienstudien zur Geschichte des 13. Jahrhunderts* (Münster, 1891), pp. 38–39.

21. The charges against Saisset and Boniface are recapitulated by A. Rigault, *Le procès de Guichard, Evêque de Troyes* (Paris, 1896), pp. 243–44.

in the thirteenth century.[22] Less familiar is another case which again displays the preponderance of such accusations and shows how they were rooted more in a state of mind than in actual fact.

In 1308 Guichard, Bishop of Troyes, who had made a number of influential enemies at the French court, was arrested and imprisoned in the Louvre. The charges against him were so scandalous that the imagination is baffled to conceive of any more horrible crimes. He was accused of being the son of an incubus and of having had a pact with the devil which led him to poison the queen's mother and to stick pins into a model of the queen's body until she herself died. When a priest refused to baptise a child the Bishop had had by a nun without knowing the name of the father Guichard had him killed immediately. In addition to other acts of homicide and sorcery he was accused of sodomy, usury, simony, counterfeiting, blasphemy, and inciting to riot.[23]

In this frightful catalogue one charge is so comparatively mild that it has gone unnoticed: among his other crimes Guichard supposedly indicted people falsely for heresy and sorcery in order to extort money from them. For example, in 1307 at Aix-en-Othe the Bishop accused one Garnier Haymer of having said that normal baked bread was as good as bread consecrated on the altar, that it was better to confess to a tree trunk than to a priest because the tree would not reveal a confession, and that it would be just as well to couple with a dog than with a woman if it were not for the fear that a dog might bite. People going to Church supposedly were greeted by Garnier with the cry that they were foolish and would be much better off going to a tavern. The accused denied all these charges but he was only freed when his son delivered a huge money payment to the Bishop.[24]

22. Above, Chapter I, Section 3. The attempt of K. Wenck, "War Bonifaz VIII ein Ketzer?" HZ, XCIV (1905), 1–66, to prove that the Pope was actually guilty of the charges launched against him was convincingly refuted by R. Holtzmann, "War Papst Bonifaz VIII ein Ketzer," *Mitteilungen des Instituts für österreichische Geschichtsforschung*, XXVI (1905), 488–98. Most recently another attempt has been made to fix the "guilt" of the Templars by G. Legman, *The Guilt of the Templars* (New York, 1966), but see the telling review of this preposterous work by R. C. Smail in the *New York Review of Books*, Feb. 23, 1967 (VII, 3), 14–15.

23. The standard work on Guichard's case is Rigault.

24. *Ibid.*, pp. 174–77.

The enlightened Third Republic historians who studied Guichard's trial believed, probably with justice, that most of the allegations against him were fabricated.[25] Yet in this particular instance it is possible to surmise that Guichard himself manufactured charges against innocent people. If so, and if Garnier Haymier's case had not been exposed at Paris but simply recounted by a chronicler of Troyes, modern historians might be writing that the Free-Spirit heresy had been perpetuated in Champagne since the days of Amaury of Bène or that heretics in the early fourteenth century were advocating sexual intercourse with dogs. If, on the other hand, Philip's lawyers made up the entire story, it is an interesting reflection on how they themselves proceeded.

Less familiar even than the trial of Guichard of Troyes is the case of a beguine who in 1304 ran afoul of the Capetian authorities. This was a woman from Metz who lived in a beguinal community in Flanders and who had gained so great a reputation at the French court for her prophecies that she had won the favor of Philip IV and his queen. In this she was reminiscent of the beguine mentioned in the last chapter who was noted for her powers of revelation at the court of Philip III; but it was safer to have a reputation for the occult in the thirteenth century than it was in the fourteenth. According to the continuator of the chronicle of Nangis, who represented a semi-official point of view, the beguine tried to murder the King's brother, Charles of Valois, at the instigation of the Flemish.[26] Her alleged plan was to send a young boy to poison the Prince, but Charles learned of the scheme, captured her, and interrogated her while burning the soles of her feet. Naturally she confessed and was imprisoned for a long time in Charles' castle at Crépy before she was finally released. This incident may be partially explained as the product of war-time hysteria, occurring as it did after the humiliating defeat of the French at Courtrai when stories of poison plots were common coin, but it is characteristic that a beguine was the victim. The continuator of the chronicle of Nangis showed his contempt for the woman from Metz by calling her a *"pseudomulier"* much in the way that eccentric characters are still today

25. In addition to Rigault, see C.-V. Langlois, *Saint Louis—Philippe le Bel, Histoire de France*, ed. E. Lavisse (III, 2) (Paris, 1901), p. 211.

26. RHF, XX, 590. On the semi-official quality of the continuation of Nangis, G. Lizerand, *Clément V et Philippe IV le Bel* (Paris, 1910), p. xviii.

often called "pseudos." Such people may be more "genuine" than most that call them "pseudos," but in times of stress and in the absence of civil liberties unions they do not have an easy lot.

Another beguine whom the continuator of Nangis called a *"pseudomulier,"* but who did not escape Capetian displeasure with her life, was Marguerite Porete, one of the most important figures in the history of the heresy of the Free Spirit. Marguerite was a woman from Hainaut who referred to herself as a *"mendiant creature"* and who was called a beguine by so many independent sources that the designation may be taken as certain. Nothing is known of her exact place of birth or early life, but we do know that sometime between 1296 and January 1306 she wrote a book which was condemned and burned in her presence at Valenciennes by the Bishop of Cambrai, Guy II, who warned her not to disseminate her ideas or writings any further under pain of being relaxed to the secular arm.[27]

The admonition, however, was to no avail. Between 1306 and 1308 Marguerite was brought before the new Bishop of Cambrai, Philip of Marigny, and the Inquisitor of Lorraine whose jurisdiction extended over Hainaut and the Cambrésis. This time she was accused of having sent her book to Bishop John of Châlons-sur-Marne and of propagating it among simple people and beghards. Instead of acting further themselves her judges apparently sent her to Paris where we know that she was taken into custody by the Dominican Inquisitor, William Humbert, late in the year 1308. There Marguerite refused to answer any questions or even to take the vows necessary for her examination and languished in prison for almost a year and a half while brother William was at any rate fully occupied with the case of the Templars. But in 1310 the Inquisitor, for want of direct testimony, extracted a list of articles from Marguerite's book and presented them for examination to twenty-one theological regents of the University of Paris. On April 11 these examiners unanimously declared the articles to be heretical. Thereafter events moved more swiftly: on May 30 Marguerite was judged "relapsed" by a commission of canon lawyers

27. Marguerite's self-designation is in her *Mirouer des simples ames,* ed. Guarnieri, 594. She is called a beguine in the consultation of canon lawyers of May 30, 1310, ed. Lea, II, 578; *Les grandes chroniques de la France,* ed. J. Viard (Paris, 1934), VIII, 273; and Jean d'Outremeuse, *Chronique,* in Fredericq, II, 64, #39.

on the questionable assumption that she had already abjured her errors at Valenciennes and was handed over to the Provost of Paris who executed her the day after at a solemn ceremony in the Place de Grève. The same fate was shared by a converted Jew who was supposed to have relapsed and to have spat in a fit of contempt on an image of the Virgin.[28]

In view of these circumstances it is most interesting to note that sometime in the course of her tribulations Marguerite sent her book to three authorities who all actually approved of it.[29] Of these the first was a Franciscan named John of Quaregnon (Hainaut) and the second was Dom Frank from the Cistercian Abbey of Villers (Brabant), a monastery famed for its direction and support of beguines.[30] Nothing more is known about either man, but the third, the secular theologian Godfrey of Fountains, was one of the most important scholastic philosophers at Paris from 1285 to ca. 1306. Like the first two, Godfrey also was associated with areas of the North close to Marguerite's sphere af activity: he was a canon of Liège and Tournai and renounced his claim to the Bishopric of the latter see in 1300 when his election was contested.[31]

Godfrey and his associates were by no means the last to have looked tolerantly on the work of Marguerite Porete, for the astonishing fact is that her book—entitled *The Mirror of Simple Souls*—has

28. The account of Marguerite's career is pieced together from the continuation of Nangis, RHF, XX, 601, and especially the two trial documents edited by Lea, II, 575–78 (reprints in Fredericq, I, 155–60, #164–66). The reference of Leff, p. 368, to "Margaret of Porète's confession in 1311" is mistaken on three counts: her surname appears in no source as referring to a place; she did not confess, and by 1311 she was no more than ashes.

29. This information comes from the prologue to Marguerite's book found in all the mss of the Latin, Italian and English translations (on which see directly below). The Latin text of this is ed. Guarnieri, 638–39, the Middle English by M. Doiron, *Archivio Italiano per la storia della pietà*, V (1968), 249–50, and a modern translation from the Middle English is by C. Kirchberger, *The Mirror of Simple Souls* (London and New York, 1927), pp. lxv–lxvi.

30. E. de Moreau, *L'abbaye de Villers-en-Brabant aux XIIe et XIIIe siècles* (Brussels, 1909), pp. 96–104, 113–24, and McDonnell, pp. 170–76. I know of nothing to substantiate the guess of Guarnieri that John of Quaregnon was actually Duns Scotus—there were many Franciscans called John!

31. On Godfrey, see R. J. Arway, "A Half Century of Research on Godfrey of Fountains," *The New Scholasticism*, XXXVI (1962), 192–218.

survived in a large number of copies and translations. The story of this transmission cannot yet be told in entirety because the evidence is still being assembled.[32] Presumably three copies exist of the original Old French version, but of these only one is accessible. This is a manuscript from the Loire valley written between ca. 1450 and 1530 which was owned by a nunnery at Orléans and which was inspected in 1530 by the Archbishop of Tours who did not record any qualms about it. It is this version that Romana Guarnieri has recently edited though it is unfortunately a late copy and seems to be corrupt. Potentially more valuable is a manuscript which might date from the fourteenth century, but which is owned by a French-speaking religious community outside of France that is unwilling to grant its use for scholarship. In addition, a seventeenth-century copy bound together with other mystical tracts was noted in the catalogue of the public library at Bourges, but was shipped to Paris where it was lost without a trace in the caverns of the Bibliothèque nationale.[33]

Unlike the French versions all the known medieval translations of the *Mirror* are currently accessible, though more are probably still gathering dust. Three complete manuscripts in the Vatican and one fragment in the Bodleian Library are copies of a Latin version translated from the French sometime in the fourteenth century. This also became the basis for two independent Italian translations: the first done in the fourteenth century and surviving in a manuscript at Florence, the second done later in the same century and now to be found in manuscripts in Naples, Vienna, and Budapest. As if this profusion

32. The identification of Marguerite Porete's book, which was previously known to students of mysticism but falsely attributed or deemed anonymous, is one of the most exciting discoveries recently made in the field of medieval religious history. It was first announced to scholarship by Romana Guarnieri in the unusual medium of the *Osservatore Romano* of June 16, 1946—an article now reprinted in Guarnieri, 661–63. The attribution is unquestioned, see Axters, II, 172–74 ("De betekenis van deze ontdekking kan dan ook niet hoog genoeg worden geschat"); and Grundmann, "Ketzerverhöre, 526–27."

33. On the three French MSS, Guarnieri, 501–504. M. de Corberon used the same MS afterwards edited by Guarnieri for a transcription, annotation, and translation into modern French in installments running in *Études traditionnelles* from Vol. LVI (1955) to LIX (1958). This project was abandoned after it reached Marguerite's Chapter 31 and thus represents less than one quarter of the original text.

were not bewildering enough, there is an indication that no less than thirty-six copies of the *Mirror* were circulating in Italy in the fifteenth century![34]

Marguerite's work also had a vigorous life in England where it was translated into Middle English directly from the French. Since all the surviving manuscripts of this version date from the fifteenth century and belonged to Carthusian monasteries it seems likely that the *Mirror* crossed the Channel after 1414 when Henry V's foundation at Sheen had close contacts with continental Charterhouses and brought over many mystical tracts including several works of Ruysbroeck.[35] Finally, in 1491 Richard Methley (1451–1528), a Carthusian of Mount Grace, Yorks., translated the *Mirror* still another time from the English into Latin and added his own glosses.[36]

All this is not to say that there was no disquiet about the book's boldness. The Middle English translator, known only by his initials as M. N., was very aware of this, as he indicated in an independent prologue. There he states that he had already translated the work once, "but now I am stired to laboure it agen newe, for bicause I am enfourmed that some wordis therof have be mystake." He also added fourteen glosses to dissuade readers from drawing wrong conclusions from daring passages because the work "is but schortli spoken, and may be taken othirwise than it is iment of hem that reden it sodeynli and taken no ferthir hede." But his own conviction was that "the boke is of highe divine maters and of highe goostli felynges, and kernyngli and ful mystili it is spoken."[37] The same judgment persisted in England

---

34. On the *Mirror's* career in Italy, a subject that lies outside of the scope of the present work, Guarnieri, 466–77, 484–86, 645–60. On the Latin and Italian translations, Guarnieri, 505–508. The first Latin translation was published as a work of Ruysbroeck in a rare Bolognese edition of 1538, see Guarnieri, 485–86.

35. Eric Colledge, "The Treatise of Perfection of the Sons of God, a fifteenth-century English Ruysbroeck translation," *English Studies*, XXXIII (1952), 49–66. Colledge's hypothesis of a Carthusian transmission is confirmed by a passage in MS Vat. Pal. 600, fol. 228v which indicates that a Latin copy of the *Mirror* existed in the Charterhouse of Strassburg. An alternate theory of transmission through the entourage of Philippa of Hainaut, to me less convincing, is proposed by Guarnieri, 434.

36. A critical edition of this text is planned for a future issue of the *Archivio Italiano per la storia della pietà*.

37. Doiron (as above, n. 29), 247. On the text and glosses of the English translation, see M. Doiron, "The Middle English Translation of Le Mirouer des Simples Ames," *Dr. L. Reypens-Album, Studiën en Tektsuitgaven van ons*

before the authorship of Marguerite Porete was recognized and accounts for the edition made under the auspices of the Downside Benedictines.[38]

This account shows that the doctrine of Marguerite's *Mirror* was by no means self-evidently pernicious. Not that the Parisian theological regents were necessarily more narrow-minded than the Downside Benedictines: unlike modern scholars they were not presented with Marguerite's entire book for examination, but only with extracts from it prepared by the Inquisitor. Two of these—the first and the fifteenth—are preserved in the procès-verbal of the theological examination among the documents of the Nogaret collection. The first declares that the "annihilated soul" can no longer be governed by the virtues because all the virtues are much more the servants of the soul, and the fifteenth argues that such a soul should not and cannot concern itself with the consolations or gifts of God because such would disturb the exclusive direction of the soul toward God.[39]

The only passage describing Marguerite's ideas in a contemporary chronicle—the continuation of the chronicle of Nangis—tries, like the first article from the procès-verbal, to portray her as an antinomian. This was written by an anonymous monk at the royal Abbey of St. Denis who habitually expressed the crown's point of view and must have been well informed since a certain Peter from the same Abbey had been on the examining commission. Perhaps the error related in the chronicle was even a direct citation of another extracted article. As we have mentioned in the Introduction, it runs that "the annihilated soul" can "grant to nature all that it desires without remorse of conscience." This, the chronicler adds directly afterwards, sounds manifestly like heresy, and he certainly seems right.[40]

---

geestelijk erf, XVI (Antwerp, 1964), pp. 131–52, and Edmund Colledge and R. Guarnieri. "The Glosses by 'M. N.' and Richard Methley to 'The Mirror of Simple Souls'," Archivio Italiano per la storia della pietà, V (1968), 357–82.

38. Mirror, tr. Kirchberger. See also the approval of E. Underhill, "The Mirror of Simple Souls," Fortnightly Review, XCV (1911), 345–54.

39. Ed. C.-V. Langlois, "Marguerite Porete," Revue historique, LIV (1894), 297. (Also in Fredericq, II, 63, #37.)

40. RHF, XX, 601. The continuation of the chronicle of Girard de Frachet, RHF, XXI, 34, is just an abridgment of this text. The later grandes chroniques de la France (cited above, n. 27) state that the beguine Marguerite erred in the articles of faith and uttered false and contemptuous words about the sacrament of the altar. This statement was probably based on another article of the

Now that we have Marguerite's book to work with we can see that it does in fact contain the statement that "the soul neither desires nor despises poverty, tribulation, masses, sermons, fasts, or prayers and gives to nature, without remorse, all that it asks." But immediately afterwards in the same sentence Marguerite explains that because of the soul's miraculous transformation nature "is so well ordered" that it "does not demand anything prohibited."[41] In other words, Marguerite's adversaries, who made moral turpitude their favorite charge, took the most sensational passages from her book out of context, as others were to do in the next decade with the writings of Meister Eckhart. We will examine the doctrine of the *Mirror* in detail in a later chapter, but here it may be said that while it reveals Marguerite Porete to have been the first identifiable Free Spirit, it does not advocate antinomianism and presents a thoroughly different picture of her thought than the Inquisition would have wished left to posterity.

The case excites particular disquiet when one considers how it was interwoven with the other sordid trials then going on at Paris. The fact that the director of Marguerite's examination, brother William, was the King's confessor and was also in charge of Philip the Fair's proceedings against the Templars does not inspire great confidence in his independence or integrity. Furthermore, Philip, the Bishop of Cambrai who apparently sent the beguine to Paris, was later the Archbishop of Sens who called the Council of 1310 against the Templars, and was the brother of Philip the Fair's notorious first minister, Enguerrand of Marigny—"the man who knew all the King's secrets."[42]

Why would Philip the Fair's minions want to convict a beguine just at the time when they were having enough trouble with the

---

Parisian condemnation and refers to a complicated theological passage in the *Mirror* best discussed by Colledge and Guarnieri (as above, n. 37), 359–61.

41. Ed. Guarnieri, 527: "laquelle Ame ne desire ne ne [sic] desprise pouvr[e]té ne tribulation, ne messe ne sermon, ne jeune ne oraison, et donne a Nature tout ce qu'il luy fault, sans remors de conscience; mais telle nature est si bien ordonnee par transformacion de unité d'Amour, a laquelle la voulenté de ceste Ame est conjoincte, que la nature ne demande chose qui soit deffendue."

42. On Enguerrand and his connections, Jean Favier, *Un conseiller de Philippe le Bel: Enguerran de Marigny* (Paris, 1963), esp. pp. 129–37 (Enguerrand was also an important witness at the trial of Guichard of Troyes). For an assessment of brother William and Philip of Marigny, Lizerand (as above, n. 26), pp. 94, 155–56.

Templars? Conceivably they saw in her book lèse majesté. In one passage Marguerite says that certain people are called kings in a country where all are one-eyed but those who have two eyes know that the former are serfs (Pierre Flote, the King's leading minister before 1302, was one-eyed). In the same breath she then compares such "kings" to the owl who mistakenly considers its offspring to be the most beautiful in the forest.[43] Both passages are similar to remarks of Bernard Saisset which led to that Bishop's arrest and as a result Philip the Fair's final struggle with Boniface VIII.[44] It is doubtful that Marguerite intended her words to have had a political connotation, but it is not impossible that someone at Philip's court took umbrage at them. A simpler and more likely explanation is that with difficulties and doubt accumulating in the matter of the Templars, Philip and his officials wished to display their unwavering orthodoxy in a case against a controversial beguine in which no base motives could be suspected. The zealous legislation of the Emperor Frederick II against heretics or Henry VIII's pious concern for doctrine are parallel cases in point.

While Marguerite was imprisoned in Paris, a certain Guiart de Cressonsacq (diocese of Beauvais) who claimed that he was the Angel of Philadelphia sent to comfort Christ's adherents tried to intervene for her—whether physically or merely verbally we do not know—but only succeeded in being taken into custody himself. His ideas, preserved in the procès-verbal of his examination, deserve fuller analysis than they have hitherto been accorded by historians of heresy, but this is not the place for such treatment because Guiart was not a Free Spirit.[45] He believed that he was a divinely-appointed "angel" given a mission to defend the "Church of Philadelphia"—in his view a body comprised of "adherents of the Lord" who desired to give away all and hold only to the rigors of the apostolic life. Previously he had

43. Ed. Guarnieri, 564: "Telles gens, dit Amour, sont roys appellez, mais c'est ou pays la ou checun est bourgne. Mais sans faillir, ceulx qui ont deux yeulx, les tiennent a sers. . . . Ilz resemblent la chouete, qui cuide qu'il n'y ait point de plus bel oyseau ou boys, que sons ses choueteaux."

44. P. Dupuy, *Histoire du différend d'entre le pape Boniface VIII et Philippes le Bel* (Paris, 1655), p. 640: "Tamen dixit ab eodem Episcopo se audivisse dici quod dictus dominus Rex male regebat regnum suum, . . . et quod in regione caecorum monoculus erat Rex." (The more famous remark about Philip being the most beautiful of birds who can do nothing but stare is on pp. 643-44.)

45. The procès-verbal is ed. Langlois (as above, n. 39), 297-98. I intend to discuss Guiart's ideas more fully in the future in another context.

defended such people against the mendicant orders in Reims and it was no doubt because he felt that Marguerite was one of their number that he tried to intervene for her in Paris.

Actually Guiart's "adherents of the Lord" were much like beghards and beguines. In addition to leading the evangelical life, they wore a special habit which Guiart also wore and called the "habit of Christ." This consisted of a tabard and tunic, exactly the same terms used to describe the habit of beghards by the council which legislated against them in Trier contemporaneously with Guiart's arrest. To this outfit he and his adherents added a fur waist-band—the same belt worn by John the Baptist in the Gospel of Mark (I, 6).[46] According to the continuation of Nangis, again the only original narrative source, when Guiart was asked to take off his offending habit he refused to do so and replied that even the pope did not have the right to deprive him of it. But in the end he lacked Marguerite Porete's steadfastness and saved himself from the Place de Grève: "moved by fear" he agreed to abjure his habit and his errors and was condemned to life imprisonment.[47] We do not know whether Guiart was directly associated with Marguerite before he came to Paris, but his testimony reveals only an intense concern for the *vita apostolica* without any of the ecstatic mysticism that was a fundamental quality of the Free-Spirit mentality.

4. THE COUNCIL OF VIENNE

Thus before 1312 beguines or beghards were charged with antinomian heresy only twice and in neither case is the evidence decisive: we know of no actual heretics examined at Cologne and it is now clear

---

46. *Ibid.*, 298–99: "requisitus si sciant aliqui quod ipse habeat illud donum, respondit quod sic, quia dixit aliquibus recipientibus habitum Christi (intelligens de tali habitu qualem ipse defert). . . . requisitus si illi qui deferunt tabardos sunt de societate sua, respondit quod non quantum ad omnia, nisi illi qui tenent et portant tunicam longam et zonam pelliceam, que zona est de essencia habitus. . . ." The decree of Trier of 1310 (as above, n. 19), refers to "tabardis et tunicis longis et longis capuciis."

47. Continuation of Nangis, RHF, XX, 601. The continuation of Frachet, RHF, XXI, 34, adds nothing. Some of Guiart's associates might have been executed: according to W. Rolewink, *Fasciculus temporum*, ed. J. Pistorius, *Rerum germanicarum scriptores* (Frankfurt, 1583–1607), II, 84, between 1304 and 1314 "beguardi multi combusti sunt in Parisiis, propter heresim pauperum de Lugduno," but it is hard to know how much to trust this self-contradictory late fifteenth-century source.

that Marguerite Porete was not so radical as her antagonists claimed. But there were other circumstances that contributed to the legislation against the beguinal movement at Vienne. One was the dislike we have already examined in the previous chapter. By the fourteenth century both secular and regular clergy regarded beghards and beguines as a threat to discipline and were anxious to deal firmly with them at an ecumenical council. Beyond that there was a very real fear of antinomian heresy stated often enough, if not in direct connection with beghards and beguines.

In 1296, for example, Boniface VIII issued a bull condemning a new sect whose members prayed in the nude. Though lay, they preached, heard confession, and wore the tonsures of priests. Boniface gave neither their name nor place of activity and his silence has permitted historians to speculate that he meant either followers of Segarelli or Clareno in Italy, or Free-Spirit heretics.[48] Whatever the Pope had in mind, it is doubtful that any heretics corresponded fully to his description, but the bull reveals the sort of practices that orthodoxy most feared. No further record of this nudist sect is preserved, but on the eve of the Council of Vienne there was renewed concern about antinomianism. The Franciscan Nicholas of Lyra, one of the theologians who had condemned Marguerite Porete's book in 1310, noted in his third *Quodlibet*, written in the same year, that there were new heretics who said that one should not obey the prophets but should live freely after the flesh.[49] According to Nicholas, the Pope had already proceeded against these hypocrites who hid their impurity under the mantle of piety. This might have been a reference to Boniface VIII's bull of 1296 or perhaps a later more explicit bull that has been lost.

What has survived is a letter of Clement V written in April 1311, requesting the Bishop of Cremona to extirpate a new sect of the "Free Spirit" in the Valley of Spoleto and elsewhere in Italy. Supposedly these sectaries, clerical and lay, and of both sexes, argued that they were free to do whatever they pleased because they were guided by

48. Text ed. J. de Guibert, *Documenta ecclesiastica christianae perfectionis studium spectantia* (Rome, 1931), p. 127, #222. On the various interpretations, Guarnieri, 387–88.

49. F. Pelster, "Die' 'Quaestio' Heinrichs von Harclay über die zweite Ankunft Christi and die Erwartung des baldigen Weltendes zu Anfang des 14. Jahrhunderts," *Archivio Italiano per la storia della pietà*, I (1951), 45.

the Holy Spirit; thus they deceived simple souls, but their presumed liberty came from the spirits of evil and not from God.[50] This is the first mention of a sect of the Free Spirit. It is improbable that these Umbrian heretics had any connection with France or the Rhineland, but Clement's letter indicates that he was concerned about antinomian heresy shortly before Vienne, and if he thought heresy was the work of the devil he might have been prone to expect pestiferous doctrines mushrooming in the North as well as in the South.

If the Pope had already expressed concern about antinomianism, there were many influential delegates to the Council of Vienne who were hostile to beguines and beghards. Among these were several associated with the case of Marguerite Porete: of the twenty-one theological regents who declared Marguerite's book to have been heretical, at least six were present at Vienne including such important members as Berengar of Landora, who became general of the Dominicans in 1312, Gerard of Bologna, general of the Carmelites, and Jacques Fournier, who was later to become Pope Benedict XII. Also present was Bishop John of Châlons-sur-Marne and most of the members of the Marigny clan: Philip, Archbishop of Sens, was at Vienne at least part of the time; his brother Enguerrand of Marigny was an emissary of the French King in secret negotiations concerning the Templars and received numerous special favors from the Pope; and lastly their cousin Nicholas of Fréauville, a Dominican who had been Philip the Fair's confessor until 1305, was Cardinal Priest of St. Eusebius and had already taken the French side against the memory of Boniface VIII.[51]

Given the state of the evidence it is impossible to say whether Philip the Fair's friends wanted to justify the execution of Marguerite

---

50. *Regestum Clementis Papae V* (Rome, 1885–88), VI, 423–27, #7506: "novam sectam novumque ritum. . . quem libertatis spiritum nominant." Leff, p. 331, mistakenly dates this bull to after the Council of Vienne.

51. On the composition of the Council, E. Müller, *Das Konzil von Vienne, 1311–1312* (Münster, 1934), pp. 79–80, and pp. 176–81 for the role of Enguerrand of Marigny. On the influence of the latter on Clement V, F. Pegues, *The Lawyers of the Last Capetians* (Princeton, 1962), pp. 57–58 and Rigault (as above, n. 21), p. 222. On Nicholas of Fréauville, S. Baluzius, *Vitae paparum Avenionensium*, ed. G. Mollat (Paris, 1914–27), II, 117–19, and Lizerand (as above, n. 26), pp. 53–54.

Porete by a general condemnation of beguines, but it is certain that some of the doctrines condemned by the Council of Vienne bear a striking resemblance to those ascribed to the beguine of Hainaut. On the other hand, the decree of Vienne against the beghards refers especially to Germany. On this basis historians argue that the legislation must have been initiated by German prelates.[52] This theory is supported by the fact that Henry of Virneburg was present at Vienne along with John of Dürbheim, the Bishop of Strassburg who shortly afterward was to be a leading persecutor of beguines and beghards. But the Archbishops of Trier and Mainz were not there and we do not know what role any of the prelates actually played because most of the acts of the Council have disappeared (some concerning the Templars may even have been intentionally destroyed). It is known that grievances concerning reform of the Church were collected from various ecclesiastical provinces and acted upon by commissions rather than in plenary sessions. It is also recorded that the decree against the beghards was the product of a long deliberation. But there is no record of who introduced or agreed to condemn their alleged errors and it can only be guessed that both French and German delegates were responsible.[53]

We have already discussed the decree *Cum de quibusdam mulieribus* which was classified under the heading of "religious houses" and was concerned primarily not with doctrine but with the beguinal way of life.[54] For us the more important decree of Vienne was *Ad nostrum* which was issued under the rubric of heresy and was exclusively doc-

52. Müller, pp. 581–82. J. Lecler, *Vienne* (Paris, 1964), p. 127, goes beyond Müller's "*Vermutung*" by saying "c'est certainement sur l'initiative des évêques allemands que la question fût portée devant le concile," but Lecler has no additional evidence for this assertion.

53. On the procedures concerning reform legislation at Vienne, Müller, pp. 117–21. (It may be pointed out parenthetically that Henry of Virneburg, the most influential German prelate at Vienne and a man who had already legislated against beghards, was a close ally of the French.) Though some of the Clementine decrees might not have been discussed at Vienne at all, *Ad nostrum*, the decree against beghards, unquestionably was drawn up at the Council. We know this from a MS in Munich (published with an introduction by Müller, pp. 679–88) that was written before the publication of the Clementines and which contains a list of articles decided on at Vienne including all eight points of *Ad nostrum*.

54. Above, p. 47.

trinal in content.[55] This listed eight errors of "an abominable sect of malignant men known as beghards and faithless women known as beguines in the Kingdom of Germany" which are generally considered to be the essence of the Free-Spirit heresy. The first tenet was the central one. This stated that man can attain such a degree of perfection in his earthly life that he is incapable of sin. In this state he can achieve no additional grace because such would give him a perfection superior to Christ. The second point followed that such a man need not fast or pray because in his state of perfection sensuality is so subordinated to reason that he can accord freely to his body all that pleases him. Similarly the third point was that such a man is not subject to human obedience or to any laws of the Church because "where the spirit of the Lord is, there is liberty" (II *Corin.* III, 17).

The following five propositions were elaborations or consequences of the first three: man can attain final blessedness just as much in this life as in the other; such men do not need the light of glory to be elevated to the vision and enjoyment of God; the acts of virtue are only necessary for imperfect men, but the perfect soul no longer needs them; a kiss is a mortal sin when nature does not demand it, but the sexual act itself is not sinful when demanded by nature; and it is not necessary to rise or show any sign of reverence during the elevation of the host because to think of the sacrament of the Eucharist or the passion of Christ would be a sign of imperfection and a descent from the heights of contemplation. The decree also claimed that the heretics did and said other things which offended the eyes of the divine majesty and were perilous to mortal souls. Therefore, it concluded, the sect should be extirpated and all who held, defended, or approved of such errors be made subject to canonical punishments.

Had beghards and beguines actually expressed such errors? The only source for *Ad nostrum* that can be established is the list of tenets extracted from *The Mirror of Simple Souls.* The sixth article of *Ad nostrum* to the effect that the liberated soul takes leave of the virtues is almost literally the same as the first tenet extracted from the work of Marguerite Porete and there is a great similarity between the eighth article that respect for the Eucharist impedes perfection and the other tenet extracted from Marguerite's work to the effect that the soul

55. In Fredericq, I, 168–69, #172, and E. Friedberg, *Corpus iuris canonici* (Leipzig, 1879–81), II, 1183–84.

does not care for the consolations of God because such would disturb the concentration on divine union. In addition, the articles of *Ad nostrum* that refer to dispensation from fasting or prayer and justify sexual intercourse if demanded by nature correspond to the statement ascribed to Marguerite by the continuator of Nangis that the annihilated soul can accord to nature all that it desires without remorse of conscience.[56] But we have already seen that all these statements were taken out of context and do not represent fairly Marguerite's views.

Though *Ad nostrum* was directed against beghards and beguines in Germany, we know of no immediate sources for that text from that area. Henry of Virneburg's legislation of 1307 ascribed an antinomian program to beghards, but its language was completely different. Much closer are the parallels between some tenets of *Ad nostrum* and the *determinatio* of Albertus Magnus against the heretics of the Ries written some forty to fifty years earlier. The first article of the former is an elaboration of Albertus' article 94 that man can so advance in this life as to become "impeccable." It is quite possible that the fathers of Vienne used Albert's text and perhaps also the Nördlingen list in drawing up *Ad nostrum*, but if they did it reflects on the artificiality of their procedure.[57]

Ad nostrum is the birth certificate of the heresy of the Free Spirit since, technically speaking, heresy is defined by the pope and the decree referred explicitly to heretics who spoke of their "spirit of liberty."[58] But, as if it were in the theater of the absurb, there is a birth certificate without it being fully clear whether there was any child. Surely there were radical mystics among beghards and beguines: in addition to those in Cologne and Marguerite Porete, there were probably others that we do not know about. Yet, so far as we can tell,

56. The similarities have already been set forth convincingly in parallel columns by Guarnieri, 416

57. Cf. *Determinatio* (ed. de Guibert, as above, n. 48, pp. 116–25), #94: "homo [in vita] sic proficere possit ut inpeccabilis fiat" with *Ad nostrum*, #1: "homo in vita presenti tantum et talem perfectionis gradum potest acquirere quod reddetur penitus impeccabilis. . . ." An example of similarity with the Nördlingen list is *Ad nostrum*, #8: "in elevatione corporis Jesu Christi non debent assurgere. . . ." compared to Nördlingen #36 (ed. C. Schmidt, "Actenstücke besonders zur Geschichte der Waldenser," *Zeitschrift für die historische Theologie*, XXII [1852], 250): "non sit assurgendum corpori domini. . . ."

58. "Tertio, quod illi qui sunt in predicto gradu perfectionis et spiritu libertatis, non sunt humane subjecti obedientie. . . ."

inveterate hostility toward the beguinal movement and unreal fears of antinomian heresy were forceful motivating factors in the shaping of the condemnation. Until we have more information about the actual deliberations at Vienne we must therefore regard *Ad nostrum* less as an accurate description of a flourishing heresy than as a document of enormous import in persecutions to come.

Chapter Four

THE INQUISITION IN
STRASSBURG

Just a few years after he left the Council of Vienne, the Bishop of Strassburg, John of Dürbheim, launched a campaign against the beghards and beguines in his diocese which other ecclesiastical officers took up intermittently throughout the later Middle Ages. In the process these officials left behind them a comparatively large number of records (a number of which have not been published). Strassburg thus makes a good test case for estimating the extent of the Free-Spirit heresy in a single place from inquisitorial sources.

1. THE CAMPAIGN OF JOHN OF DÜRBHEIM

John of Dürbheim acted in 1317, before the publication of the Clementines, by ordering an inquisition to examine certain "false Christians" of both sexes in Strassburg and he reported the results to his clergy in a letter of August 13. This contains an excellent description of the appearance of the accused as well as an extensive exposition of their errors classified under seven headings: God, Christ, the Church, the sacraments, heaven and hell, the Gospels, and the saints. Because of its structured detail and its claim to be based on actual testimony it is one of the most frequently cited descriptions of the heresy which the document itself calls "of the Free Spirit."[1]

1. On John, N. Rosenkränzer, *Johann I von Strassburg, genannt von Dürbheim* (Trier, 1881). The letter was first published by Mosheim, pp. 255–61, and fre-

The first rubric begins with the contention that God is all that exists and that man can be so united to Him that everything he does and wills is identical to divine action and will. Man can become God "by nature" without distinction, in which state he cannot sin. Such men comprise the kingdom of heaven and are unmovable: nothing can cause them to rejoice or be disturbed. They have no need to pray and since they are God they should be adored like God.[2]

As for Christology, the heretics allegedly said not only that every perfect man is Christ "by nature," but that any man could transcend Him in merit. They did not revere His body; asserted that He was crucified not for mankind but for himself; and blasphemed against the consecration of the host, saying that a perfect man should be free from all acts of virtue and should not meditate on Christ's passion or on God.

The tenets under rubrics three and four could be summed up by the heretics' alleged claim that the Catholic Church and Christianity were foolish. The perfect man is free from all ecclesiastical precepts and statutes. He need not honor his parents nor work with his hands, and he can receive alms, even if not in orders, or indeed steal, since all property is held in common. Any good layman is as able to confer the Eucharist as a sinful priest; Christ's body is found equally in all bread as much as in that of the altar; and confession is unnecessary for salvation. Under the same heading, though not directly related, is the interesting tenet that all sexual relations in marriage except those leading to offspring are sinful.

The list goes on to deny the existence of hell, purgatory, and last judgment.[3] Man is judged on death, when his spirit or soul returns

---

quently reprinted; the most convenient edition for purposes of citation (with numbered lines) is in *UB der Stadt Strassburg*, ed. W. Wiegand (Strassburg, 1879–1900), II, 309–13, #358. This, like all the editions, is just a copy of Mosheim's text because no one could find the original MS. Recently, however, it has been located in MS Wolfenb., Helmst., 311, fol. 107ra–108rb by Dr. Alexander Patschovsky, to whom I owe the greatest thanks for informing me about his find. The frequent citations of this MS throughout this chapter reflect its prime importance.

2. These last two tenets were overlooked by Mosheim in his reading of MS cit., fol. 107va. They belong in *UB Strassburg*, II, 310, 27 (after "liberare") thus: "Item quod debent adorari sicut deus dicentes vis adorare deum adora me. Item quod ratione huius perfectionis non tenentur orare."

3. Correct *UB Strassburg*, II, 311, 12–13, after MS cit., fol. 107va, thus: "quinto errando *circa* infernum et regnum celorum" and "*quando* moritur."

from whence it came, and nothing is left except God who exists eternally. Not even Jews or Saracens are damned, because their spirits too return to God. Thus a man should follow his own interior instincts rather than the Gospels. The Scriptures have many purely poetical passages which contain no truth at all, and if all the books of the Catholic faith were destroyed they could be easily replaced with better ones. Lastly, the heretics supposedly claimed that they could surpass the saints, were more perfect than the Virgin, could neither increase nor decrease in holiness, and had no need of the three theological virtues.[4]

Bishop John's description has survived in only one copy, but there is another record of the examination in Strassburg surviving in two manuscripts and entitled: "articles and errors which were found in the inquisition made by lord John, Bishop of Strassburg, among those of the sect of Beghards and among those who adhere to them and shelter them."[5] Though it lacks coherent organization it lists all the general points found in John's letter with one important exception: the first document contains the tenet that sexual relations even in marriage were sinful unless they led to propagation, but the inquisitorial list contains the contradictory statement that the free in spirit can do whatever they wish with their bodies without sin.

On the matter of freedom the second list also adds some details. The free in spirit need not observe the fasts of the Church and may eat meat on Fridays. A perfect woman need not obey her husband concerning acts of matrimony. Men, though healthy and strong, do not have to engage in bodily labor, even though by receiving alms they take that much away from the truly poor. And the state of free-

---

4. Correct *UB Strassburg*, II, 311, 24, after MS cit., fol. 107vb, thus: "*circa sanctos viros errando*."

5. "Isti sunt articuli et errores qui inventi sunt in inquisitione facta per dominum Johannem Argentinensem episcopum esse inter illos qui sunt de secta Beghardorum et inter eos qui eis adherent et eos fovent." Published by C. Schmidt, "Actenstücke besonders zur Geschichte der Waldenser," *Zeitschrift für die historische Theologie*, XXII (1852), 247–48 from MS Strassburg B 174 (subsequently destroyed in the fire of 1870), and, with numerous errors, by Döllinger, 389–91 from MS Clm 14959, fol. 231va–232ra. Leff, pp. 366–67, recapitulates this document, but uses the poor transcription of Döllinger and mistranslates "non debent obedire prelatis ecclesie nec statutis eorundem" as "priests can flout the decrees of the Church."

dom releases all from servitude including those who had been previously bound to a king or other lord.

What are we to make of these two lists, so rich in scandalous propositions and far exceeding in detail the prior condemnations of Cologne and Vienne? Were beghards, known until the fourteenth century for their extreme piety, really uttering all these outrageous tenets summed up by the statement that Christianity was mere foolishness? On the face of it, it appears astonishing that a group hitherto criticized primarily for unlicensed religiosity should so suddenly become avowedly anti-Christian.

An alternate explanation for the content of the Strassburg lists is that they were influenced by texts which the inquisitors used as materials to examine the accused. For example, the Bishop's letter has as its first point the belief that "God is formally all that is." This is contradictory to the heretics' belief that only some men could become God and is a technical proposition more likely to be debated in the schools than to be maintained with any ardor by wandering mendicants. Possibly John's inquisitors, some of whom were probably Dominicans, already knew St. Thomas' statement of the pantheism of Amaury of Bène[6] or some other source and used it as a basis for their examination. Similarly, the view that the body of Christ can be found in all bread just as well as in the bread of the altar was attributed to the Amaurians of Paris in 1210 and reappeared in the trial of Guichard of Troyes a century later.[7] Perhaps the beghards of Strassburg said the same thing independently, but it is just as likely that the inquisitors suggested it to them, especially remembering the fact that the Bishop of Troyes had been accused of using the very same words to convict an innocent victim in 1307.

The Strassburg tenets bear most similarity to the articles of the "new spirit" found in Nördlingen.[8] The Strassburg pantheism cor-

6. *Summa Theologica*, I P, qu. III, art. 8, c. a. Text in G. C. Capelle, *Amaury de Bène* (Paris, 1932), p. 95.

7. *UB Strassburg*, II, 311: "corpus Christi equaliter est in quolibet pane sicut in pane sacramentali." *Contra Amaurianos*, in Capelle, p. 93: "sicut Corpus Domini adoratur in pane consecrato in altari, ita adoratur in pane simplici apposito comedenti." A. Rigault, *Le procès de Guichard, Evêque de Troyes* (Paris, 1896), p. 174: "Guichard accusa Garnier Haymer, de Charmoy, d'avoir dit que le pain de la huche était aussi digne que le pain consacré sur l'autel." (Rigault does not give the original Latin.)

8. See above, Chapter I, Section 2.

responds to the statement from Nördlingen that all creatures are "full of God" and that "God is everywhere;" the contempt for Christ corresponds to the earlier statements that man can be greater than the son of God and that Christ was not wounded nor suffered in his passion. Even such details as the denial of hell and the justification of theft appear first in the Nördlingen list.[9]

9. It is easiest just to present the following parallel columns with extracts from the Strassburg inquisitorial list and Nördlingen list as edited by Schmidt. (Döllinger's transcription of MS Clm 14959 is so unreliable that I cite directly from the MS when it has important variants from Schmidt's reading of the now lost MS of Strassburg):

Strassburg 1317	*Nördlingen*
Deus sic est in omnibus quod omnia sunt Deus	(8) omnis creature plene sit Deus. (36) Deus ubique est
Ex hac perfectione unionis aliquorum cum Deo dicunt aliqui quod sint impeccabiles	(4) ita homo possit uniri Deo quod quidquid de cetero faciat non peccat
sunt realiter et naturaliter ipse Christus	(32) ita Deo sunt uniti quod sanguis eorum sit sicut sanguis Christi
Christus non pro nobis sed pro se ipso passus sit	(3) nullo modo sit credendum Christum in passione fuisse laceratum nec quidquam doluisse
ipsi meritum Christi . . . transscenderunt	(2) etiam homo precellat filium Dei
non reverentur sacramentum ewkaristie in ecclesiis vel alibi sicut deberent	(14) dicunt se elevari cum corpore domini in missa, nec surgunt nec flectunt genua quando elevatur vel portatur, sed tantum propter homines, ne scandalizentur
	(36) non sit assurgendum corpori domini
ex hoc nituntur concludere quod nec malum nec demones nec infernus	(6) non sunt demones nisi vita hominum (7) non sit infernus
dicunt furtem eis licitum (this is from the Bishop's letter)	(18) sine peccato possunt retinere rem alienam invito domino
dicunt quod quamvis sint sani et fortes non debent laborare corporaliter	(16) boni homines non debent insistere laboribus sed vitare (Clm 14959, fol. 231vb: vacare) et videre quam suavis est Deus

Either the heretics in the Ries around Nördlingen promulgated their unusual doctrines with amazing consistency for upwards of fifty years and spread them to Strassburg without ever being noticed, or else the beghards of Strassburg were examined on the basis of the earlier list. The first hypothesis taxes the imagination; the second is entirely in keeping with known inquisitorial practice and in addition is confirmed by the state of the manuscripts. Both surviving copies of the Strassburg inquisitorial list have the Nördlingen tenets immediately appended. Neither manuscript explains this, but it seems that the inquisitors must have given their results along with the texts that they used for their interrogations to the scribes. This was the way that inquisitorial handbooks were compiled.

A final document that must have influenced the Strassburg examinations of 1317 was the Clementine decree *Ad nostrum*. It is true that the latter had not yet been published at the time of John of Dürbheim's action, but the Bishop had attended the Council of Vienne and was definitely aware of the actions taken there.[10] The use of *Ad nos-*

Strassburg 1317	*Nördlingen*
dicunt orationes non esse necessarias	(17) orationes non valent que fiunt infra opera hominum
dicunt quod quidam eorum non tenentur quocunque tempore confiteri	(14) bonum hominem non oportet confiteri peccata quantumcunque magna, nisi alteri bono homini
	(20) non sit necesse in confessione narrare gestus peccatorum, sed sufficit dicere: ego peccavi
negant veram resurrexionem	(13) non sit resurrectio
quidquid faciunt cum corpore nunquam peccant; unde quamvis exerceat actum incontinentie vel cujuscunque vitii alterius non reputant hoc peccatum	(12) unitus Deo possit explere libidinem carnis per quemcunque modum licite
de facto frangunt libere ieiunia ecclesie, et aliqui comedunt carnes sextis feriis. . . .	(11) diem diei non preferunt in ieiunio (Clm 14959, fol. 231vb: diem dici non preferunt in ieiunia)
	(15) homines impediant bonitatem suam propter orationes suas, ieiunia, et flagella, et alia quecunque bona opera.

10. This is shown by the reservation in John's letter: "salvis nichilominus

trum, or at least knowledge of its contents, explains a number of further similarities. Indeed, of the eight points of the decree only the fifth and the seventh are not directly reflected in the texts of Strassburg.

All these sets of parallels notwithstanding, it would be going much too far to contend that there was no objective basis for John of Dürbheim's campaign. We have seen earlier that beghards and beguines had previously been arrested for heresy in Alsace in 1290.[11] Whatever they may have believed, it is clear from several surviving texts which we will examine later that unregulated mysticism had gained a tenacious foothold in Strassburg in the first half of the fourteenth century. Finally, we know that Meister Eckhart was preaching there just about the time of John of Dürbheim's actions and some of the tenets recorded seem to reflect his influence, though of course in a very distorted way. Such, for example, is the statement that those unified with God are "unchangeable" because they neither rejoice nor upset themselves.[12]

Another statement that is not in the earlier lists is the claim that on death all human spirits or souls return to God from whence they came. This is reported as an heretical belief in a sermon delivered in Cologne at roughly the same time as the Strassburg examinations,[13] which makes it more likely that it is authentic. The belief that parts of the Bible are only to be understood "poetically" fits in with this because the illustration chosen is the passage from Matthew (XXV, 34) that promises everlasting life for the "sheep" and eternal punishment for the "goats." From this it can also be seen that the heretics of Strassburg had not the slightest interest in chiliasm because they stressed the here and now rather than the future.

Beyond these suggestions there is no infallible way of winnowing out the wheat from the chaff in the two documents. The matter is

---

aliis sententiis atque penis in tales per sedem apostolicam promulgatis" and the formula in the inquisitorial document: "que et quos prohibuit sancta mater ecclesia, tam romana in generali, quam maguntina de consilio omnium suffraganiorum in speciali." Grundmann's inference ("Ketzerverhöre," 533 and n. 43) that John knew *Cum de quibusdam* but not *Ad nostrum* seems improbable.

11. See above, p. 62.

12. MS Wolfenb., Helmst., 311, fol. 107rb: "sunt etiam immutabiles, quod de nullo gaudent, et de nullo turbantur." On the marginal note to this passage see below, p. 210.

13. P. Strauch, "Kölner Klosterpredigten des 13. Jahrhunderts," *Jahrbuch des Vereins für niederdeutsche Sprachforschung*, XXXVII (1911), 44.

greatly complicated by the circumstance that people of different views must have been examined. This helps explain how one tenet categorically denies hell and purgatory, but shortly afterwards another says that it is useless to pray for those in purgatory. There probably were also different opinions about sexual morality that account for the attack on all nonprocreative sexual relations in the Bishop's letter as opposed to the justification of license in the inquisitorial list. There must have been mystical extremists in Strassburg, but the suspicion that they were not so outrageously anti-Christian as they were reported to be is confirmed by independent and more reliable evidence to be examined in a separate chapter of this book.

More credence can be placed in the non-doctrinal points of the Bishop's letter because these have nothing to do with stereotyped descriptions of earlier heretics. According to John, the accused were commonly called beghards and sisters (*"swestrones"*). This is the first known example of the term "sister" as a designation for heretical beguine, but it is not the last. It is confirmed by the heading of the most famous Free Spirit tract: *"Daz ist swester katrei meister Ekehartes Tohter von Strâzburc"* and it reappears consistently in fourteenth-century writings from Germanic speaking lands.[14] The fact that John used it in preference to the term beguine indicates that he wanted to distinguish between the "dishonest" and the "honest" and reserved the term beguine, as we will see, for those whom he wished to protect.

In contradistinction to their nicknames, the accused called themselves "youths or brothers or sisters of the sect of the Free Spirit and voluntary poverty."[15] This self-designation reflects the union between mystical and apostolic strivings that was a major trait of the movement. Despite the oft-repeated assertion of modern scholarship that the term "Free Spirit" was seldom used, there are in fact many examples of it, and this one is a clear indication that some alleged heretics

14. For the use of this term as far north as the Netherlands see Fredericq, II, 153, #106 (Utrecht, ca. 1393).

15. Mosheim mistakenly read *"parvos fratres vel sorores"* and saw therein a similarity to the terms *"Fraterculus"* or *"Fratricellus"* (p. 262), but the correct reading from MS *cit.*, fol. 107ra is: "nonnulli qui sub nomine cuiusdam ficte et presumpte religionis quos vulgus Begehardos et swestrones Brot durch got nominant ipsi vero et ipse se de secta liberi spiritus et voluntarie paupertatis pueros sive fratres vel sorores vocant."

used it themselves. According to John's account, the beghards and sisters had followers in the city and diocese of Strassburg. These included, to his horror, many in sacred orders as well as married people and men of various conditions.

The beghards themselves wore tunics which were cut away in the front from the belt downwards and short hoods which were not joined to their tunics. This description varies somewhat from that of Trier seven years earlier and it is likely that the beghard habit differed in details throughout northern Europe; but whether hoods were long or short they must have been regarded as an irritating imitation of the mendicant orders. Likewise, according to the Bishop's description, the women covered their heads with their cloaks. This later became a recognized beguinal practice: for example, a German edict for nuns of 1406 ordered that "no sister shall wear her coat over her head because only the condemned beguines wear their coats this way."[16]

Relying on the advice of "wise and elected men," and citing the decisions taken against beghards at Mainz in 1310 (the diocese of Strassburg belonged to the province of Mainz), the Bishop condemned all the errors, ceremonies, conventicles, and dress of the "sect." He ordered that the heretics be driven from their dwellings and assembly places, which were to be confiscated for the use of the Church and the poor. Books containing the heretical doctrines and songs were to be delivered up within fifteen days to be burned. For the sake of the unity of the Church, John gave the accused three days to discard their habits and refrain from crying "Brot durch Gott." If they did not comply, they and all those that aided them were to be excommunicated. The condemnation expressly exempted Franciscan tertiaries, "honest secular beguines," and any others who were under the governance of the approved mendicant orders, a concession that must have resulted from the influence of the friars.[17]

---

16. Cited by Mosheim, p. 265.

17. Mosheim's mistaken reading (p. 260): "sed eos iuxta modum servatum in aliis provinciis perdurare" led McDonnell, p. 528, to believe that Bishop John thought beguines could be tolerated in certain provinces—"presumably a reference to Belgium." But the correct reading is very different: "Per hanc autem nostram sententiam. . . Religiosis qui sunt de tertia Regula fratrum Minorum, aut Beginis honestis secularibus, vel etiam quibuslibet aliis familiaribus fratrum approbatorum ordinum, et secundum eorum consilium se regentibus, nullatenus

Two months later Pope John XXII promulgated the Clementine decrees and at the end of 1317 he issued the bull *Sancta Romana* which seemed to be directed against the Third Order of St. Francis. John of Dürbheim, who already had not confined himself to mere threats, was now at a loss as to how to proceed because he had excluded "honest" beguines and tertiaries from his own legislation but was not sure how the Papacy stood on the issue. Thus, in a letter he wrote to his clergy on July 22, 1318 to explain the important measures taken by the Council of Vienne he entirely ignored the two Clementine decrees against beguines and beghards.[18] At about the same time he wrote to the Pope for advice.

This letter has not survived, but we know its contents from John XXII's answer. The Bishop complained that many prelates and rectors in various dioceses (he does not speak of his own) made no distinction between "good" and "bad" beguines but applied the provisions of *Cum de quibusdam* indiscriminately. The good beguines, whom the Bishop extravagantly numbered at more than 200,000 (presumably throughout Germany), were compelled to remove their habits and return to secular life. In some cases, recluses who had been living in cells for fifty years were driven out into the world. In view of this situation, John appealed for further instructions.[19]

The Pope's answer was twofold. First, he replied directly to the

---

volumus praejudicium generari, sed eas iuxta modum servatum ab eis permiciis perdurare" (from MS cit., fol. 108rb).

18. S. A. Würdtwein, *Nova subsidia diplomatica* (Heidelberg, 1781–92), XIII, 301–10 (this important document was unfortunately overlooked by the editors of the *Strassburger Urkundenbuch*). It is instructive to compare John's letter to a similar document of Bishop Frederick of Utrecht, dated March 31, 1318, which asks his clergy to enforce both *Cum de quibusdam* and *Ad nostrum* (ed. J. G. C. Joosting and S. Muller, *Bronnen voor de geschiedenis der kerkelijke rechtspraak in het bisdom Utrecht, 4–5: provinciale en synodale statuten* [The Hague, 1914], 104).

19. John XXII's answer to the Bishop's letter exists in two versions. A short one was published by Mosheim, pp. 630–32, from a MS that can now be identified as Wolfenb., Helmst., 315, fol. 203v–204r; a longer and more detailed one was published by S. Baluzius, *Vitae paparum Avenionensium*, ed. G. Mollat (Paris, 1914–27), III, 353–56, # LXVI, from the inquisitorial archives of Carcassonne. Neither version is dated; Baluze-Mollat hazard "[1321?]" but, as noted in *UB Strassburg*, II, 332, n. 2, there can be little doubt that the Bishop's letter was written shortly before the papal bull *Racio recta* of August 13, 1318, which then clarified the issue.

Bishop to say that the "good" beguines should not be molested on the pretext of the decrees of Vienne, but should be allowed to retain their habits and their former way of life. On the other hand he insisted that those wanderers who call themselves "youths and brothers or sisters of the Free Spirit and voluntary poverty" be sought and punished on the basis of the Clementine decrees with all dispatch and severity. At the same time, in *Racio recta* of August 1318, he applied the same instructions to the treatment of all beguines, "especially those in German parts."[20]

In the meantime, John of Dürbheim did his utmost to convert or extirpate "bad" beguines and beghards and was praised for his actions in this regard by the pope.[21] The Bishop sought out heretics wherever he could find them and pressured them to abjure their errors. Those who did so were released, but were forced to wear crosses as signs of their penitence; those who did not were handed over to the secular arm for punishment. There are no reports of any executions, but the persecution was severe enough to cause many to flee, as we know from a letter that John wrote to a neighboring prelate, the Bishop of Worms, warning him to be on his guard for any heretics escaping down the Rhine, and adding that many were fleeing to other cities and dioceses.[22] The memory of John's actions was still alive half a century later.

20. Papal letter to John of Dürbheim, ed. Baluze-Mollat, III, 355. *Racio recta* is in Fredericq, II, 72–74, #44 (on this subject, see further above, pp. 48–49). MS Wolfenb., Helmst., 311, fol. 108vb–109rb and 109vb–111ra, contains important new documents about the further treatment of "good" beguines and Franciscan tertiaries at Strassburg, including a letter dated January 18, 1319 concerning the beguines, and the episcopal promulgation of the bull *Etsi apostolici* concerning the tertiaries (dated June 18, 1319). This material supplements the account of Haupt, "Beiträge," 521–24.

21. Ed. Baluze-Mollat, III, 355: ". . . tuam, quam circa exterminationem dictorum errorum et errantium habuisti, sollicitudinem dignis in Domino laudibus commendantes."

22. John's letter to the Bishop of Worms containing the description of the persecution was published by Mosheim, pp. 268–69, from MS Wolfenb., Helmst., 311, fol. 108va–vb. Mosheim dated it "1318, VI, Kal. Julii" (i.e. June 26, 1318), but the letter in the MS is in fact undated. The date 1318, V, Kal. Julii (i.e. June 27, 1318) appears only in the next document in the MS; because the compiler of this section worked chronologically it is safe to say only that the letter was written sometime between August 13, 1317 and June 27, 1318. The conclusion that there were no executions is made by C. Schmidt, "Über die Secten zu Strassburg im Mittelalter," *Zeitschrift für die historische Theologie*, X (1840), 61,

2. THE SECOND WAVE OF PERSECUTIONS

After the campaign of John of Dürbheim there was a long lull, as there was throughout Germany, in persecutions of heresy. Only in 1359 did the subject reappear in official records. These tell of three men who were permanently banished from the city for claiming that they were breaking off God's legs and scratching His eyes out by striking and scratching a chair. One of them similarly threw a knife into the sky saying that he wanted to strike God with it. If this account has any substance, it must relate to the conduct of eccentrics. The men were not called beghards and were not charged with belonging to any organization.[23]

Seven years later the Papal Inquisition, invigorated by the reforming Pope Urban V, went to work for the first time in Strassburg and brought about the first known execution for heresy there since the early thirteenth century. On June 6, 1366, Henry de Agro, Inquisitor for the province of Mainz, relaxed a certain Metza of Westhoven to the secular arm because she had already recanted during the persecutions of John of Dürbheim almost fifty years earlier but had relapsed into heresy. Since John's campaign had been levelled against alleged antinomianism Metza was probably charged with such errors, but the habit of calling her a beguine derives only from an assumption made in the eighteenth century. The church historian Mosheim, who found her sentence, published it with the title: *Sententia diffinitiva contra Metzam de Westhoven, Beguinam,* but now that the manuscript has been rediscovered it can be said that the last word appears nowhere in the original text.[24]

It is impossible to say to what degree Metza was guilty since there is no surviving protocol of her trial and the sentence does not list any of her errors. But it does appear that her execution was a staged spectacle. Punishment must have been carried out a few days after the sentence of June 6, and we know that John of Luxemburg, the newly

---

on the basis of the sixteenth-century account by the Strassburg architect Daniel Specklin. The MS of this work was destroyed in the disaster of 1870, but Schmidt, 64–65, n. 72, reproduces a large part that shows that Specklin must have had access to original documents.

23. *Heimlich Buch* of the Strassburger Stadtrat, CdS, IX, 1021–22.

24. Cf. Mosheim, p. 333, with MS Wolfenb., Helmst., 311, fol. 42vb–43ra.

named Bishop of Strassburg, was received ceremonially into the city on the tenth of the month.[25] John was a relative of the Emperor Charles IV who had used his influence at Avignon to secure the appointment. The Emperor was as dedicated to the persecution of heresy as the Pope, so it was probably not accidental that his protegé was greeted at Strassburg by the auto-da-fé of a defenseless old woman.

So far as we know, Metza was the only victim of that year, and two years later an inquisition commissioned by John of Luxemburg to investigate the beguines of Strassburg found them guiltless.[26] But, in a letter of August 19, 1374, a new Bishop, Lambert of Burn, launched a campaign against beguines (without mentioning beghards) for ignoring the prohibitions of the Council of Vienne and the ruling against new orders.[27] Even though he quoted from *Ad nostrum*, he included no charges of doctrinal error, but complained only of their way of life. According to him, they begged without need, wore habits unique in form, color, and cut, held conventicles, and elected their own superiors whom they called mistresses. They confessed to these or to each other, and received penances in the form of prayers or blows. Instead of receiving the Eucharist from parish priests they took it from the religious (i.e. mendicant orders) in violation of canon law. For these and other reasons, the Bishop ordered his clergy to preach against them for the next three Sundays and Feast-days and gave the beguines fifteen days to disband or face inquisition.

What prompted Lambert to these measures when others seemed convinced of the beguines blamelessness? One answer might be found in his close relations with Charles IV, the patron of persecutors. Lambert "belonged without a doubt among the most trusted and influential advisors of the Emperor."[28] As Bishop of Speyer he had accompanied the latter on a trip to Italy, and, as no one has yet noticed, he was a witness to one of the imperial edicts of 1369 against beghards

25. Jacob Twinger von Königshofen, *Chronik*, CdS, IX, 675–76.
26. All we know about this comes from an oblique reference in ms *cit.*, fol. 105ra.
27. Ed. Haupt, "Beiträge," 562–64 from ms Colmar 29, and Döllinger, 378–81 from ms Clm 14216. A third version in ms Wolfenb., Helmst., 311, fol. 103va–104ra has too many variants to list here, but none are crucial.
28. J. Looshorn, *Die Geschichte des Bisthums Bamberg* (Munich, 1891), III, 343. According to Königshofen, 676, Lambert became Charles IV's Chancellor after he left Strassburg for the bishopric of Bamberg.

and beguines.[29] Thus he was fully cognizant of imperial policy on this subject, and he was no doubt anxious to please.

Further motivation can undoubtedly be found in the tangled local ecclesiastical politics of Strassburg, though this is a subject beyond the present writer's competence and one that should be treated separately on the basis of a newly rediscovered manuscript dossier.[30] All that can be said here is that the Dominicans, who were overseers of certain beguinages, were one of the objects of the Bishop's attack and were already on the defensive in the matter of a struggle with their own nuns.[31] Lambert chose a good moment to proceed against them, especially since the Dominican provincial was far away at the time.[32] The wording of his edict, as well as the fact that his campaign allegedly uncovered many heretics among Franciscan tertiaries, shows that Lambert, no friar himself, was challenging the Franciscans as well.[33] The result was a rare inquisition not conducted by the mendicant orders but actually levelled in part against them.

The friars did their best to defend themselves and the women in their charge. A month after Lambert's edict the Dominicans presented to the episcopal court a papal privilege of 1287 that entrusted them with the supervision of certain beguines.[34] Also, together with the Franciscans, they issued a long complaint in which they protested the fact that all beguines without distinction had been banned from par-

29. Fredericq, I, 213, # 211, confirmed by MS Wolfenb., Helmst., 315, fol. 212r. On the imperial legislation of 1369, see below, pp. 133–34.

30. Wolfenb., Helmst., 311, fol. 103r–107r, from the collection of Flacius Illyricus, and familiar to Mosheim (see his p. 399), who planned to make use of it before his death intervened. The presumed loss of the MS was lamented by Schmidt, (as above, n. 22), 62, n. 70, who mistakenly thought that the documents pertained to the persecution under John of Dürbheim. For this reason, Schmidt's "Die Strassburger Beginenhäuser im Mittelalter," *Alsatia*, VII (1858–61), 149–248, goes no further than Mosheim in its discussion of charges of heresy.

31. W. Kothe, *Kirchliche Zustände Strassburgs im 14. Jahrhundert* (Freiburg, 1902), pp. 71–74.

32. *UB Strassburg*, V, 2, 846–47, #1120; 857, #1150.

33. The statement that his campaign uncovered heretics among the tertiaries is in MS Clm 14216, fol. 178rb, ed. Döllinger, 378.

34. MS Wolfenb., Helmst., 311, fol. 103r. The heading, in a later hand, terms this "Privilegium fratrum predicatorum super beginas ad turrim in argentina apud predicatores residentes," but the text itself refers only to the "mistress and sisters in Molsheim." For other legislation pertaining to Strassburg issued in 1287 by the papal legate, John Buccomatius, see *UB Strassburg*, II, 86–94, #125–132.

taking of the sacraments. They insisted that the women were guilty neither of the excesses attributed to them by Lambert nor of the errors contained in the Clementines and pleaded with him to revoke his edict.[35]

A few months later the Dominicans also tried to bring to their advantage the fact that the Papacy was concurrently re-examining its position on beguines. At the end of 1374 a delegation that included a vicar of the Dominican provincial[36] brought to Strassburg a bull of Gregory XI that ordered the suspension of actions against beguines until reliable information about them could be gathered.[37] It is not known what effect this bull had, but new evidence shows that procedures against beguines were resumed (probably in the next decade) by Lambert of Burn's successor, Frederick of Blankenstein.[38]

The most valuable part of the dossier concerning the beguine controversy under Lambert is a formulary that was meant to be used in inquisitorial interrogations. This is the only such list extant and it reveals how people could be found throughout the later Middle Ages who always confessed to the same errors. The questions fell into several categories, the first of which aimed at obliging arrested beguines to admit that they were violating the papal ban on new orders. They

35. MS *cit.*, fol. 104ra–105ra: "Contradictio ordinum mendicantium." Fol. 104va: ". . . mulieres innocentes cum nocentibus, si que cum nocentes fuerunt, quod non credimus neque scimus, a . . . sacramentorum perceptione segregata sunt et excluse et cottidie segregantur ac excluduntur. Hinc est quod dictum processum cum eius penis supplicamus et petimus nostri et dictarum mulierum nomine revocari. . . ."

36. Hugo de Zabern. The conclusion that he was the provincial's vicar can be drawn from *UB Strassburg*, V, 2, 846, #1120 and 952, #1306.

37. Fredericq, I, 228–31, #220, reprinted from Mosheim, 394–98. Since Lambert had already left for the bishopric of Bamberg, the bull was presented to the episcopal Official, Reinbold of Gmünd, who might have been the motive force in the proceedings against the beguines. On him, see H. Heimpel, "Stadtadel und Gelehrsamkeit. Die Vener von Schwäbisch Gmünd und Strassburg, 1162–1447," in *Adel und Kirche: Festschrift für Gerd Tellenbach* (Freiburg, 1968), p. 422. On Gregory's bull, see above, pp. 53–54.

38. John Mulberg, *Materia contra beghardos, beginas, lolhardos, et swestriones*, MS Basel A. IX. 21, fol. 106r: "Item Episcopi argentinensis Johannes, lampertus, fridericus in suis. . . processibus contra beginas . . . ." Also MS Clm 14216, fol. 179rb (overlooked by Döllinger): "Dominus quoque fridericus Episcopus argentinsis prefati domini Lamperti successor consimiles processus contra ipsas Beginas fulminavit." These brief statements are the only ones I could find regarding Frederick's activities against the beguines.

were asked "whether, and to whom, and in what manner did they promise obedience?" and "did they profess any rule approved by the apostolic chair?" If they said that they followed the Third Rule of St. Francis, they were to describe their mode of living and say from whom they received this rule.[39] These queries were carefully phrased to offer the accused only two alternatives: either they followed no approved rule and could be condemned ipso facto, or else they had to implicate the mendicants, who, in the eyes of the secular clergy, had no license for directing beguines.

The second set of questions was based on the Clementine decree *Cum de quibusdam*, and provided a transition from questions concerning organization to those concerning heresy: did the witness "ever dispute, or hear others dispute, about the highest Trinity, the divine essence, the articles of the faith, or sacraments of the Church? did she hold or introduce, or hear anyone else hold or introduce, singular opinions about the articles of the faith or sacraments of the Church? did she ever preach, or hear any other women preach?"[40] These questions led directly to the next set, which asked *ad separatim* if the beguines believed in any of the eight articles of *Ad nostrum*.[41]

The final group of questions, with one exception were worded like charges contained in the Bishop's edict: did the beguines consciously wear a special habit? did they hold congregations and conventicles, or have a superior, or mistress, or "Martha?"[42] (The latter term was used frequently by beguines as a synonym for mistress.) The last question, which was the only one of the set that did not correspond to a passage from Lambert's edict, is the most interesting: did the witness "have, or ever have, or know anyone to have a German book entitled *de novem rupibus*, known in the vernacular as *bûch*

---

39. MS Wolfenb., Helmst., 311, fol. 105va–vb: "utrum et cui et qualiter promittant obedientiam;" "utrum professi sunt aliqua regulam approbatum per sedem apostolicam;" "si dicant se professas regulam tercii ordinis sancti francisci, queratur ab eis quis sic modus vivendi earum et an et qualiter et per quem ad huiusmodi regulam sint recepte."

40. *Ibid.*, fol. 105vb: "an unquam disputaverit aut disputari per alias audiverit de summa trinitate aut de divina essencia aut de articulis fidei aut de ecclesiasticis sacramentis. Item an aliquas opiniones singulares circa articulos fidei et ecclesiastica sacramenta tenuerit vel introduxerit vel per alias teneri aut introduci audiverit. Item an unquam predicaverit vel alias predicare audiverit."

41. *Ibid.*, fol. 105vb–106ra.

42. *Ibid.*, fol. 106ra–rb.

von den nùn feilsen. . . ?"[43] This is a clear reference to vernacular literature among the beguines, a subject we will treat in a later chapter. The formulary ends with the instruction that other questions should be asked according to the quality of the witnesses, the exigencies of their responses, and other varying circumstances.

A note prefacing one of the manuscript copies of Lambert's edict tells us that the Bishop called in a certain Martin, "a priest from Bohemia," to direct his inquisition.[44] The latter was to become in subsequent decades a notorious Inquisitor and Strassburg seems to have been the place where he first won his spurs, for, as the same note tells us, he was there able to find many heretics among the Franciscan tertiaries. The surviving formulary shows that he must specially have been looking for them because the Bishop's edict mentions only matters of discipline while the formulary asks witnesses to comment on all eight articles of *Ad nostrum.* As we will see in the next chapter, the mere posing of tenets from *Ad nostrum* to suggestible women could yield results satisfactory to an inquisitor and this probably happened in Strassburg, though no protocols survive to illuminate the case further. Still, the signal absence of any reference to male heretics or outside agitators along with the facts that the Bishop did not refer to heresy and the representatives of the mendicant orders heatedly denied such a possibility makes it seem that the heresy of the Free Spirit was not flourishing in Strassburg at the time of Martin's activities.

3. THE CASE OF JOHN MALKAW

As the fourteenth century waned and the Babylonian Captivity gave way to the Great Schism, unfounded charges and countercharges of heresy proliferated. The best example in Strassburg was the case of John Malkaw, who was thoroughly orthodox and had nothing to do with either beguines or beghards, but was charged with being a heretic of the Free Spirit.[45]

43. *Ibid.,* fol. 106rb: "an habeat vel habuerit vel sciat habentem quemdam librum theotunicum qui intitulatur de novem rupibus, wlgariter dicendo debet bûch von den nùn feilsen in quo dicuntur multa fidei katholice dissona contineri."

44. See above, n. 33. Since the Munich MS mentions this "Martinus presbiter de Bohemia" as an executor of a bull of Boniface IX it is almost certain that he is identical to the Martin of Prague whose activities are described below, pp. 146–48.

45. His turbulent career is described in admirable detail by H. Haupt, "Jo-

Malkaw was a secular cleric who was a fanatic adherent of the Roman Pope. In 1390 he journeyed through the Rhineland toward Rome and stayed in Strassburg for about a month to preach against the Avignonese schismatics. These he unhesitatingly called an heretical and satanic congregation, and he made more enemies by excoriating the morals of the mendicant orders. Unfortunately for him, the Dominicans had come back to power in the city with the result that, according to Malkaw's own account which may certainly have been embellished, he was threatened with punitive action. Specifically, the Dominican inquisitor, Nicholas Böckeler, an associate of the leader of the Avignonese party in Strassburg, warned Malkaw that he would seal his mouth as a troublemaker.

This he nearly did. Malkaw continued on to Rome, but in 1391 he returned the same way. As soon as he was over the Alps he was arrested by the Bishop of Basel who had been urged to do this by some friars who had found out that Malkaw was no longer carrying documents to prove that he was a priest. Either he escaped from his captivity in Basel (the story of his enemies) or else he was released by the Bishop with a warning to return home (his own account), but then, still spoiling for a fight, he went right back to Strassburg and returned to the pulpit. Not surprisingly, he was arrested shortly afterwards by the Dominican inquisitor, incarcerated in an episcopal prison, and charged with heresy. After two preliminary hearings Böckeler deemed it wiser not to give the peppery Malkaw a chance to protest his orthodoxy, but instead presented a clerical assembly, composed mostly of friars, with a list of articles that made his victim look like a Waldensian, a disciple of Olivi, a Free Spirit, a blasphemer, and a thorough reprobate, all in one!

It is hard to decide which of the charges was the most preposterous. A good example is the article which stated that Malkaw had absolutely no discipline because he spoke shamefully to women about menstruation. His answer to this was that he never did so, unless perhaps in confession when he urged abstention from marital intercourse during the menstrual period. Similarly, Böckeler charged Malkaw

hannes Malkaw aus Preussen und seine Verfolgung durch die Inquisition zu Strassburg und Köln (1390–1416)," ZfK, VI (1884), 323–65, with an appendix, 365–89, containing extracts from John's lengthy self-defense.

with belonging to "the sect of Lollards" because he allegedly left his own diocese without episcopal permission, and called him a Free Spirit because his followers ate what he had already chewed. Malkaw, in his defense, not only denied these allegations but included some of his own refutations of Free-Spirit error.[46]

That the hostile assembly called by the inquisitor knew that the accused was not with any shadow of doubt a heretic is reflected in the fact that it demanded only his expulsion from Strassburg. The Bishop apparently granted this request and Malkaw matriculated without incident at the University of Cologne in 1392 despite the fact that only a year before he had been accused of upholding the most scandalous heresies. In July 1394 the University of Heidelberg cleared him of all the charges that had been lodged by Böckeler, though one could well imagine that in slightly different circumstances he might have been burned at the stake.[47]

4. THE THIRD WAVE OF PERSECUTIONS

In 1400, in the midst of a campaign against heresy that encompassed most of Germany, which we will have occasion to return to, the same Dominican inquisitor who had acted so unscrupulously against Malkaw proceeded against Waldensians. An insight into his mixed motives is shown by trial records which indicate that he accepted a bribe of thirty gulden for reducing one of the convicted Waldensian's penance.[48] Since he was clearly looking for heretics of any variety, and since we know from Malkaw's case that Böckeler was informed about "lollards" and "Free Spirits," it is noteworthy that only one of some thirty people he arrested, a mistress of a *"Gotzhuse,"* was a beguine.[49] More importantly, the trial records indicate that none of the

---

46. *Ibid.,* 366–67, 370–71, 385, 387–88.

47. The decision of Heidelberg (unknown to Haupt) in E. Winkelmann, *UB der Universität Heidelberg* (Heidelberg, 1886), II, 9, #62. Long ago, Lea, III, 206, noted that Malkaw's case reveals "how easily the accusation of heresy could be used for the destruction of any man."

48. Timotheus Wilhelm Röhrich, *Mittheilungen aus der Geschichte der evangelischen Kirche des Elsasses* (Strassburg and Paris, 1855), I, 3–77, discusses the episode and publishes the trial records. See also the record of a condemnation and execution for heresy in 1400 in *UB Strassburg*, VI, 786–87, #1541. The Waldensians in Strassburg were known as *Winkelers*.

49. Röhrich, 64.

accused were antinomians or even mystics. By 1400, then, even a zealous inquisitor could find no Free Spirits in Strassburg.[50]

But in the meantime the fiery Dominican preacher John Mulberg, prompted by hostilities against the Franciscans, was conducting a campaign against the beguines and Franciscan tertiaries of neighboring Basel.[51] This led the town council of Strassburg around 1404 to ask a local commission of canon lawyers for a ruling on the legal status of beguines. When the answer came that beguines and beghards had been outlawed by several papal bulls, the councillors ordered that "notwithstanding the Third Rule of St. Francis," all beguines and beghards should abandon their habits and give up their begging.[52] This shows that some of the victims, like many of Mulberg's campaign in Basel, were Franciscan tertiaries rather than unaffiliated beguines.

The prohibition forced some women to flee down the Rhine to Mainz, a route, it may be recalled, taken by refugees from Strassburg almost a century earlier. There they met another persecution in 1406 and were incarcerated.[53] But the campaign of 1404 was, like previous ones, only temporary, and soon afterward the beguinages again filled up with inhabitants, to continue in existence until the Reformation. At the end of the fifteenth century, which saw no further harassment, the preacher Geiler von Kaysersberg referred to the errors of the sect of beghards and beguines in the past tense.[54]

The three campaigns in Strassburg produced sharply diminishing returns. There can be no doubt that in 1317 Bishop John of Dürbheim found numerous heretics among beguines and beghards, but in 1374 Bishop Lambert of Burn attacked the beguines only for their alleged violation of the papal ban on new orders and had nothing to say either about doctrinal heresy or about beghards. An inquisitor invited

---

50. *Ibid.*, 23: "Endlich muss bemerkt werden, dass in dem Documente, welches dieser Untersuchung über die Winkeler zum Grunde liegt, auch nicht die leiseste Andeutung sich finde, dass diese der Speculationen oder auch der fleischlichen Verirrungen der Secte des freien Geistes u. A. verdächtig gewesen seien."

51. See below, pp. 154–57.

52. Christian Wurstisen, *Baszler Chronick* (Basel, 1580), pp. 205–206. A translation in the Alemannic dialect of this ruling is in MS Karlsruhe, Reichenau (Augiensia) 116, fol. 356r–357r: "Es ist ain frag ob der beghart und der beginen stät vor der hailigen gottes kilchen verworfen und verbotten sig. . . ."

53. *Chronicon Moguntinum*, ed. C. Hegel, SRG, XX, 62.

54. *Ausgewählte Schriften*, ed. P. de Lorenzi (Trier, 1881–83), II, 279.

to Strassburg by Lambert supposedly did find heresy, but there is manuscript evidence for the supposition that he succeeded only by asking pointedly leading questions. In 1404 when the town council (which by this time had usurped much episcopal jurisdiction in ecclesiastical matters) became concerned with the legal status of beguines there was no mention of heresy at all. Ulterior motives played a great role in the later persecutions. Even though John of Dürbheim ordered beguinages to be confiscated for the use of the Church, material interests were probably not his greatest concern, but in 1374 the rivalry between secular and regular clergy seems to have had a dominant influence on the persecution of beguines governed by the friars, and in 1404 beguines were victimized as the result of a struggle between Dominicans and Franciscans. In between, in 1366 there was an auto-da-fé most likely for political reasons and in 1391 and 1400 motives of vengefulness and avarice were clearly at play. The high point of the Free-Spirit heresy must then have been in the first half of the fourteenth century when Strassburg was also the home of famous mystical preachers. Indeed, authentic Free-Spirit writings from Strassburg show how the heresy there came from a beguinal milieu strongly influenced by the thought of Meister Eckhart.[55] But by the second half of the century there was a cooling off of mystical and apostolic fervor in these circles, and as early as 1352 Rulman Merswin lamented that the beguines of his day did not have the great "inner zeal" that they used to have, while the beghards had forgotten "the right inner way."[56]

55. See below, pp. 208–13, 215–21.
56. *Merswins Neun-Felsen-Buch*, ed. P. Strauch, *Altdeutsche Textbibliothek*, 27 (Halle, 1929), pp. 36–38. The translation of Thomas S. Kepler, *Mystical Writings of Rulman Merswin* (Philadelphia, 1960), pp. 76–77, is inadequate (e.g. Kepler translates "*beggehart*" as "monk," and "die brüder die after wege löffent" as "the brothers in orders").

Chapter Five

THE INQUISITION IN THE EAST

The evidence from Strassburg gives us some impression of the extent of the Free-Spirit heresy in the fourteenth century and some insight into the nature of inquisitorial procedure but includes no legal testimony of any beghard or Free Spirit. Confessions or protocols are without question the most valuable sort of inquisitorial documents and these we meet first in east-central Europe. There the Papal Inquisition sought heretical beghards and beguines much earlier than in the West[1] and the result was that two of the most extensive documents describing the heresy of the Free Spirit were produced in the first half of the fourteenth century in the east. Up to now we have heard about antinomians and heretical beghards only from their enemies: in this chapter, for the first time, we can analyze their own accounts.

1. JOHN AND ALBERT OF BRÜNN

As we saw in the first chapter, the Bishop of Prague who in 1318 offered resistance to the Inquisition was imprisoned by order of the Pope; thereafter, Inquisitors in Bohemia were subject to no restraints. As early as 1319 a beguine was brought to trial in Prague for refusing to accept the Eucharist from her parish priest.[2] Later, in 1335, Pope

1. First in a papal order for the Polish diocese of Wladislaw, ed. A. Theiner, *Vetera monumenta Poloniae et Lithuaniae* (Rome, 1860–64), I, 150–51, # 231.
2. J. Emler, *Regesta diplomatica nec non epistolaria Bohemiae et Moraviae* (Prague, 1855–1954), III, 220.

Benedict XII appointed the ruthless Dominican, Gallus of Novo Castro, as Inquisitor for Czech lands. The latter was so zealous that in 1339 the populace in part of southern Bohemia revolted against the Inquisition and caused the Pope in 1340 to grant crusading indulgences for all who fought against this insurrection. A year later the pontiff urged Margrave Charles—later to be Emperor and persecutor of heretics in his own right—to aid the Inquisition and also ordered the Bishop of Prague to put his prisons at its disposal because the number of those arrested was so large. In 1346 a new Pope continued to express concern about the lack of prison space for Bohemian heretics and some time after 1350 the Inquisitor Gallus was badly wounded by an assassin. Since this is the last we hear of him he might have died from these injuries.[3]

In view of all this violence it might be assumed that heresy was widespread in Bohemia well before the time of Hus, but such a conclusion is premature. Gallus' closest ally was Ulrich, lord of Neuhaus in southern Bohemia, who used the Inquisition to repress political and economic grievances in his locality. Whatever heretics there were were mostly Waldensians, as is shown by two fragments of trial records.[4] The only mention of beghards in either is indirect. In 1337 one Henzlinus confessed that he doubted the power of sinful priests to grant absolution—a basic Waldensian tenet. He also mentioned beghards and helpfully supplied whatever scraps of information concerning their beliefs he could think of, but the cryptic and perhaps garbled tenets he reported reflect none of the autotheist or antinomian mysticism thought to be characteristic of the Free-Spirit movement.[5]

---

3. The details of Gallus' career and the Czech Inquisition are best presented by J. Koudelka, "Zur Geschichte der böhmischen Dominikanerprovinz im Mittelalter," AFP, XXV (1955), 86–88.

4. The first was published by F. Menčik, "Výzlech Valdenských r. 1340," *Sitzungsberichte der königlichen böhmischen Gesellschaft der Wissenschaften, philosophische-historische-philologische Klasse* (1891), pp. 280–87. A German summary and interpretation is by H. Haupt, "Deutsch-böhmische Waldenser um 1340," ZfK, XIV (1894), 1–18, who shows that the document concerns Waldensians exclusively.

5. From the second fragment, ed. I. Hlaváček, "Inkvisice v Čechách ve 30. letech 14. stoleti," *Československý časopis historický*, V (1957), 535–36: "Henzlinus filius Petri dicti Hereticus dixit: Quid potest me sacerdos, qui est peccator, absolvere. Item a Bernhardo nec non dicto P ipse audiverit de Beghardis qui-

Gallus of Novo Castro surely wanted to find heretical beghards in order to justify his persecutions, but it seems that he would have had a very hard time had he not been able to produce two unusually cooperative witnesses: John and Albert of Brünn. Their undated testimony is not transmitted in trial records but comes to us in the form of confessions taken when John had already been accepted into the Dominican Order. His detailed account must therefore have been his passport into the Order, of which Gallus was a leading member.[6]

John was a man of substance who lived with his wife in Brünn when he was seized with the desire to achieve a life of perfection. A century earlier he might have become a Franciscan but now he was advised by a friend that the beghards lived in the most perfect state because they imitated evangelical poverty more than any priests, friars, or laymen. Since John's wife was not of like mind he gave her half of his property and left with his mentor for Cologne. There he entered a "house of the poor" (*"domus pauperum"*) near St. Stephen in the new city, where he lived as a simple beghard for twenty years.

His description of this period in his life is conventional and credible. The house at Cologne was governed by the principles of voluntary poverty and obedience. John's superiors obliged him to surrender his remaining wealth because "the truly poor have no property but must be as free of all temporal things as Christ on the cross." Then they stripped him nude and gave him a tunic of one hundred shreds to remind him of Christ's humiliation. They ordered him to beg for a living and warned him that even though he might be derided and called a heretic the more patiently he suffered the holier he would become. When any poor brother came from the road John was to receive him kneeling and then wash his feet after the model of Christ. If ordered on any mission he was to go humbly, and at night instead

---

busdam, quod Corpus Domini, si esset verum corpus, iam esset per sacerdotes consumptum ut sicut mons materialis. Item dixit se audivisse ab aliis Beghardis quod si beata virgo Maria in hoc seculo adhuc fuisset, vix debet fuisse publica mulier forma." The remark about the "mountain of matter" turned up again in a list of errors attributed to Thuringian flagellants in 1414. See A. Stumpf, "Historia Flagellantium, praecipue in Thuringia," *Neue Mittheilungen aus dem Gebiete historisch-antiquarischer Forschungen,* II (1835), 29: "Si verum corpus Christi esset in sacramento, diu devoratum esset, si ingens mons magnus esset."

6. Both confessions were first published from a fifteenth-century MS by Wattenbach, 529–37, and are reprinted in Leff, pp. 709–16.

of simply entering an inn he was to shout for admission; if not received he was to sleep on the doorstep and patiently endure attacks by robbers.

This uncompromising imitation of the apostolic life was accompanied by a contempt for the clergy and sacraments. John's superiors ordered him not to go to confession even if he had spent the night with a woman because they taught that priests did not understand true poverty and deemed it unfitting for the "poor of Christ" (*"pauperes Christi"*) to submit to them. He only had to witness the elevation of the host once rather than make an outward show of sanctity and was ordered to meditate inwardly on Christ's passion by remaining in one spot rather than by wandering through the Church. Nor was he to feel remorse if he fell asleep during the divine service.

After twenty years of abnegation John achieved "liberty of the spirit" and became one of the "perfect" for eight more years. In this state he was entirely freed, according to his account, from the moral law. He could violate all the fasts of the Church without confessing and could lie or deceive. If he found any money he could spend it with his brothers in the service of Christ and if anyone claimed it he could answer with words and blows. Indeed, he could even murder the claimant because anyone who opposed the free in spirit was worthy of death.

In matters of sex he could feel equally free. The perfect were allowed to satisfy their lust with women in the most sacred of nights, for "perfect freedom" consisted in "grasping with the hands all that the eye sees and desires." Men and women who had reached this state had a series of signs by which they could express their wishes: one of these signals represented the desire for intercourse which was always granted immediately because the free in spirit could indulge in works of the flesh freely and without any sin. Likewise, if a sister who had just been to communion asked a brother to have commerce with her he should satisfy her "with vigor two or four times" and he should have the same freedom in homosexual relations. If the perfect happened to conceive a child they could drown it with a clear conscience like they would any worm.

The much shorter confession of Albert lacks autobiographical details and refers to beghards of Brünn rather than Cologne, but it is similarly shocking. Albert held that anyone in "true liberty" could say mass and that frequent communion does not make man holy since priests who celebrate many masses are worse than those who seldom go to Church. Like John he stressed inner response to outward show. He said that the beghards called those who concerned themselves too much with Christ's passion "blocks of wood" (*"blochwerg"*), but said that man must rise above himself in self-contemplation and then could do all that he wished without fasting or good works. According to him all beghards believed that man could achieve a state of liberty, or freedom of the spirit, that made all mortal sins become venial. They did not consider any act of the flesh, including sodomy, to be sinful and Albert himself witnessed a beghard of Brünn lie with a beguine all night and then grant her communion.

These two accounts have met with a mixed reception. Some scholars consider them to be honest confessions that rank among the most reliable sources for the history of heretical beghards, while others dismiss them as worthless, going so far as to characterize John's confession as being "of no more value than the account of a highly wrought man who has been to a séance."[7] Both positions appear too extreme. Certainly the confessions contain kernels of fact: John's account of the apostolic conduct of beghards and parts of his description of the state of liberty correspond to other trustworthy sources. His expression that freedom is achieved after "the exterior nature is annihilated" and his claim that bodily abnegation and inner contemplation can lead the soul to total unification with God is typical of actual Free-Spirit literature that we will examine in a later chapter.

But John's report begins to lose credibility when it reveals inconsistencies and malice. For example, he says that during his twenty years of abnegation he was ordered to eat surreptitiously under his hood, but this fits with the hostile stereotype of beghards as hypocrites rather than with the picture of extreme asceticism that John himself otherwise portrays. Moreover, it appears from his description that John entered the beghard house *"zur Lunge"* near the chapel of St. Stephen in Cologne which, despite numerous campaigns against

7. Rufus Jones, *Studies in Mystical Religion* (London, 1909), p. 215, also Haupt, "Zwei Traktate gegen Beginen und Begharden," ZfK, XII (1891), n. 1, who suspects that torture was used in obtaining the confessions, though there is no evidence for this and it was probably easier for the Inquisitor to use a carrot (i.e. entrance into the Dominican order) than a stick. The positive evaluations are by Wattenbach, 528, and Leff, p. 371.

beghards in the fourteenth century, was not only never dissolved but was supported by some of the most prominent families in the city.[8] This fact hardly coincides with John's account of depravities: he speaks of two hundred beghards who believed in all the most extreme articles he reported but that number is incredibly large and even if there only had been a few libertines in the house "*zur Lunge*" their scandalous conduct could not have gone unnoticed.[9]

One must thus agree with the verdict that John went out of his way to cooperate with Gallus of Novo Castro in order to be accepted as a Dominican and, depending on how one interprets John's reference to Albert as his "brother," similar considerations may have motivated the confession of the latter.[10] If this is true, both witnesses may have been coached by the Dominican Inquisitor. Albert's assertion that whatever man does "under the belt" is not sinful was earlier recorded as an heretical tenet by the Dominicans Albertus Magnus and Anselm of Alessandria and it is less likely that the slogan was relayed by thirteenth-century heretics in the Swabian Ries and Italy to Albert of Brünn than that it was the common property of Dominicans who read each other's works.[11] In addition, a large number of the excesses that John and Albert reported can be found *in nuce* in *Ad nostrum*, a document that Inquisitors carried with them as a matter of course. Indeed, the correspondence between their confessions and *Ad nostrum* was even noted by the fifteenth-century compiler of the handbook in which John and Albert's confessions are preserved.[12] In the last analysis the decision of how much confidence can be placed in these sources is largely subjective, but modern experience has instructed

8. J. Asen, "Die Begarden und die Sackbrüder in Köln," *Annalen des historischen Vereins für den Niederrhein*, CXV (1929), 169–70, 175–78.

9. This was already pointed out by Haupt, "Zwei Traktate," 86, n. 1.

10. Leff, p. 375, n. 3, argues that John's reference to "fratre meo Alberto" only indicates that both called each other brothers as beghards. But would John have used the term in that way if both had already converted? (Would an ex-Communist still call another ex-Communist "comrade"?) To me it seems more probable that either Albert too had become a Dominican, since Dominicans too were "brothers," or that the two were actually brothers.

11. Cf. Albert of Brünn, ed. Wattenbach, 536: "quidquid facit homo infra cingulum, non est peccatum," with Albertus Magnus' *determinatio*, #63: "hoc quod fit sub cingulo a bonis non est peccatum." For Anselm of Alessandria and other citations of the phrase, see above, Chapter I, section 3, n. 18.

12. Ed. Wattenbach, 537: "Hic nota errores in Clementinis c(apite) de he (reticis)."

us to be wary of lurid confessions of paid state's witnesses or political converts and common sense might indicate that if heretical beghards did believe in the possibility of supernatural perfection they did not seriously advocate drowning children like worms.

2. THE BEGUINES OF SCHWEIDNITZ

The other important document concerning the Free-Spirit heresy came from Silesia, which in the fourteenth century had become a possession of the Bohemian crown. There, in 1315, the Bishop of Breslau had ordered Dominicans and Franciscans to conduct an inquisition which led to the burning of fifty alleged heretics including women and children in Schweidnitz and the execution of others in Breslau, Neisse, and elsewhere in the region. We know nothing about the beliefs of these victims, though it is possible that a good number were innocent since secular and even clerical circles opposed the persecution.[13] Then the Papacy assumed direction of the Inquisition in Silesia as it had in Bohemia. Between 1330 and 1341 the papal Inquisitor was the Dominican John Schwenkenfeld who was murdered in the latter year by assassins who approached him in a cloister under the pretense of coming for confession. Like Gallus of Novo Castro, John had overextended the use of his inquisitorial powers for political purposes and consequently, like Gallus, paid with his blood.[14]

In September of 1332, well before his violent end, John conducted an examination of women who called themselves "hooded nuns" (*"moniales caputiatae"*) in Schweidnitz, a small town in Silesia. The protocol of this trial, which was held in the refectory of the Dominican cloister in the presence of John and ten other clerics (eight of whom were friars), fortuitously survives in the original and is gratifyingly extensive.[15] Sixteen different women testified, some at great length, and since most of them were anxious to help the Inquisition, no torture was necessary. The result was that they drew a picture of intense, if certainly heterodox, religiosity which tells us

13. Haupt, "Waldenserthum," I, 310.
14. The story is told in detail by Koudelka (as above, n. 3), 92–93.
15. The original is MS Vat. lat. 13119, unaccountably overlooked by all historians of heresy. The published version, ed. B. Ulanowski, *Scriptores rerum Polonicarum* (Cracow, 1874–1908), XIII, 5, 239–55, is from a copy in Krakow. This is reprinted by Leff, pp. 721–40. I quote from the Vatican MS whenever its text differs significantly from the Krakow version.

more about the Free-Spirit mentality than any other trial document that we possess.

The community of "hooded nuns" at Schweidnitz was regulated, like all medieval coenobitic communities, by principles of subordination and obedience. The "supreme mistress" was one Heylwig of Prague (also called "de Molendino") who was not present at the trial because she did not always live at Schweidnitz but travelled between several houses. Her contacts were so wide that she was able to send one of the Schweidnitz inmates to stay for a year in Erfurt, presumably at a similar community.[16] One of the witnesses explained that Heylwig took superfluous funds from one house and gave them to another like the Franciscan *custos*, an official who also supervised numerous houses.[17] Though Heylwig had great power she assumed an image of apostolic humility: she was called "maid servant" by one of the older inmates and said of herself that the most noble work she could do was to carry tubs of excrement.[18]

In Heylwig's absence a senior member of the house acted in her stead but was considered a sister rather than a mistress.[19] Then there were elders who often sequestered themselves and were regarded as sources of authority, though sometimes with resentment, by the younger members. These elders were far fewer than the recent entrants: of those questioned, two said that they had been in the house twenty-six and twenty-four years; a third inmate had dwelled at Schweidnitz for four years, but all the others had only been there for a year or less. New entrants were shorn of their hair and were required to take vows of absolute obedience unto death. They had to receive permission to do anything or go anywhere, even to church.[20] To ensure submission meetings were held on Fridays during which the novices knelt to confess their sins and be beaten.

16. ms Vat. lat. 13119, p. 4 (the ms is paginated): "suprema magistra earum sit Heylwig;" "Heilwig etiam alias esset magistra;" "heylwig margaretham de lichenow emiserit in Erfordiam. . . quod debuit ibi manere uno anno."

17. *Ibid.*, p. 3: ". . .ab heylwig de Praga que est inter eas veluti Custos inter minores et pecunias superfluas unius domus, si sunt, defert ad alias sue secte."

18. *Ibid.*, p. 2: "Nobilius opus quod possum facere est ut portem Tinam plenam cum fecibus seu cervicia ultima per platheas. . . ."

19. *Ibid.*, p. 4: "Heylwig sit suprema et modo Gerdtrudis de Olsna preest quam tamen non nominant magistram sed sororem."

20. *Ibid.*, p. 4: "quod non audet ire ad ecclesiam, nec ad sermones, nec ad alia divina officia sine licencia magistre vel ea contradicente," *et passim.*

Like John of Brünn at Cologne, the women of Schweidnitz pursued lives of voluntary poverty and harsh, one must say barbarous, asceticism. One of the elders named her community "the congregation of the poor" (*"congregacio pauperum"*) in striking resemblance to John's "house of the poor" in Cologne. The novices had to renounce all their possessions and were adjured to overcome their natural desires for food, drink, and clothing. To achieve this goal they underwent cruel fasts and tortures. One woman said that she beat herself with the hide of a hedgehog and that others did the same to themselves with barbed chains and knotted thongs. Another, who had only been in the house for eleven months, said that she underwent such brutal exercises that she now was horribly disfigured and could hardly recover from her injuries even though she had entered as a beautiful young girl.[21]

Because they practiced such severities the inmates of the community self-confidently believed that they were more perfect than all others. They thought that they had better knowledge than many priests or doctors and preferred their own prayers to attendance at church. When a novice had such a desire her request for permission was often treated with insults and though the inmates sometimes went to confession they always confessed to their own mistress first. During the time when they should have been in church, especially on Sundays and feast days, they stayed in their house and worked. Indeed, next to self-flagellation, hard work like sewing and spinning was the most distinctive trait of the community.[22]

Though their choice of the term "hooded nuns" shows that they were anxious to be taken for regulars the women were particularly hostile to the mendicant orders. One older inmate insisted that even though her house had no official recognition its members could be saved just as well as the Preachers and Minors and another even boasted that she had interrupted a public sermon against heresy in

21. *Ibid.*, p. 4: "Item percussit se cum pellibus ericii et pectenavit se etiam cum cartonibus sed alie verberaverunt se cum chatenulis accuatis et corrigiis nodosis;" Ulanowski, 251: "extenuerunt eam ieiuniis, vigiliis ac aliis exerciciis tam irracionaliter, quod cum prius esset puella speciosa, parvo tempore fuit in tantum destructa, quod vix nuncquam recuperabit."

22. Ulanowski, 241: "quod diebus dominicis et festivi operantur opera similia nerendo, suendo et alia opera similia faciendo," *et passim.*

Breslau and called the Dominican preacher a liar.[23] This is another in-dication of the tension between the beguinal movement and the men-dicant orders that we have noticed in earlier chapters and it helps to explain why not only the Dominican Schwenkenfeld, but three Fran-ciscans and five other Dominicans participated in the case against the women of Schweidnitz.

Still, the insistence on asceticism, poverty, and labor, or even the sharp anticlericalism of the "hooded nuns" was not what made them "Free Spirits" since these were all characteristics, to a greater or lesser degree, of the trend toward lay piety that gathered momentum in the later Middle Ages in proportion to the travails of the hierarchical Church. What made them distinctive was their conviction that their austerities led them to a supernatural state. For example, novices claimed to have heard an older member say that "just as God is God, so she was God with God, and just as Christ was never separated from God, neither was she," and "when God created everything . . . I cre-ated everything with him, and I am God with God, and I am Christ, and I am more." Later the Inquisitor asked the older woman whether she ever had said such things and she replied that she "had heard them preached but never taught much more herself"—an oblique confirma-tion of the novices' reports.[24] Another novice said she heard that the community followed not only the Ten Commandments and Gospels, but was also guided by the Holy Spirit. She also spoke of an inmate

23. Vat. lat. 13119, p. 4: "quod nos in secta nostra possimus ita bene salvari sicut predicator vel minor, si ita bene vivimus et servamus;" Ulanowski, p. 241: "quod una in Sweidnitcz sit, que vocatur Gerdrudis de Olsna, que publice contra quendam fratrem predicatorem, quando predicavit de hereticis et de eis, insurrexit, et dixit sibi in faciem: Vos menciemini;" 254: "Hedwigis fatetur se audisse ex ore Gerdrudis de Olsna super hoc se iacticare, quod in Wratislavia in publico sermone surrexerit de predicanti verbum dei in faciem cunctis audientibus, qui aderant et audire poterant, dixeret: Vos mentimini."

24. Ulanowski, 241: "interrogata dixit se frequenter audisse de ore Girtrudis de Civitate, que est hic: Sicut deus est deus, ita ipsa esset deus cum deo; et sicut Christus nunquam separatus a deo, sic nec ipsa;" 243: "Adelheidis dixit iurata, quod audivisset de ore Gertrudis de Civitate, que est inter eas hic, ista verba: Quando deus omnia creavit, tunc ego concreavi sibi omnia vel creavi omnia cum eo, et sum deus cum deo, et sum Christus, et sum plus;" 253: "Item interrogata, utrum nunquam dixisset: quando deus creavit omnia, cum eo omnia concreavi et sum deus cum deo etc. respondit: audivi predicare, sed non multum ulterius docui."

who underwent such tortures that she went mad and when asked when lying ill why she did not eat replied that she had no need to because she had reached such a state of perfection that Christ would feed her. This picture is all too vivid.

Modern examiners might have been satisfied with these insights, but the Dominican Inquisitor wanted to show that the women were exponents of errors condemned by the pope and therefore confronted them with the decree *Ad nostrum.*[25] But the notary only occasionally indicated this fact. The first witness reported, as if spontaneously, that the sisters said that man can become perfect and can reach such a state of spiritual liberty that he does not have to obey anyone. The next witness repeated these statements and added that she had also heard it said that perfect souls do not need to practice acts of virtue and that it is not necessary for them to show reverence for the body of Christ. These are points one, three, six, and eight respectively of *Ad nostrum.* Had the notary not indicated later that the papal decree was used as a basis for the examination it would have seemed from these answers that the women of Schweidnitz were saying exactly the same things that German beghards were reputed to have said decades earlier.

The notary does mention that the fourth witness was asked to comment on the Clementine articles. When she said that the older members of the community met separately, the Inquisitor, who was quick at drawing conclusions, asked her if they also subscribed to the second point of *Ad nostrum* which stated that the perfect can grant to their bodies all they desire. To this the novice, who had been in the house for only half a year, replied that she never heard this tenet *"expresse verba,"* but had heard similar things and was suspicious of the conduct of the senior members because of the suggestive nods and signals they gave to each other and because they would not reveal what they did in secret.

The same novice testified about several of the other points of *Ad*

25. Inquisitors' handbooks sometimes contained not only *Ad nostrum,* but the gloss on it written in 1322 by the legal glossator John Andreae of Bologna. An east-central European example of this is in MS Greifswald, Kirchenbibliothek St. Nicolai, XXIII E 100, fol. 148r–154v, described by W. Wattenbach, "Über das Handbuch eines Inquisitors. . . ," Abh. Berlin, IV (1889), 19. Another copy of John Andreae's gloss under the title *Reprobacio secte peghardorum et Beginarum regni Alimanie et errorum eorundem* in MS Clm 15177, fol. 275r–282r, was noted by Leff, p. 367, who was unable to identify it.

nostrum. She said that the community followed the fourth tenet in believing that their exemplary life made them equal to the apostles in heaven and that they followed the spirit of the eighth point in only paying reverence to the body of Christ so as not to attract attention. But she was less clear about the antinomian tenets: she said that man can achieve a state of union with divinity that renders him free from the virtues *after death*, but this is entirely different from the purport of *Ad nostrum* which talks about such a state in this life. And though she repeated her guesses that the secret meetings of the elders were occasions for scandalous behavior she admitted that neither she nor any of the other neophytes really knew what transpired at them.

The question of antinomian conduct is indeed the most perplexing one posed by the protocol. According to the novices, the older women thought themselves so perfect that they gave up the austerities that they imposed on the others. They allegedly regaled themselves on butter and lard and drank the best beer, leaving an inferior brew for the neophytes and the worst for the poor, to whom they said that they had nothing better. Worse, they supposedly indulged in sodomy and every other type of sexual licence. A novice told of hearing how beghards celebrated orgies with them in secret and how the men and women even petted each other and had their tongues in one anothers' mouths in church during sermons and mass.

But the trouble is that all these reports came from novices who may have harbored the sort of resentments that arise in any hierarchical organization, let alone one that is based on principles of humiliating submission and bodily torture. The witnesses were encouraged by leading questions, such as citations from *Ad nostrum*, and all their stories of shocking sexuality came at second hand. Thus the novice who spoke of orgies and obscene caresses in church could only say that she knew about them from another woman who had experienced such things; but she did not identify this source by name (though she did so for other less scarlet allegations) and no such woman confessed to any such practices in the extensive protocol that we possess.[26]

26. Ulanowski, 242–43: "quod inter tales Beghardos et huiusmodi mulieres portantes ymaginem sanctitatis maxime et artissime paupertatis committuntur opportunitate nacta quasi omnia genera peccatorum Sodomiticorum et inmundiciarum, hec dicit de certa sciencia, quia audivit ab illa, cui talia acciderunt, et

Later another novice admitted that she had heard about such things from others and suspected the worst but never actually witnessed any obscene conduct herself.[27]

One might guess that many of these young girls, who had starved and flagellated themselves to the point of deformity, were in a highly wrought if not to say hysterical state. By their account beghards were always incorrigible lechers and scoundrels. One novice claimed that a beghard told her when they were alone that to resist or to have shame at sexual contact was a sign of grossness of spirit but that she could have the greatest spirituality if she exhibited herself to a man. The witness who made the most colorful charges of sexual scandals told somewhat paranoically of how the beghards drove her away when they wished to confer with other women in her house.[28] She also claimed that they were so crafty that they were able to convince prelates, friars, and priests that their sexual liberties, even their obscene kisses and fondlings in church, were holy and she told of a beghard of Cologne who was so infamous that he stole wooden images from churches and burned them to keep warm. Surely this sort of testimony must be treated with scepticism.

This is not to say that the elders might not have acted strangely or accorded to themselves certain privileges. Unaccountably the Inquisitor, so far as the protocol shows, did not question the two elders who testified on the subject of antinomian conduct, perhaps because he did not want to mar the picture that his star witness had painted

---

eciam de certo ab alys est experta, quod abutuntur se mutuo lateraliter et in anum tangentes se mutuo impudice et linguas suas in ora sua ad invicem pre delectacione mittentes oportunitate habita eciam in ecclesia sive infra sermonem sive Missam sive alia divina officia celebrata. . . ."

27. Vat. lat. 13119, p. 3: "Item interrogata super hoc, quod Adelheydis confessa fuit de inmundiciis, inpudiciis ac Sodomia exeuncium ab eis et usque ad libertatem spiritus veniencium, dicit se talia audisse ab aliis sed non vidit, nisi quod suspicabatur talia de quodam cum quadam in osculis et in tactibus inpudicis quia in tenebris frequenter convenerunt et illa iacebat in lecto simulans se oculos dolere." (The reading of *quia* in the Vatican MS in place of the *ac* in the Ulanowski version makes this answer a great deal more intelligible, although I still find the last clause obscure.)

28. *Ibid.*, p. 2: "Item iurata dixit se hic in Sweydnicz in domo earum Beghardis ministrasse commedere et quod dicti Beghardi volebant postea aliqua ad ipsas loqui ista repellebatur ab aliis huiusmodi verbis: Recede hinc, hic non habes aliquid facere." (This sentence only makes sense with the Vatican MS reading of *repellebatur* for *repellebantur.*)

so vividly. But the notary did record his impression that one of the two answered obscurely ("ad omnia interrogata per inquisitorem involute et quasi sub glosis respondit") and indicated that the other was uncooperative ("et statim mutavit verba sua dicens, quod nesciat, si umquam dixerit"). This suggests that these two, in contradistinction to the novices, were hostile to the authorities because of their conviction in their own perfection and perhaps capable of abnormal conduct, though we can say no more unless we are satisfied with the evidence of hearsay and guesses. The fact that the house was not a clandestine community makes it seem doubtful that it sheltered a nest of perverts: one of the older women insisted that her organization had no enemies in Schweidnitz, and since it had existed at least twenty-six years without dissolution she could not have been entirely wrong.

The women of Schweidnitz, no matter what they called themselves, were clearly beguines insofar as they were semi-regulars devoted to the apostolic life. Both their testimony and the confessions of John and Albert of Brünn show the connection between the beguinal movement and mystical heresy, for both reveal the belief that voluntary poverty and abnegation led the way to spiritual perfection. The conviction that the depths of asceticism could be a preparation for the heights of perfection was common in the later Middle Ages, but the extremes of self-torture and certainty of oneness with God that we see in the cases of John of Brünn and the women of Schweidnitz must be regarded as traits of the heresy of the Free Spirit.

3. THE HUSSITE PROBLEM

We cannot leave east-central Europe without considering whether the Free-Spirit heresy had any role in the Hussite Revolution in Bohemia. The best recent studies of that Revolution conceive of a "Free-Spirit phase" that in 1419 succeeded a "Waldensian phase" and played itself out in the excesses of the "Adamites" of 1421. Indeed the leading authority, Howard Kaminsky, has even said that the Hussite Revolution might not have taken place without the heresy of the Free Spirit and that "it was in Hussite Bohemia that the Free-Spirit. . . reached its highest medieval development."[29] Since I know no Czech, it is

---

29. "The Free Spirit in the Hussite Revolution," *Millennial Dreams in Action,* ed. Sylvia L. Thrupp (The Hague, 1962), pp. 166–86 (quotation p. 168). In addition to this important article, Kaminsky makes his argument for a Free-

scarcely possible for me to swim into the mainstream of the discussion of Hussite ideology. Still, it is possible to offer some reasons why the theory of Free-Spirit influence is open to criticism.

To begin with, there is a total lack of evidence that there were any indigenous Free-Spirit heretics in Bohemia or neighboring parts at the time when the Hussite Revolution broke out. The only known Bohemian Free Spirit was Heylwig of Prague, the travelling mistress of the community of Schweidnitz, but she was last heard of in 1332, more than three-quarters of a century before the outbreak of revolution in Bohemia. The two documents we have previously examined in this chapter do reveal the existence of Free Spirits in neighboring Moravia and Silesia, but they were separated from the Hussite outbreak by the same amount of time. Further, while the Hussite revolutionaries were of course Czech, both documents indicate by the occasional Germanic words that the scribes left in the vernacular that the heretics were Germans and both show that the real center of Free-Spirit activity was farther west: John of Brünn went to Cologne to become "perfect" and the women of Schweidnitz referred to kindred communities in Leipzig and Erfurt as well as to beghards and beguines in Aachen, Cologne, Mainz, and Strassburg.

Of course there were beguines in fourteenth-century Bohemia, perhaps native, but there is no reason to believe that they were unorthodox. A Czech student song of the fourteenth century attacks them for studying Scripture according to their own tastes, arguing with all about religious matters, and defending their absence from sermons with the claim that they understood the Bible better than priests even though they knew no Latin.[30] This shows intense hostility to beguines

---

Spirit phase in the Hussite Revolution in "Chiliasm and the Hussite Revolution," *Church History*, XXVI (1957), 43–71, and in his *History of the Hussite Revolution* (Berkeley and Los Angeles, 1967), pp. 352–59. Similar positions are taken by E. Werner, "Die Nachrichten über die böhmischen 'Adamiten' in religionshistorischer Sicht," in Theodora Büttner and Ernst Werner, *Circumcellionen und Adamiten* (Berlin, 1959), pp. 73–134, and by Robert Kalivoda, *Das hussitische Denken im Lichte seiner Quellen* (Berlin, 1969), pp. 62–81. The latter's views are presented in greater detail in Czech in his major work, *Husitská ideologie* (Prague, 1961). All these works make further reference to the earlier literature on the subject.

30. Czech text ed. J. Fejfalik in Sb. Vienna, XXXIX (1862), 174–75, summarized by E. Werner, *Nachrichten über spätmittelalterliche Ketzer aus tschechoslovakischen Archiven und Bibliotheken* (Leipzig, 1963), p. 259.

and for that reason it is significant that it does not charge them with hypocrisy, let alone with specific doctrinal errors. In 1388 the Archbishop of Prague supported King Wenceslas in ordering the expulsion of "beghards" from that city,[31] but this could have meant any number of things ranging from an attack on orthodox beghards to a generic expression of abuse. As an example of the latter, conservatives called the pious reformer Milič of Kroměříž and his followers beghards because they sought frequent communion. Later even Hus was accused of accounting himself to be a priest of the Free Spirit, which shows how careful we must be about taking such terms literally.[32]

If it is impossible to prove the existence of indigenous Free Spirits in pre-Hussite Bohemia, is there any evidence that the Free-Spirit heresy was imported from the outside during the Hussite Revolution? Most modern scholars answer affirmatively on the basis of an oft-repeated passage in the Taborite chronicle of Laurence of Březová.[33] This reports that in 1418 almost forty *"Picardi"* and their families were warmly received in Prague after they explained that they had been forced into exile by their own prelates "on account of the Law of God." It is argued that these refugees must have been Free-Spirit heretics from Picardy, where the existence of the heresy is supposedly attested by a trial record of 1411, and that even though the original group did not long remain intact, its members had enough time to infect Bohemia with their extremist doctrines. The result was the Taborite radicalism of 1419–1421.

This theory may be questioned on several grounds. First there is the question of geographical origins. One can by no means take for granted that Laurence's *"Picardi"* came from Picardy because *pikard* was a south-German spelling of "beghard."[34] In other words, Laurence might just have wished to say that the refugees were beghards

---

31. Ed. R. E. Weltsch, *Archbishop John of Jenstein (1348–1400)* (The Hague and Paris, 1968), pp. 233–34.

32. Kaminsky, *History*, pp. 12, 22, 86–87. Kaminsky's careful search for Free Spirits in Bohemia directly before Hus (pp. 352–53) brings to light only Waldensians infected with chiliasm. The view that the term beghard was used loosely in the later Bohemian instances was first stated by Haupt, "Waldenserthum," III, 344–45.

33. See the works cited above, n. 29. The passage from Laurence's chronicle is ed. J. Goll, *Fontes rerum Bohemicarum* (Prague, 1873–1932), V, 431.

34. See above, p. 39.

rather than that they came from Picardy. If one does take the road to Picardy, the results are by no means so conclusive as many scholars believe. The trial of 1411, as we will see, concerned an allegedly anti-nomian sect not in Picardy, but in Brussels, the capital of Brabant, and the only alleged heretic whose record survives was a Carmelite friar who adjured and ended his career as a respected member of his order.[35] Putting that case aside, it is true that one Gilles Mersault of Tournai is known to have been in Prague in 1420, but even Tournai, while closer to Picardy, is in Hainaut and Mersault seems to have been a Waldensian, not a Free Spirit.[36] Closest to Picardy of all is Artois where in 1420, as Hussite scholars have not noticed, the Bishop of Arras uncovered an heretical sect that must have existed several years before. But the documents concerned with this case make clear without a doubt that the accused were Waldensians.[37] Thus if Laurence's *"Picardi"* really did come from the region of Picardy it is far more likely that they were Waldensians than Free Spirits.

This conclusion is confirmed by other evidence that Laurence presents. He says that the *Picardi* had families, but most Free Spirits we know of had no family life (they usually lived in semi-regular communities or wandered alone). Waldensians, on the other hand, usually were found in sedentary communities that existed for hundreds of years because the faith was passed down through families and by leaders much like the *"vir latinus"* who, according to Laurence, read to the *Picardi* in their own language. More important, Laurence tells us that the refugees' doctrine was simply the denial of a real presence in the Eucharist rather than any errors usually associated with the heresy of the Free Spirit. The heretics found in Artois in 1420 also questioned the Eucharist, so Laurence's term *"Picardi"* might have referred to members of a similar northern French congregation. If not, he must have used it as a generic term of abuse for heretics rather than as a designation of Free Spirits.

The final argument against speaking of a Free-Spirit phase in the Hussite Revolution concerns the ideology of the Revolution itself.

35. This trial is studied in detail below, pp. 156–62.

36. This is conceded by Kaminsky, *History*, p. 357, who summarizes the thesis concerning Mersault of the Czech scholar F. M. Bartoš.

37. Paul Beuzart, *Les hérésies pendant le Moyen Age et la Réforme. . . dans la région de Douai, d'Arras et au pays de l'Alleu* (Le Puy, 1912), pp. 46–48, 476–78.

The decisive ingredient in the supposed Free-Spirit phase was revolutionary chiliasm, first noticeable in late 1419. Laurence does not say that his *Picardi* had anything to do with this development. Furthermore, real Free Spirits were seldom chiliasts and most of them had no interest in historical theories at all.[38] Free Spirits were interested in a program of mystical perfection for the individual, apart from the course of history; whereas Taborite chiliasts foresaw material as well as mystical perfection for their community at a certain stage of historical development. There is thus no reason to turn to the Free-Spirit heresy to explain the ideological shifts within the Taborite camp in 1419–1420.

That leaves us with the "Adamites" of 1421, the extremists who in the account of Norman Cohn have exerted enormous fascination on the "now" generation and who in the latest Communist historiography are denigrated as typical left-deviationists.[39] These supposed fanatics, driven out of Tabor, allegedly ran about naked like Adam and Eve, danced wildly around fires, abandoned themselves to sodomy, fornicated by day and murdered by night. But did they? The major source for their antics is the hostile chronicle of Laurence of Březová who presents a list of errors supposedly sent to Prague by John Žižka, the soldier who destroyed the Adamites.[40] It might be overly suspicious to think that Laurence himself may have taken liberties with the list, but it can hardly be so to wonder how Žižka compiled it in the first place. We do know that he so hated his victims that he slew all his prisoners, and it is doubtful that under these circumstances he would have written back to Prague that his enemies were anything other than monsters of iniquity. If the list he sent was based on someone's confession, torture must certainly have helped in eliciting it, but

38. See my conclusions on this subject below, pp. 236–38.

39. Norman Cohn, *The Pursuit of the Millennium*, 3rd ed. (New York, 1970), pp. 214–22. Sharpest on the Communist side is E. Werner, "Der Kirchenbegriff bei Jan Hus, Jakoubek von Mies, Jan Želisvský und den linken Taboriten," *Sitzungsberichte der deutschen Akademie der Wissenschaften zu Berlin, Klasse für Philosophie etc.*, X (1967), 53–54, who goes so far as to say that the Adamites' antagonist John Žižka was "not only subjectively, but also objectively" right in proceeding against them.

40. *Fontes rerum Bohemicarum*, V, 517–19. The list is in Czech; a German translation is in Kalivoda, *Das hussitische Denken*, pp. 327–29. The other sources that describe the Adamites are hostile chronicles that are not directly contemporary.

there is no clear indication (at least not in the German translation of the passage from Laurence at my disposal) that it was a confession instead of a piece composed by Žižka and his aides on their own. When it is remembered that descriptions of immoral "Adamites" were *topoi* in hostile medieval accounts of heresy, reservations about the veracity of the list seem even more justified.[41] The inclusion of proper names does not eliminate the possibility that we are dealing here with a patchwork of *topoi*. Finally, even if not, as many no doubt will continue to believe, there is no proof that any known Free Spirits murdered or practiced ritual love feasts and therefore no reason to connect the Czech incident with the Free-Spirit heresy. The events of 1421 should be understood as an ideological and social development within the context of Tabor rather than as a demonstration of previously clandestine Free Spirits who waited until then to tear off their masks as well as their clothes.

41. See above, pp. 31–34.

Chapter Six

THE INQUISITION IN THE WEST

Although the evidence from Strassburg and east-central Europe indicates that mystical heresy reached a peak in the first half of the fourteenth century, very little additional inquisitorial material survives from that period. This is no doubt because the Papal Inquisition was quiescent in the West until the middle of the century and Free Spirits, even at their worst, did not trouble local authorities very much. Once the Papacy started to persecute heretics in earnest, inquisitorial records proliferated, and since Inquisitors were commissioned to look specifically for heretical beghards and beguines they usually managed to find them. At least they maintained that they did. In actuality they dredged up an ill-assorted assemblage in their nets, as we will now see.

1. HERMANN KUCHENER AND CONSTANTINE OF ERFURT

Before the Papal Inquisition went to work, only two western Free Spirits called so much attention to themselves that local authorities were obliged to proceed against them. The first was one Hermann Kuchener who was examined in Würzburg in 1342 and readily confessed to a number of outrageously heretical tenets. According to the surviving notarial instrument,[1] when he was about twenty years old

1. Published in *Monumenta Boica* (Munich, 1763–1932), XL, 415–21, from MS Staatsarchiv Würzburg, Standbuch #2 (Codex "Liber copiarum Luppoldi de

he was seized by a state of supernatural insensibility for half a year in which he could not think about the passion of Christ or pray but could only say the two words, *"Pater noster,"* and meditate on the divinity. In this condition he felt that there was something "uncreated" in man and that he himself had become deified.[2] He thought he was so illuminated that he could have offered instruction to all the theological masters of Paris and it even seemed to him that he was walking on air and could cross the Rhine without getting his feet wet. Thereafter he did not believe in hell or purgatory and refused to accept the authority of the pope; he also said that fornication was natural and was a sin only when it hurt![3] But he never said that he had ever actually violated the moral law.

The document calls Kuchener "a beghard in the sect of beghards,"[4] but was he really that? He himself claimed that he was a priest of Nürnberg, though the authorities believed that he had forged his certificate of ordination. Even if that were true, real beghards never even claimed to be priests. They might have tried to rival the mendicant orders, but they had only contempt for the secular clergy. There is no reference in the record to any sort of mendicancy and it must be

---

Bebenburg"), pp. 461–66. The text was copied often in the later Middle Ages, e.g. MS Staatsarchiv Würzburg 6, fol. 27v–28v (I am most grateful to Oberregierungsarchivrat Dr. H. Hoffman of the Bayerisches Staatsarchiv, Würzburg, for calling my attention to this fourteenth-century copy, which might very well be the best that we have). It is also in MS Wolfenb., Helmst., 279, fol. 282r–284v, and MSS Würzburg, Universitätsbibliothek, M. ch. f. 51 and M. ch. q. 96. I have used the first three of the listed MSS and have not made a search for any others. A critical edition might be in order since there are more MSS of this notarial instrument than of any other document relevant to the heresy of the Free Spirit.

2. *Mon. Boica*, XL, 417: "Item censetur sentire quod in homine sit aliquid increatum, cum in illo lumine crediderit se non purum hominem tunc fuisse sed hominem deificatum et raptum in divinitatem. . . ."

3. This is the only sense I can make of *ibid.*, 417: "unkusche ist ein naturlich werk, und ist als sunde als we es tůt." (The three MSS that I have read all have more or less the same text here.)

4. MS Staatsarchiv Würzburg, Standbuch #2, p. 462, has "quod ipse Hermannus fuit Beghardus et in secta Beghardorum cuius quidem secte errores in iure expressi sunt per sedem apostolicam condempnati," but the better reading is probably that of MS Staatsarchiv Würzburg 6, fol. 28r, followed by MS Wolfenb., Helmst., 279, fol. 282v (=WH): "quod ipse Hermannus fuit Beghardorum huius (WH: cuius) quidem secte erroribus (WH: errores) in iure expressi sunt per sedem apostolicam condempnati."

concluded from this that Kuchener was not a beghard properly so called.

Why, then, did the authorities term him so? The answer must be that they found it easiest to classify him as a beghard because his errors appeared similar to those allegedly held by beghards in texts that they were familiar with. Hermann of Schildesche, an Augustinian theologian who directed Kuchener's examination, had written a tract a few years earlier wherein he had refuted mystical heresies with the appropriate passages from *Ad nostrum*[5] and in the trial of Kuchener he must have been glad to put his theoretical knowledge to use. The examiners probably also had at their disposal a tract "against the eight errors of the beghards" written by the Augustinian Gerard of Siena and sent by him to the canon Lupold of Bebenburg at Würzburg between 1326 and 1328.[6] That the authorities knew about *Ad nostrum* is confirmed by the statement in the instrument that the errors of the beghards had been "condemned by the Apostolic Chair," and that they classified Kuchener as a beghard because he maintained things that beghards were supposed to say is shown in the instrument when it records him as declaring that Adam did not sin because he possessed "indifference," with the following verdict that he was "therefore suspected of adhering to the doctrine of the beghards who say that he who possesses the light of indifference is not able to sin."[7]

Thus it would be a mistake to believe that Kuchener belonged to a sect, especially since his description of his conversion makes it sound as if it had been generated entirely from within. But sometime in his career he seems to have come under the direct or indirect influence of the great mystic Meister Eckhart as evidenced by his avowal of the Eckhartian doctrine that there is something "uncreated" in man, and

5. *Tractatus de vitiis capitalibus duplex*, MS Klosterneuburg 352, fol. 205r-v. A. Zumkeller, *Die Schriften und Lehre des Hermann von Schildesche* (Würzburg, 1959), pp. 58-59, dates the composition of this tract to 1335 or shortly thereafter.

6. *Tractatus super octo erroribus begardorum beghinarum in Clementinis constitutionibus condemnatis*, unpublished and consequently unfamiliar to most historians of heresy. The tract survives in two MSS: Olomouc 385, fol. 17r-24v, and Milan, Ambrosiana, S. 58. SUP, fol. 87r-96v. It has no historical information but discusses the errors of *Ad nostrum* from a theological point of view.

7. *Mon. Boica*, XL, 418: "Unde suspectus redditur de doctrina beghardorum, qua dicunt quod habens lumen indifferencie peccare non potest."

his belief in his earthly deification made him a Free Spirit if we use that term loosely, as we must, to include eccentrics who had picked up a few mystical terms.

A second eccentric Free Spirit who has mistakenly been called a beghard was Constantine of Erfurt. Fortunately we know a good deal about him because a copy of the protocol of his examination has recently been discovered and it is supplemented by two independent contemporary chronicle reports.[8] Constantine, who came originally from Arnheim in Holland, was condemned for heresy in Erfurt in August of 1350 by two local clerics deputized as inquisitors by the Archbishop of Mainz. These two examined Constantine three times and conferred about his errors with "religious and secular doctors of the orthodox faith," even though there could be no doubt that he was a bold heretic. When he refused to recant and rejected their urgings to return to the bosom of the Church as "diabolical," they had no choice but to hand him over to the secular arm which executed him the next day.

It is remarkable that Constantine's inquisitors did not ask him whether he believed in the tenets of *Ad nostrum* but questioned him instead about the power of priests and the efficacy of the sacraments. On both subjects his views were rabid. He insisted that he had been baptized by pharisees, refused to take the oath necessary for his examination because he had no more respect for the pope, bishops, priests, and officers of his trial than for devils, and dismissed the sacraments as diabolical, false, or useless. Furthermore, he denied the existence of purgatory—though he acknowledged hell—and rejected the Athanasian Creed.

Most of these denials, though no doubt distinguished by their vehemence, were characteristic of all late medieval antisacerdotal heresy. Constantine emerges from his protocol as a Free Spirit in the pas-

---

8. The protocol is edited by M. Erbstösser, *Sozialreligiöse Strömungen im späten Mittelalter* (Berlin, 1970), pp. 160–63. (This book came to my attention after my own book was in the press and I have been unable to address myself to the problems of interpretation it raises. Constantine's protocol is the only new documentary material it presents.) Tho two chronicles are the *Gesta archiepiscoporum Magdeburgensium*, MGH SS, XIV, 435, and the *Chronica S. Petri Erfordensis moderna*, continuations II and III, in *Monumenta erphesfurtensia*, ed. O. Holder-Egger, SRG, XLII, 381 and 396. Unless otherwise noted, my account is taken from the protocol.

sages where he talks of his own powers. Just as he was sure that he was baptized "carnally" by a "pharisee," so he was sure that he was baptized "spiritually" by the Holy Spirit and was equal to Christ "in grace." For these reasons he believed that he had the same power as Christ to bind and loose and could act like a priest in baptizing and absolving others from sin. But as radical as Constantine was, it should still be noted that he thought himself a Christian whose miraculous powers came from grace.[9] It should also be added that he did not believe that the sacrament of marriage licensed marital intercourse and argued that such commerce was a diabolical act. Moreover, nowhere did he say that he had the right to indulge in sexual activity himself or allow others to do so, and nowhere did he in any way suggest violating any moral law, for the real burden of his argument, as that of many paranoids, was that he was pure and all those who were supposed to be were not.

The comparison to paranoids is made advisedly since even Constantine's examiners felt prompted to ask whether he spoke from "bodily debility or dementia." Of course he answered that he was sound in body and mind, but it is hard to imagine him answering otherwise. It is impossible to diagnose the state of his psyche with any precision, but it seems highly likely that he was in some way disturbed, especially when one remembers that the terrible Black Death, the worst of all medieval plagues, had just passed through Erfurt a few months earlier, leaving behind it, according to one estimate, as many as 12,000 dead.[10] Constantine's at least giddy condition can be inferred not only from his violent attacks on his judges, but from a statement he made that John and Matthew were holy men whose gospels should be believed but Luke and Mark were not. Before the protocol of his trial was discovered some historians who had read about this bizarre tenet from the chronicle reports tried to find some sense in it, but the protocol strongly suggests that it was capricious: when asked about it again, Constantine changed his mind and conceded that all the gospels could be believed when they agreed with each other.

It is doubtful that Constantine, who never spoke about being

9. Erbstösser, *Strömungen*, p. 160: "sum christianus et baptizatus in gracia dei"; p. 161: "sum carnaliter baptizatus a quodam phariseo, et spiritualiter a spirito sancto. . . . et addit se esse Christum in gratia."

10. Philip Ziegler, *The Black Death* (New York, 1969), p. 84.

initiated into his beliefs by others, belonged to any sect. The chronicles —but not the protocol—called him a "beghard," but like Kuchener he was not a beghard in the sense of being a wandering mendicant. Rather, he was a professional copier of books who apparently was so good at his work that his judges genuinely wished to save him.[11] He did allow the possibility in his trial that other "sons and daughters of God" could have the same power of remitting sins as he had, but this possibility was proposed to him by his examiners and his affirmative answer by no means proves the existence of such "sons and daughters." Certainly it is striking that there were no further arrests for heresy made in Erfurt or its vicinity for another seventeen years.

Perhaps the inquisitors did not even consider Constantine to have been a Free Spirit, a possibility suggested by the fact that they did not question him about *Ad nostrum* and perhaps confirmed by the writings of Jordan of Quedlinburg, one of the theologians who conferred in Constantine's case.[12] Jordan wrote an entire tract about the heresy of the Free Spirit which unfortunately is lost and also included many polemics against the heresy in two of his sermon collections. These show that he had knowledge not only of *Ad nostrum*, but also of Marguerite Porete's *Mirror of Simple Souls*, but they make no mention of Constantine of Erfurt even though they were written at about the same time or after Jordan was involved in his trial.[13]

---

11. *Chron. S. Petri*, cont. II, 396: "datis sibi induciis VIII septimarum, ut si esset ex litargia. . . quia bonus scriptor fuerat."

12. Jordan's participation is not mentioned explicitly in the protocol (which mentions none of the theologians involved by name) but is reported by the *Gesta archiepisc*. There is every reason to accept this since in 1350 Jordan was Augustinian Provincial of Saxony whose headquarters were in Erfurt.

13. Jordan refers to his tract, *De spiritu libertatis*, in passages cited by Guarnieri, 445, 450. See also Jordanus de Quedlinburg, *Sermones de sanctis* (Strassburg, 1484), serm. 146G, fol. 179rb: "De talibus etiam habentibus legem scriptam in cordibus suis habes supra in tractatu de spiritu libertatis sermone primo"; *idem, Opus Jor* (a work which takes its strange title from Jordan's conceit of designating it by the first syllable of his name—his *Sermones de sanctis* are subtitled *Opus Dan*), MS Göttingen, Universitätsbibliothek, Lüneburg 38, fol. 49vb: "require in tractatu de spiritu libertatis sermone duodecimo, secundo membro principali"; and *idem, Opus postillarum et sermonum de tempore* (Strassburg, 1483), serm. 188 bis. Pater A. Zumkeller, the authority on writings of medieval German Augustinians, informs me that he has not come across any MSS of this lost work since compiling his *Manuskripte von Werken der Autoren des Augustiner-Eremitenordens in mitteleuropäischen Bibliotheken* (Würzburg,

2. THE REVIVAL OF THE PAPAL INQUISITION

All the other relevant trials that we know of took place after the resuscitation of the Papal Inquisition in the second half of the fourteenth century. While bishops only had to deal with heresy when it was a clear and present danger, commissioned Inquisitors were obliged to justify their existence by producing heretics. Thus it was not accidental that heretical beguines and beghards were found in east-central Europe by Papal Inquisitors and that Inquisitors found more in Germany in the second half of the century when they began to look for them. The Avignonese Papacy was always doctrinally vigilant and anxious to spread the Inquisition, but it was first prevented from doing so in Germany by incessant civil wars and the hostility of the Emperor Ludwig of Bavaria. The new Emperor Charles IV, however, restored peace and willingly cooperated with Papal Inquisitors.

The story begins in 1348, a year after Ludwig of Bavaria's death, when Pope Clement VI commissioned the Dominican lector of Strassburg, John Schadeland, as Inquisitor for Germany.[14] Clement's successor Innocent VI renewed this appointment in 1353 and ordered all German officials to cooperate with the Inquisitor especially in providing prison space since the Inquisition had none of its own. Innocent's letter is noteworthy for us because it singled out the "pestiferous madness" of beghards as an object for special concern.[15] Schadeland was claiming expenses as late as November 1357 and, though no records survive from any trial he may have conducted, it does appear that he, or his associates, managed to turn up at least one suitable victim. This was Berthold of Rohrbach, who, we are told, first spread his errors in Würzburg where he was arrested, recanted out of fear, and

---

1966). Selections from *Opus postillarum* and *Opus Jor* are edited by Guarnieri, 444–50. Further pertinent passages are in *Opus postillarum*, serm. 264B, fol. 252ra, and serm. 360B, fol. 337r. The *Opus postillarum*, like the *Opus Jor* (for the dating of which see above, Chap. II, n. 52) was written over a long span of time in the middle of the fourteenth century: though it was published after the *Opus postillarum* on which Jordan was still working in 1365, one passage (ed. Guarnieri, 444) refers to Clement VI (1342–52) as reigning Pope.

14. *Nomen est omen*: later, as Bishop of Augsburg, Schadeland was notorious for his severity. Thus MS Cgm 2026, fol. 6v: "Bischoff Schadlands (welcher denn Nahmen nicht vergebens gehabt: dann er in der Wahrheit ein schadlicher Bischoff gewesen). . . ." On his entire career, McDonnell, pp. 558–59.

15. Fredericq, I, 204–205, #206.

subsequently was released.[16] From there he went to Speyer and sup-posedly continued to teach heresy, but in 1356 he was seized by the Inquisition and this time burned. The two chroniclers who described his case wrote about 150 years later and there is thus not much to be gained by dwelling on it. What is worth pointing out is that the more reliable of the two chroniclers drew a distinction between the errors Berthold spread in Würzburg and those that he was convicted of teaching by the Inquisition at Speyer. The former were idiosyncratic: e.g. Christ cursed Mary on the cross and cursed the earth that ab-sorbed his blood. The latter, on the other hand, were typical "beg-hard errors" and correspond, in some cases almost literally, to portions of *Ad nostrum*.[17] From this evidence it seems likely that Berthold of Rohrbach was a harmless individualist who was turned into a "beg-hard" by the Inquisitors at Speyer.

Schadeland's undistinguished record as a heresy hunter did not discourage the Papacy. In the following decade Urban V ascended to the Throne of Peter on a platform of reform that resulted in a return to Rome. Since reform was also associated with the fight against her-esy, Urban renewed his predecessor's support of the German Inquisi-tion, this time to more effect. By October 1364 he had appointed four new Dominican Inquisitors and ordered that they be provided for and assigned to specific territories.[18] We have already seen how one of them, Henry de Agro, convicted Metza of Westhoven in Strassburg in 1366.[19] We know that the second, Louis of Caligula, was commis-sioned for the provinces of Cologne and Trier, but we know little about what he did there,[20] and we know nothing at all about the ac-

16. Johannes Nauclerus, *Chronica. . . ad annum 1500* (Cologne, 1544), pp. 898–99; J. Trithemius, *Annales Hirsaugienses* (St Gall, 1690), II, 231–32.

17. Cf. Nauclerus, p. 899: "homo in hac vita in tantum proficere possit, quod nec orare, nec ieiunare eum oportet" with *Ad nostrum*, #1: "homo in vita presenti tantum et talem perfectionis gradum potest acquirere quod reddetur penitus impeccabilis et amplius in gratia proficere non valebit" and #2: "quod jejunare non oportet hominem nec orare."

18. Ed. P. Kehr and G. Schmidt, *Päbstliche Urkunden und Regesten aus den Jahren 1353–1378. . . .* (*Geschichtsquellen der Provinz Sachsen*, XXII) (Halle, 1889), 173–75, #632, 634, 635, 637. One of the officials Urban wrote to was John Schadeland, now Bishop of Hildesheim, an appropriate man to turn to.

19. See above, pp. 96–97.

20. An indication that Louis might have been quite active is found in a hitherto unnoticed passage from Hermann Korner (O. P.), *Chronica Novella*, ed. J. Schwalm (Göttingen, 1895), 285: "Excommunicata est secta Baghardorum

tivities of the third, John of Moneta. But the fourth, Walter Kerlinger, was so efficient in finding heretics that he deserves a section of his own. Before we proceed to that, we must indicate how Kerlinger was aided by his benefactor, the Emperor Charles IV, who fully earned his nickname of *Pfaffenkönig*. Charles has supported the Papal Inquisition from his youth in Bohemia, where the murder of John Schwenkenfeld and the attack on Gallus of Novo Castro might have made an indelible impression on him. Whether he moved from conviction, policy, or a mixture of both, there can be no question that he supported the persecution of heresy with more legislation and determination that any German Emperor since the time of Frederick II. Indeed, it was probably he who inspired the virulent campaigns not only of Walter Kerlinger, but of Lambert of Strassburg examined previously.

The occasion for Charles' legislation was his trip to Italy. Urban V had renewed the commissions of the German Inquisitors from Rome in April 1368[21] and must have discussed the matter with Charles when the two were together in the Eternal City in the fall of that year (the first time that Emperor and Pope were together in Rome since 1220). Then, at Lucca in June 1369, Charles issued four edicts in support of the German Inquisition. These are of great importance in the history of the Inquisition as an institution, but since they have been described at length,[22] it is only necessary to discuss the points relative to the "beghards."

The only heresy that Charles specifically mentioned was that of the beghards. More precisely, in his first edict he referred to the "sect of Beghards and Beguines or conventual sisters who are popularly called *wilge armen* or *convent swestern*, or who, while begging, say *Brot dorch god* [sic]."[23] From this we can see that people still termed

---

et Beghinarum sive sororum eorundem ab hereticorum inquisitoribus. . . quia multitudo maxima talium succreverat et specialiter in Colonia Reni et Erphordia terre Thuringorum, prout habetur in libris inquisiconis." Louis' excommunication of a priest of Soest for heresy is described by R. Wilmanns, "Zur Geschichte der römischen Inquisition in Deutschland während des 14. und 15. Jahrhunderts, HZ, XLI (1879), 203-204. For what else is known about his career, see McDonnell, p. 562.

21. Published in Fredericq, I, 206-208, #209, from Mosheim, pp. 336-37. I can now identify one MS as Wolfenb., Helmst., 315, fol. 199ra-rb.

22. E.g. Lea, II, 387-91 and McDonnell, 563-65.

23. Edict of June 9, 1369 in Fredericq, I, 208-210, #210, from Mosheim, pp. 350-55 (=MS Wolfenb., Helmst., 315, fol. 212v-213v. Fol. 212v differs slightly

beghards the "voluntary poor" a half-century after beghards called themselves that in Strassburg. The third edict is the most interesting for the historian of the Free Spirit. This was an instruction addressed to Kerlinger and the other Inquisitors in Germany, which, in effect, initiated an office of censorship. According to the Emperor, the German beghards and beguines were spreading errors and blasphemies against Christ, the Virgin, and the Catholic faith by means of sermons, tracts, and other books written in the vernacular. They allegedly disseminated these among the "lay and almost lay" whom they thereby infected with heresy.[24] In recognizing the existence of a beghard literature, which Charles ordered the Inquisitors to seek out and burn, the edict rested on fact, but how blasphemous these books really were is another question. The final edict aided Kerlinger most of all by ordering that the houses of beghards and beguines be confiscated by the Inquisition.[25]

3. THE CAMPAIGN OF WALTER KERLINGER: JOHN HARTMANN AND THE BEGUINES OF THURINGIA

Walter Kerlinger was a Dominican master of theology who came from a patrician family of Erfurt and was chaplain to Charles IV. His

---

from Mosheim in having: "sectam beghardorum et beginarum seu *swestronum* conventualium que *vulgariter wilge armen* vel convent swestern dicunter vel que simul mendicando dicunt *Brot dorch god*"). J. F. Böhmer and A. Huber (eds.), *Die Regesten des Kaiserreichs unter Kaiser Karl IV*, Regesta imperii, VIII, 1 (Innsbruck, 1877), 394, #4756, list another MS copy in the Stadtarchiv zu Mühlhausen. The second edict, published on June 10, suggests that some resistance was being offered to the Inquisition because it named German princes as protectors and ordered the strongest penalties for anyone who attempted to obstruct the inquisitorial procedures (Fredericq, I, 210–14, #211).

24. Edict of June 17, 1369 in Fredericq, I, 214–17, #212, from Mosheim, pp. 368–75 (=MS Wolfenb., Helmst., 315, fol. 206ra–207vb. Fol. 206rb differs from Mosheim in having: "Quod in partibus Alamannie propter sermones tractus [sic] et alios libros in vulgari scriptos inter personas laicos vel pene laycos dispersos. . . ."). Böhmer and Huber, 395, #4761, list another copy in the Stadtarchiv zu Erfurt.

25. Edict of June 17, 1369, mistakenly dated June 18, in Fredericq, I, 218–21, #213, from Mosheim, pp. 356–62 (=MS Wolfenb., Helmst., 315, fol. 199rb–200vb). Another copy, from a MS of Vienna, was edited by J. Caro, "Aus der Kanzlei Kaiser Sigismunds. Urkundliche Beiträge zur Geschichte des Constanzer Concils," *Archiv für österreichische Geschichte*, LIX (1889), 168–72.

sphere of activity was central Germany and it was probably he who came across three female heretics in Wittenberg who were clearly Waldensians.[26] We know definitely that in the same period he was in Magdeburg, where a chronicler says that he extirpated the heresy of the beghards and beguines, and that he was active in Bremen at the beginning of 1367, with unknown success.[27] Later in the year he went to his native city of Erfurt, which thereafter became the center of his campaign. One report has it that early in 1368 two hundred beghards and beguines escaped from Erfurt while an equal number recanted and wore penitential garb. These figures might be exaggerated, but it appears from other reports that many did do public penance and that a few were even executed: one for trying to persuade a girl to let him have intercourse with her "from the rear, in the manner of a dog," two for relapsing, and at least two others for obduracy.[28]

An inquisitorial protocol, which is generally considered to be one of the most valuable sources pertaining to the heresy of the Free Spirit that we have, records the case of one of the latter, John Hartmann of Ossmannstedt, whose trial was conducted by Kerlinger in Erfurt in 1367, on the day after Christmas.[29] No torture was necessary: the accused was highly cooperative and answered all questions extensively and with obvious relish. By his own declaration he was "free in spirit" and he apprised his interrogator that no one could express such truth as one so free as himself. He even admonished him that he ought to be grateful for his answers because they were more valuable than all the money in the towers of the town council. Kerlinger must have been taken aback by this self-confidence and gave John a chance to escape dire punishment by asking if he suffered from insanity, but Hartmann denied that he was ill in any way and even insisted that he had never been sick during the nine years in which he had been free in spirit.

26. On Kerlinger's career, Erbstösser, pp. 108–10. On Wittenberg, references given by D. Kurze, "Zur Ketzergeschichte der Mark Brandenburg und Pommerns vornehmlich im 14. Jahrhundert," *Jahrbuch für die Geschichte Mittel-und Ostdeutschlands*, XVI/XVII (1968), 66.

27. On Magdeburg, *Gesta archiepiscoporum Magdeburgensium, continuatio*, MGH SS, XIV, 441. On Bremen, Erbstösser, pp. 109 and 154–55.

28. *Detmar Chronik von 1101–1395*, CdS, XIX, 539; Korner (as above, n. 20), p. 285; *Gesta arch. Magdebg.*, 441.

29. A critical edition, based on the three surviving MSS, is in Erbstösser, pp. 136–53.

The protocol contains no mention of his having recanted and it may therefore be assumed that he was executed. The Inquisition could have had no other choice, for John's testimony shows him to have been the most outspoken and unashamedly radical Free Spirit of whom we have reliable record.

Unfortunately, Hartmann was not allowed to speak entirely for himself but was examined, like the beguines of Schweidnitz, on the basis of *Ad nostrum*. Furthermore, the inquisitorial document, as valuable as it is, cannot be equated with a modern stenographic record: because certain words were left in the original we know that John was examined in German and that a protocol was then drawn up in Latin. Thus when John is quoted as saying, for example, that man in the present life can reach such a state of perfection that he can no longer sin in any way ("talis homo tantum et talem perfectionis gradum acquirit quod redditur penitus impeccabilis"), we know that Kerlinger or his notary simply borrowed the phrase from *Ad nostrum* and inserted it into the record. The entire protocol follows this text point by point and John readily confessed to believing all eight tenets. It would be interesting to know whether he could have named them himself if they had not been supplied.

Because we cannot answer that question it is only when John's testimony goes beyond the language of *Ad nostrum* that it becomes really useful. Fortunately, that is often enough: John was particularly expansive about the effects of being free in spirit. According to him, one who is "truly free" can be subject to no authority because he himself is king and lord of all creatures. Since everything belongs to him he can take whatever he pleases and kill whoever tries to stop him.[30]

30. Erbstösser, p. 111, has already noticed that this is one of several striking similarities between Hartmann's testimony and that of John and Albert of Brünn. It must, however, be questioned if this arose from a transmission of ideas from Brünn or Cologne to Erfurt and their perpetuation over a period of two generations, or if Kerlinger did not simply confront Hartmann with the earlier testimony. The case of Conrad Kannler, to be discussed below, shows that inquisitors did use more than one document as bases for their examinations. Furthermore, the only MS that contains the confessions from Brünn also includes the testimony from Erfurt directly following. Conceivably Kerlinger had the Brünn materials in his handbook and transmitted it for another copy along with his own hearing of John Hartmann. The most impressive correspondences between the two texts are as follows:

Here Kerlinger intervened with leading questions. He asked John if one free in spirit could seize a golden chalice from someone for his own use and he answered yes, that it was better to receive a golden chalice than a coarse cloth. Then he asked him if he would kill even the Emperor if he stood in his way and John answered that it depended on whether the Emperor was free in spirit: if he were not, he would certainly kill him. In such ways Kerlinger, Charles IV's chaplain, gathered material that would be certain to insure further imperial support.

John's testimony on sexual matters was so unrestrained that leading questions were not at all necessary. He maintained that if the nature of a free spirit (*"ein frey geist"*) inclined toward the sexual act he could have intercourse with his sister or his mother in any place, even on the altar, and that it would be "more natural" to have sex with one's sister than with any other woman. Nor would a young girl lose her virginity after sexual intercourse, but if she had already been robbed of it she would regain it by having relations with one free in spirit. Even if a girl had successive intercourse with ten men, if the last of them was a free spirit she would receive her virginity back. Just as calves and oxen were created for men to eat, so women were created for the use of the free in spirit. When asked what would happen if two of the latter desired the same girl simultaneously, John answered that the one who was "more free" should satisfy himself first, but if they were equally free they would have to cast dice!

When Kerlinger asked John if Christ had been a free spirit he

---

Hartmann, ed. Erbstösser	*John and Albert of Brünn, ed. Wattenbach*
quia occidendo eum remitteret ipsum ad originale suum principium (p. 140)	et si homo iste moritur fame, quia ei non plus fecisti nisi ad suum originale Principium transmisti (p. 533)
Nec Maria nec angeli possent discernere inter deum et ipsum propter perfectam unionem ipsorum (p. 142)	angeli in speculo Trinitatis non possunt discernere inter Deum et animam que in libertate spiritus vixerit propter prefatam unionem ipsorum (pp. 533–34).

Hartmann and Albert of Brünn both used the term *grossi homines*, but this seems to have been a favorite pejorative expression among beghards and beguines, as noted in the discussion of the beguines of Mühlhausen directly below.

obtained the answer that Christ first became truly free on Good Friday, after the Crucifixion, which is why people call the day Friday (*"freytag"*)! When Kerlinger asked if Christ, after the Resurrection, had had sex with Mary Magdalene—a question which shows that the Inquisitor's imagination was not much paler than the heretic's—John replied, almost coyly, that that was a lofty and profound sentence and said that although he well knew the answer he preferred not to expound on it. Then he added, as the protocol tells us "smiling," that some people believe there will be the same sexual relations in the future life as in the present, because if there were not, men would prefer to remain with their wives on earth. As for the sacraments, a Free Spirit did not have to confess because he was without sin and a game of chess could reveal God as well as the Eucharist if one took more delight in it because God is found in pleasure!

There are some personalities that so enjoy being in the spotlight that they will do or say anything to remain bathed in it. John might have been of this type, or he might have been slightly deranged. His avowals to the contrary prove nothing since few madmen believe that they are mad. One's suspicions are whetted by the fact that Kerlinger asked him why he was so pallid, but he refused to disclose the cause.[31] On the other hand, extravagant or unbalanced as his testimony was, he never once said that he actually did the things a Free Spirit theoretically could do. He delighted in providing shocking examples of the consequences of divine union, but it was that union itself which interested him most. His language in describing it, moreover, shows that he was the representative of a tradition and not a mere lunatic. At one point he sounds like a mystical theologian, albeit an heretical one, when he says that "the nobility of the spirit is essentially one with God from the outflow of divinity and its return flow in the deity," adding that "no multiplicity can be placed between the divinity and the free in spirit."[32] Such difficult concepts he must have had from other heretics or books.

Unlike Hermann Kuchener, Constantine of Erfurt, or Berthold

31. Ed. Erbstösser, p. 148: "Interrogatus an talia dixerit ex demencia cordis vel debilitate capitis seu ex aliqua infirmitate corporis, respondit quod nullo istorum morborum sed ex fundo suo talia dixit. . . ."

32. Ed. Erbstösser, pp. 142–44: "quod nobilitas spiritus ex effluxu divinitatis et refluxu in deitate essencialiter est unus cum deo. . . . nulla multiplicatio est ibi ponenda in divinis et inter talem liberum spiritu."

of Rohrbach, John Hartmann was probably a real beghard. Not only was he called this in the protocol, but his surname "de villa Astmanstete" indicates that he was not born in Erfurt but did some travelling. The protocol also records that he was called John "Spynner" among the beghards. This could refer to the profession of weaving, or, more likely, a special mystical quality. In the modern German vernacular *spinnen* sometimes means to imagine improbable or fantastic things— a quality well displayed by John's testimony. That the word had a similar connotation centuries earlier is shown by Luther's "gott hatts yhn nicht befolhen sondern sie spinnen es aus yhrem eygen kopffe."[33] It is hard to see why John would be called a weaver only among the beghards, whereas an esoteric name used by his confederates would be thoroughly fitting. In either event his testimony is of very real value in illustrating the perpetuation of heretical mysticism among some German beghards in the second half of the fourteenth century.

The survival of another document, this time one that has hitherto escaped the notice of scholarship, illuminates Kerlinger's activities in Thuringia in the months directly following the trial of John Hartmann.[34] It records his absolution of a beguine named Aleydis of Nürnberg at Mühlhausen on February 7, 1368, and is prefaced by a list of errors that were presumably taken from her confession. The latter is divided into articles concerning the sacrament of penance, the sacrament of the altar, and excommunication. Unfortunately, the pertinent part of the manuscript is a palimpsest so badly mutilated that it is difficult to piece together whole sentences. But it is clear that the errors primarily concern discipline, which is why the decree *Cum de quibusdam* is explicitly cited and *Ad nostrum* is not mentioned at all.

The document alleges in particular that beguines could not go to confession without the license of their congregation and their "Martha" or mistress. If one of them did so, she had to seek pardon in the beguinage by prostrating herself on the ground in the form of a cross. Then the beguines would try to find out what she had confessed, even by the use of force. On the other hand, the "Martha" would hear confessions herself and grant absolution on the condition of such penances

33. Grimm, *Deutsches Wörterbuch*, X, 1 (Leipzig, 1905), 2525.
34. MS Schloss Pommersfelden 141 (2743), fol. 1r–1v, in a cursive of the fifteenth century. *Incip.*: "Isti sunt errores in quibus quedam Begine circa sacramentum penitencie erraverunt."

as making an inmate take care of the house and not go to church with the others. Similarly, the women supposedly showed contempt for the Eucharist and defied excommunication.

It may be recalled that the beguines examined in Schweidnitz in 1332 revealed their contacts with beguinages in central Germany and the evidence of Kerlinger's examination three decades later shows that such houses continued to exist. The beguines of Mühlhausen had an organization similar to that found in Schweidnitz and they even used the pejorative adjective *"grossus"* found not only in the protocols from Schweidnitz but also in the confessions of Albert of Brünn and John Hartmann. But what is missing is any reference to a doctrine of mystical illumination. The Thuringian beguines might have arrogated to themselves certain sacramental functions, but this came from excessive lay religiosity rather than any claims to a special mystical state. The best example from the examination of 1368 is a reference to the desire of certain beguines to receive communion every Sunday, at that time still an outrageous demand for the laity. Their urge was so great that they stole the host from a church by concealing it under one of their habits and then used it for their own service.[35] The document cited this as an example of disrespect for the Eucharist, but others might see it as evidence that such women were holier than those who kept them from participation in the Mass.

In 1369 Kerlinger arrested more than forty suspects of both sexes at Nordhausen in Thuringia, of whom several remained obdurate and were burned. The only source that mentions this does not indicate whether any of those arrested were beguines or beghards, nor does it say what they believed.[36] In the same year Charles IV's legislation was promulgated in Germany and Kerlinger, armed with the Emperor's fourth edict, was able to terminate his campaign against the beguines of Mühlhausen on February 16, 1370 by ordering the magistrates of the town to confiscate four beguinages for pious uses.[37] But this was the high point of his career. In 1371 or 1372 he requested the

<hr/>

35. *Ibid.*, fol. 1rb: "Isti articuli alibi inter eas sunt inventi. Nam quedam volentes singulis dominicis diebus communicare. . . . Invente sunt quod corpus christi de Ecclesia domum portaverunt, et sub peplo absconderunt, et domum venientes proicerunt super mensam ante se. . . ."

36. Korner (as above, n. 20), p. 285.

37. B. C. Grasshof, *Commentatio de originibus atque antiquitatibus S. R. I. liberae civitatis Muhlhusae* (Leipzig and Görlitz, 1749), pp. 69–70.

new Pope, Gregory XI, to approve the provisions of the fourth imperial edict; the Pope did this, but in 1372 he also limited Kerlinger's
authority.[38] The latter died in 1373 and nothing more is heard about
persecution of beghards in central Germany for another generation.

4. CONRAD KANNLER

Innocent beghards and beguines continued to be persecuted in Strassburg and Cologne for a few years afterwards,[39] but the promulgation
of *Ad audientiam nostram* in 1377 in favor of "good" beghards and
beguines, the death of Charles IV in 1378, and the uncertainties related to the opening of the Great Schism in the same year brought
about a comparative lull in inquisitorial activity.[40] The Papal Inquisi-

38. Gregory's approval of the imperial legislation is in a bull published by
Fredericq, I, 221-22, #214, from Mosheim, pp. 364-66. There, and in MS Wolfenb., Helmst., 315, fol. 200vb-201ra, it has the dating "pontificatus nostri anno
primo" (i.e. 1371), but see Kehr and Schmidt (as above, n. 18), 282, #1030, who
date the same document to 1372. Gregory's limitation of Kerlinger's authority is
in Fredericq, I, 222-24, #215, from Mosheim, pp. 380-83 (see also Kehr and
Schmidt, 285-86, #1043).

39. See above, pp. 54, 97-101. It may also be added that Pope Gregory XI
strengthened the Inquisition in the Rhineland, Brabant, and Holland by a number
of bulls issued in January of 1372 or 1373 because beghards were fleeing from
central Germany to the West (Kehr and Schmidt, 295, #1081-84), and in 1372
he wrote to all clerical and secular officials in Germany, Silesia, and Poland to
say that beghards and beguines were escaping to the Duchy of Stettin, Silesia,
and the city and diocese of Breslau (Mosheim, pp. 647-49; Kehr and Schmidt,
286-87, #1044). In 1375 a man named Löffler was condemned at Bern by the Official of the Bishop of Lausanne for adhering to "dem bösen ketzerschen glouben,
den die haltend, die man nempt des fryen geistes," but this case is unfortunately
known only through a brief entry in the *Berner Chronik* of Conrad Justinger,
ed. G. L. Studer (Bern, 1871), pp. 147-48, which gives no further information
about Löffler's beliefs.

40. On *Ad audientiam nostram*, see above, p. 54. Even that bull did not curtail
the work of the Papal Inquisition as is shown by an order of Charles IV previously thought to have been issued in 1373 but actually dated February 17, 1378,
which refers to the fact that Gregory XI had just commissioned the imperial
chaplain, the Dominican John of Boland, as Inquisitor for the dioceses of Trier,
Cologne, and Liège to examine beghards and beguines (no other heretics were
even mentioned). In this order Charles commanded that John be given all the
rights specified in the imperial legislation of 1369. The document was first misdated by Mosheim, pp. 388-92, who was followed by Fredericq, I, 225-28, #218.
The correct date was noted by J. F. Böhmer and A. Huber (eds.), *Erstes Ergän-
zungsheft zu den Regesten des Kaiserreichs unter Kaiser Karl IV*, Regesta
imperii, VIII, 2 (Innsbruck, 1889), 773, #7461, and is unmistakably clear in the
MS copy of Wolfenb., Helmst., 315, fol. 202ra. The false dating misled Lea, II,

tion did not dissolve, but in the 1380s it exercised its functions fitfully while jurisdiction in heretical cases was often reassumed by local authorities.

In 1381, for example, a layman named Conrad Kannler was brought in Eichstätt before Eberhard of Freyenhausen, a canon who was appointed inquisitor by the local bishop. Thanks to the preservation of the trial protocol, Conrad has become one of the most noted of "heretical beghards," but a recent analysis by Herbert Grundmann has thrown his testimony into a completely new light.[41] For one, Conrad neither called himself, nor was ever called, a beghard, and belonged to no sect or religious community. Despite this, as Grundmann has shown, he was examined on the eight tenets of *Ad nostrum* and also on the testimony of John Hartmann, which the inquisitor must have had in a handbook. Though Kannler must have spoken German, his answers were recorded in Latin, sometimes in the form of quotes from the Clementine decree or Hartmann's confession. Before Grundmann's work, scholars seized on these passages as examples of the continuity of Free Spirit thought and organisation, but it is now clear that Kannler had his own ideas and that the most interesting parts of his testimony are not those which repeat, but those which diverge from the earlier models.

Kannler was first asked if he were "free in spirit" and when he answered in the affirmative, his reply was enough to send the inquisitor to *Ad nostrum* and Hartmann's protocol. These texts then governed the proceedings. Asked to define "freedom of spirit," Kannler supposedly answered in words exactly the same as Hartmann's. But actually he was far less radical. When the inquisitor reached the second point of *Ad nostrum* and asked him if his perfection came from his own merit or the grace of God, Kannler replied only from grace, since even the angels and saints could reach perfection through divine

---

394–95, McDonnell, p. 570, and Leff, p. 347, into believing that *Ad audientiam nostram* alone was a milestone in the treatment of beghards and beguines, but it was obviously that along with the concurrent deaths of Charles IV and Gregory XI in 1378 and then the outbreak of the Great Schism that initiated an ebb in the wave of persecution.

41. Grundmann, "Ketzerverhöre," 535–50. The protocol was originally published by H. Haupt, "Ein Beghardenprozess in Eichstätt vom Jahre 1381," ZfK, V (1882), 494–98, but Grundmann, 561–66, has re-edited it with indications of all the borrowings from previous texts.

grace alone. Later he added that what God was from nature, he him-self was from grace,[42] in both cases showing the independence of his thought and repudiating the Pelagianism that the inquisitor was trying to pin on him.

Kannler differed the most from Hartmann in his answer to the fourth and fifth points of *Ad nostrum*. He responded affirmatively to the words of the decree that he could attain final beatitude on earth, but then he added that this blessedness could not be obtained "essen-tially" or "face to face," but only as "through a glass, darkly." Here Grundmann exclaims, with full justice, "is this really the same heresy that was condemned in Erfurt and at the Council of Vienne?"[43] As for the fifth point, that the soul does not need the light of glory to see God, Kannler answered, directly to the contrary, that if the soul has any blessedness it has it from God, not from itself, and it *needs* the light of glory to be elevated to God! This reply fully answers Grund-mann's rhetorical question.

Kannler also took an independent position concerning the sexual claims made by John Hartmann. If a virgin had intercourse with one free in spirit she would indeed lose her virginity "according to the flesh," though God would be indulgent and give it back to her for the sake of spiritual freedom. On the other hand, he agreed with Hart-mann that, if nature so inclined, one free in spirit could have sex with his mother and sister, but he was careful to add that he did not believe that God would let such a thing occur for one so perfect.[44] Thus, where Hartmann preened himself on theoretical perversities, Kannler

42. Grundmann, 562: ". . . nuncupat se fratrem Christi per graciam et, quod deus est per naturem, hoc ipse foret et esse posset per graciam. . . ." Leff's mis-translation, p. 380, "As free in spirit he was one with God, calling himself Christ's brother by grace and God by nature" entirely alters the real meaning of Kannler's answer.

43. Grundmann, 543. The text is 563: "sed essencialiter huiusmodi beatitudi-nem non potuerit apprehendere, sed tantum enigmate et speculo, sed non facie ad faciem." The attempt of Leff, p. 380, n. 2, to dismiss this as a "faulty transcrip-tion or an error in the text" is unconvincing in light of Kannler's entire testi-mony which Leff admits (p. 382) "shows a tendency to modify the more ex-treme statements of the Free Spirit on three occasions."

44. Grundmann, 562: ". . . non peccaret cum matre et sorore, si huiusmodi actum cum ea exerceret, si natura inclinaret, sed tamen non credit, quod deus hoc permitti fieret a tam perfectis et spiritu liberis." Leff's mistranslation (p. 380) "he did not believe God would permit it for the imperfect" again produces a dia-metrically opposite meaning.

allowed them in principle alone and probably would not have mentioned sexual matters at all had not the inquisitor introduced them.

What he himself wanted to talk about was his self-centered theory of history—his greatest preoccupation. He said that he was a second Adam, or Antichrist, called by God to preach and perform miracles for thirty years. He would not be Antichrist in an evil sense (Grundmann points out that he probably used the German term *endekrist* which had a positive connotation),[45] but would initiate a third age of paradise on earth, to last until God, at the will of Christ, would bring the new generation of men to heaven. Then he added, perhaps as an afterthought, that he would preside at the last judgment because he was cast in the image of the innocent lamb. If these speculations had anything to do with Joachism the relation was distant since Kannler explained that the third age would come after the last judgment, not before it as in Joachim's prophecies. Kannler's scheme either shows how easily Joachism could become garbled, or else it represented an original phantasy.

Kannler, in fact, insisted on his own independence. He declared that all his beliefs came directly from the Holy Spirit and he explained that nine years earlier (was this figure also taken from Hartmann's confession?) he had had a supernatural experience in the Cathedral of Eichstätt. At that time he was seized by ecstasy and a divine voice said to him "Friend, all your sins are forgiven because of your contrition." (This shows that abnegation rather than scandalous conduct was for him the prerequisite for deification.[46]) Like John Hartmann he was asked if he were sick or insane, but he denied being so.

---

45. The popular positive understanding of the term is manifest in the following fictional exchange between Franz von Sickingen and Karsthans the prototypic peasant in Martin Bucer's *Gesprechbiechlin neüw Karsthans* of 1521, ed. R. Stupperich, *Martin Bucers Deutsche Schriften, I: Frühschriften* (Gütersloh and Paris, 1960), p. 441: "Franz: Was meynst du, das der Endtchrist sey?/ Karsthans: Ich weiss es warlich nit, dann das die pfaffen und münch predigen, er werd ein neüwer gott sein und wann er komm, so werd die welt bald darnach zergeen./ Franz: Ja lieber Karsthans, Es hatt vil ein andere meynung. Er heiss nit Endchrist, als der am ende der welt kommen werde, sunder heisst er Antchrist, das ist ein Kriechisch Wort...."

46. Grundmann, 564: "Amice, sint tibi dimissa omnia peccata tua propter contricionem per te habitam." H. S. Offler, *English Historical Review*, LXXXIV (1969), 576, has called attention to Leff's mistranslation of this as "Friend, all your sins have been forgiven you because of your condition."

Nor did he think that he was a heretic: before his arrest he confessed and took the Eucharist just to prove the contrary, and in his first hearing he refused to recant because he was still convinced that he was divinely inspired. As he said, if he were a heretic so were the Father, the Son, and the Holy Spirit. Despite this obduracy the local authorities were not quick to burn him. A week later they examined him again and this time he withdrew all his former statements, saying that they had after all not been inspired by the Holy Spirit, but by an evil spirit and by dullness of mind. Because of this reversal the Bishop of Eichstätt later absolved him on the condition of unknown penances. His case shows us another unstable personality, this time captivated by his presumed eschatological role, whose ideas were otherwise much less outrageous than the inquisitor thought that they would be.

In the same year as the examination of Kannler there was an unrelated incident in nearby Augsburg. There, in the month of May, an epileptic beggar by the name of "brother Hans," attracted crowds of the ill who thought that he was a thaumaturge. When the authorities arrested Hans and put him under torture he confessed to being a perverter of young boys and implicated two beghards in his crimes. These, along with Hans and two others were then burned for heresy, although doctrine does not seem to have been at issue at all. Directly afterwards "a great wind ripped up trees and blew away roofs."[47] This story, with its scent of brimstone, indicates that beghards undoubtedly would have been burned as witches had they survived into the sixteenth century since they were such obvious subjects for an unfortunate epileptic to name under torture as his accomplices in maleficence.

5. THE CAMPAIGNS OF MARTIN OF PRAGUE, PETER ZWICKER, AND EYLARD SCHOENVELD

After the lull of the 1380s, the following two decades—a time of political chaos and the desperate attempt of the Roman Papacy to hold its own in the Great Schism—witnessed the most sustained and bloody

---

47. MS Cgm 2026, *Modus Procedendi wann Malefiz Recht gehalten wird in Malefiz Sachen*, fol. 8v–9r. This is more extensive than the published sources, the *Augsburger Chronik von 1368–1406*, CdS, IV, 68, and the *Chronik von der Gründung der Stadt Augsburg bis zum Jahre 1469*, CdS, IV, 313.

campaigns against heresy that Germany and Central Europe had yet known. The most zealous directors of these campaigns were the Papal Inquisitors Martin of Prague, Peter Zwicker, and Eylard Schoenveld who between them conducted scores of investigations in cities and hamlets throughout the German Empire. We already met Martin when he was called to Strassburg in 1374. About 1380 he appears to have been in Regensburg[48] and afterwards in parts east, but in the 1390s he returned to Germany where, together with Peter Zwicker, he persecuted primarily Waldensians and occasionally beguines and beghards. The monastic compiler Tritheim, writing a century later, tells us that in 1392 Martin found several *"Fraticelli"* (a term Tritheim used interchangeably with beghards) in Würzburg whom he forced to recant and join a crusade against the Turks, and that in 1393 he found numerous beghards and beguines in Erfurt, some of whom he had burned.[49] There is probably some substance in this report because we know that Martin's campaign in Bamberg in 1399 led to the abjuration of at least seven beghards and beguines. Whether these were really heretics is another matter: all that is recorded is that one of them, a certain Margaretha de Rottenburg, supposedly preached "a good word" in her convent.[50]

It might also have been Martin of Prague, or his colleague Peter Zwicker, who in the late fourteenth century conducted an examination of a beghard in the Bavarian town of Cham in cooperation with the Duke of the region. Whoever the Inquisitor was, he left behind

48. Indicated in trial records published by Timotheus Wilhelm Röhrich, *Mittheilungen aus der Geschichte der evangelischen Kirche des Elsasses* (Strassburg and Paris, 1855), I, 63. The basic account of the campaigns of Martin of Prague and Peter Zwicker is still Haupt, "Waldenserthum," III.

49. J. Trithemius, *Annales Hirsaugenses* (St. Gall, 1690), II, 296. There are two ironies here: one is that Martin and Peter Zwicker had been together in Erfurt in 1391 without finding any heretical beghards; the other is that in 1389 the papal legate Cardinal Philip of Alençon had renewed the provisions of Gregory XI's bull *Ad audientiam nostram* meant to protect orthodox beguines. For the renewal see G. Schmidt, *UB der Stadt Halberstadt*, I (*Geschichtsquellen der Provinz Sachsen*, VII) (Halle, 1878), 522–23, #637, and the unpublished remarks in MS Clm 14216, fol. 177va.

50. I owe this information to Mr. Peter Biller of Oriel College, Oxford, who has it from a catalogue entry describing lost MSS that he intends to publish. On this entry see for the time being E. Werner, "Die Nachrichten über die böhmischen 'Adamiten' in religionshistorischer Sicht," in Theodora Büttner and Ernst Werner, *Circumcellionen und Adamiten* (Berlin, 1959), p. 112.

him a description of his findings mixed with formal charges from *Ad nostrum*.[51] Unfortunately the document recounts actual testimony at only one point, and all this shows is that the examined beghard could not (or perhaps would not) recite the Lord's Prayer. But there are many other vivid and apparently genuine details. According to the anonymous Inquisitor, the "beghards and beguines of voluntary poverty" considered themselves to be more perfect than all religious orders because of their rigorous mendicant life and their total rejection of property. They tried to suppress all their natural desires for food, drink, and sleep, and went so far in their asceticism as to eat the cadavers of dogs, cats, and dormice. Like the friars they wore habits and tonsures; the men called their superiors "father" and the women their officers "Martha" (those who had special functions were called "Shoe-Martha," "Kitchen-Martha," or the like). They had a special way of murmuring their prayers and the perfect among them did not pray orally at all, but only did so internally, from the heart. For this reason those who did not move their lips during prayers in church supposedly could be identified as beghards.

The very fact that these beghards could be found praying in church shows that they could not have been thoroughly rebellious antinomians. The Inquisitor tries to maintain that they were by claiming that they sought a state of primal innocence and gave themselves over to fleshly delights without fear, but this contradicts another of his statements that they tried to overcome sensuality by means of reason. That his former claim was based on the Clementines is indicated by his report that the beghards justified their immorality with the biblical quote "ubi spiritus domini est, ibi libertas" because this was cited explicitly in *Ad nostrum* and he mentioned that decree himself in support of his final claim that the beghards refused to rise for the

51. H. Haupt, "Zwei Traktate gegen Beginen und Begharden," ZfK, XII (1891), 85–90, first described and published the document from a fifteenth-century MS of Michelstadt. Subsequently a better copy from Prague was published by Ernst Werner, *Nachrichten über spätmittelalterliche Ketzer aus tschechoslovakischen Archiven und Bibliotheken* (Leipzig, 1963), pp. 280–81. Werner's attempt, pp. 257–58, to date the examination to the spring of 1399 does not include numerous other possibilities because there is no assurance that the Inquisitor was, as Werner believes, Martin of Prague, and Martin himself was in Bavaria on other occasions. Haupt, "Zwei Traktate," 87–88, describes another anonymous polemic from the MS of Michelstadt, a *Tractatus contra Lolhardos* that attacks beghards exclusively on the grounds of their voluntary poverty.

elevation of the host. Clearly some beghards thought they could reach a state of perfection, but this document does not go beyond old stereotypes in describing that state.

Perhaps from the same period or even by the same Inquisitor is a laconic note found by Mr. Peter Biller in an inquisitorial handbook from the monastery of Garsten in Styria. Notes in the same hand appear in a sister manuscript which was written after 1368, and since we know that the Inquisitor Peter Zwicker resided at Garsten in the 1390s, it is possible that this note was his (although his only documented inquisitions were against Waldensians). The text is so short that it may be reproduced in entirety: "primus gradus perfeccionis beghardice dicitur: primus—swenkerat; secundus—ckulslak; tertius—gluncz; quartus—ehygluncz. Et iste est perfectissimus gradus qui reddit hominem in vita presenti inpeccabilem."[52] The last words quote the first error of *Ad nostrum*, showing that the Inquisitor was still working with that text, but the four mystical states of "beghard perfection" are incomprehensible. The note does suggest that some beghards were using esoteric terms to describe four mystical states, but we do not know who the beghards were nor even exactly where and when they lived.

The activities of Martin of Prague and Peter Zwicker were encouraged by the Roman Pope, Boniface IX. At first Boniface had adopted a conciliatory policy toward beghards and beguines, but in 1396 he revoked all concessions ever granted to "beghards, lollards, or sisters," declaring that they had spawned heresy for the past hundred years.[53] In keeping with this he ordered proceedings against all of them and issued a number of bulls strengthening the organization of the German Inquisition, one of which, issued in 1399, ordered

52. MS Linz 177 (old 69), unfoliated; there is a copy in MS Vat. lat. 4265, fol. 101r. The remarks that follow the quoted passage in the Linz MS are in a different hand and do not seem related to the beghards (the first sentence introduces the old stereotype of heretics who do not think usury a sin); it is no doubt for this reason that they were not re-copied in the Vatican MS. I am most grateful to Mr. Biller for informing me of his find and hope that his own publications will cast more light on the subject: my own consultations with experts in Slavic languages have yielded no positive results.

53. Fredericq, I, 256–57, #241, from Mosheim, pp. 409–410. MS Clm 14216, fol. 177va–178ra, contains the text of the same bull with significant variations from the published edition. It also adds a brief note about the motives for its composition and fixes the date to 1396 (cf. Haupt, "Beiträge," 527).

officials to cooperate with the Dominican Inquisitor Eylard Schoen-veld.[54] Though he was one of the last Inquisitors who systematically sought beghards, Eylard was one of the most ruthless. Around 1400 he attacked the orthodox Brethren of the Common Life, whom he insisted on calling the "sect of Gerardites" after their founder Gert Groote. But Holland, then as later, was not fertile ground for the Inquisition. The Brethren had influential supporters including the Bishop of Utrecht, who in 1401 upheld an earlier ruling by theologians and canon lawyers in their favor, thus preventing Eylard from convicting the pious followers of Groote as heretics.[55]

From there the Inquisitor moved on to the north German Hanseatic cities where he had more success. In 1402 he was in Lübeck conducting the examination of a certain "beghard" named William. Again we have only the chroniclers to guide us, but they suggest that this "beghard" was either a Waldensian or an isolated religious megalomaniac.[56] William was a wanderer who first arrived in Lübeck dressed in long white robes and called himself one of Christ's new apostles. He had a long brown beard and he distinguished himself by his upright, ascetic life, gathering a large following among the men and women of the city. But in Eylard Schoenveld he met his nemesis. After the Inquisitor came to Lübeck some "good honest women" denounced William to him as a heretic and a lecher. The town authorities rapidly arrested the suspect who then confessed to eighty (!) heretical or

54. Fredericq, I, 259–61, #244, reprints this bull from Mosheim, pp. 225–28, but misdates it. (Mosheim's correct date is corroborated by Wilmanns [as above, n. 20] 205.) That Boniface had a final change of heart and went back to the policy of distinguishing between "good" and "bad" beguines is indicated by bulls in *UB Halberstadt* (as above, n. 49), I, 565–66, #681, and Haupt, "Beiträge," 565–67. Another text of the latter is edited by Döllinger, 381–83, from MS Clm 14216, fol. 179rb–180rb. The fact that both versions break off at the same point without giving a date indicates that they stem from a common exemplar.

55. The documents are most conveniently found in Fredericq, II, 176–85, 190–93, #113, 114, 119. A later chronicler, Dier de Muden, claimed that Eylard tried to proceed against communities of the Common Life ca. 1393–94 (Fredericq, I, 251, #236), but there is no confirmation of this although another Dominican Inquisitor, Jacob of Soest, did attack Groote's followers at that time (Fredericq, II, 153–56, #106). On this subject see further below pp. 198–99.

56. The sources are three versions of the chronicle of Korner (as above, n. 20), pp. 99, 364–65, 546–47 (only one of these versions has been used—in an antiquated edition—by historians of heresy up to now), and *Die sogennante Rufus-Chronik von 1395–1430*, CdS, XXVIII, 29–30.

blasphemous articles. Eylard condemned him to life imprisonment, but in his dungeon he allegedly ripped off his penitential yellow cross and trampled it under foot. Eylard had meanwhile left in search of other "beghards" but he returned to Lübeck to declare William relapsed, deliver a "glorious" public sermon on the text *Reus est ghehenne ignis*, and send the unfortunate to the stake.

The chronicles report only a sampling of William's eighty condemned articles, but they are a sufficiently bizarre assortment. Supposedly William rejected the fasts and commandments of the Church, maintained that he was as perfect as John the Baptist, and taught that fornication was not sinful (this, as we have seen, was a *topos* in medieval attacks against heresy[57]). To this he added "insults to God and his mother" such as the claim that Christ fornicated with Mary Magdalene, and that the Virgin was the paramour of John the Evangelist.

How are we to reconcile these blasphemies with William's apostolic conduct and use of the term "apostle?" Heretics examined eight years earlier in Pomerania and Brandenburg called their teachers "apostles" and the term was also used by heretics found in Augsburg in 1393.[58] All of these were definitely Waldensians who in no case were suspected of immorality. William was probably similar, for even the hostile chroniclers admit that he was outwardly ascetic. Only when the Inquisitor arrived in town did people have seconds thoughts, and the fact that some women charged him with immorality probably says more about them than about him.

Even the chroniclers were not sure of what to make of William. The same narrator who called him a *"Baggerd"* (which could simply have been meant as a generic term for heretic) elsewhere termed him a disciple of Gerard Segarelli because both wore white clothing and called themselves apostles![59] (It made no difference that Segarelli was executed more than one hundred years earlier and had no known influence North of the Alps.) With this sort of source material one should not jump to conclusions on the basis of William's alleged con-

57. See above, Chapter I, Section 3.
58. On Pomerania and Brandenburg, W. Wattenbach, "Über Ketzergerichte in Pommern und der Mark Brandenburg," Sb. Berlin (1886), p. 51; on Augsburg, J. Gair, *Brevis historia annorum 1392 et 1393*, ed. A. F. Öfele, *Rerum Boicarum scriptores* (Augsburg, 1763), I, 620.
59. Korner, 176–77. The same similarities have led Guarnieri, 464, and Leff, p. 195, to draw the same conclusions.

fession, for it is impossible to know what really transpired. All our sources are variants of a Dominican chronicle and certainly place William's supposed testimony in the worst light. Unless the trial records are discovered there can be no final judgment, but it is hard to believe that a man who wore white and called himself an apostle actually taught that the holiest figures in the Bible were fornicators.

In the following year, 1403, Eylard visited three more north German ports and left behind the ashes of his victims in each. In Wismar he condemned as a hardened heretic one Bernard, who, according to the only account, was a comrade of William of Lübeck. In Stralsund his victim was a priest named Nicholas Ville, who refused to recant after his examination and was stripped of his orders and burned. Since he was a priest he could not literally have been a beghard, but there is no record of what he believed. Finally, Eylard brought a woman to the stake for heresy in Rostock. All we are told about her is that as the flames were rising her son, a Cistercian monk, pleaded with her to recant, but she turned him away. Her death was the last that concerns us in northern Germany.[60]

6. NICHOLAS OF BASEL AND THE CAMPAIGN OF JOHN MULBERG

While persecutions were going on elsewhere, Nicholas of Basel, an elusive figure whom scholars used to portray as Rulman Merswin's mysterious *Gottesfreund*, was attracting disciples throughout the Rhine valley by his messianic pretentions.[61] We know about him from several different sources, but the evidence is contradictory. To begin with the most scandalous specimen we may examine the sentence (preserved in three manuscript copies) of Nicholas' disciple Martin of Mainz who was burned in Cologne in 1393.[62] Martin's examiners were

60. On all three cases, Korner, pp. 365–66, and *Die sog. Rufus-Chronik*, 31. As late as 1414 Schoenveld proceeded against flagellant heretics in Sangerhausen (Thuringia), by the authority of the Margrave of Meissen. See on this, A. Stumpf, "Historia flagellantium, praecipue in Thuringia," *Neue Mittheilungen aus dem Gebiete historisch-antiquarischer Forschungen*, II (1835), 26–32.

61. The theory expounded by K. Schmidt, *Nicolaus von Basel* (Vienna, 1866), that Nicholas was Merswin's *Gottesfreund* was soon after demolished by H. S. Denifle but is still repeated by some modern scholars. See above, pp. 12–13.

62. The mss are: Strassburg B174, destroyed in the fire of 1870 but fortunately edited before then by Schmidt, *Nicolaus von Basel*, pp. 66–69; Mainz 247, described by Haupt, "Beiträge," 509–10; and Clm 14959, fol. 230va–231rb.

a Dominican Inquisitor named Albert or Anthony and John of Cervo, the Official of the Archbishop of Cologne. Ironically the latter had been appointed in 1378 as overseer of the local *"pauperes"* (i.e. beghards and beguines) whom the pope at that time had ordered to be protected.[63] Perhaps this office had made him an expert on the beghard question.

Strictly speaking, however, Martin of Mainz was not a beghard but a former monk from the Benedictine cloister of Reichenau on Lake Constance. As the sentence reveals, he confessed to fifteen errors inspired by his devotion to Nicholas of Basel, who, according to Martin, taught that he understood the Gospels better than the apostles or St. Paul, assumed ecclesiastical functions, claimed superiority to masters of theology, and demanded obedience from his followers above loyalty to all prelates and the pope. As Martin had it (and we must remember that his master was not there to contradict him), Nicholas claimed that he could order his followers to murder and fornicate, and could release them from obedience to the Church into a state of primal innocence.[64] The perfect man (presumably any one who agreed to be his disciple) did not have to pray to go to heaven and the Lord's Prayer should read "lead us *into* temptation."[65] This all sounds as if Nicholas was as radical as John Hartmann but we should not come to conclusions until we examine the other evidence, especially when we bear in mind that we have no indication of how Martin's confession was extracted.

The sentence indicates that some of Nicholas' other followers

63. J. Asen, "Die Beginen in Köln, I," *Annalen des historischen Vereins für den Niederrhein*, CXI (1927), 107–108. John of Cervo had a long career. He was first listed as Official of the Archbishop of Cologne in 1376 (L. Ennen and G. Eckertz, *Quellen zur Geschichte der Stadt Köln* [Cologne, 1860–79], V, 159, #126) and remained in this post at least until the trial of Martin in 1393. He was active as late as 1407, by which time he had become a professor of law (see MS Wolfenb., Helmst., 299, 1, fol. 1r–1v).

64. The best reading is in MS Clm 14959, fol. 230vb: "9. quod ex iussione eiusdem Nicolai nullo modo, etiam interficiendo hominem vel cognoscendo mulierem carnaliter, posses peccare; 10. quod per talem dimissionem Nicolao perfecte sine formis et ymaginibus factus, fuisit liberatus ab obedientia ecclesie, intrans statum prime innocentiae."

65. *Ibid.*, fol. 231ra, similar to Haupt, "Beiträge," 509, reads: "non debet stare sic: et ne nos inducas in temptationem, sed sic: inducas nos in temptationem. . . ." Schmidt, p. 68, must have overlooked a line.

were burned earlier in Heidelberg and we know that the master himself met his end at Vienna sometime between 1393 and 1397. There the noted theologian, Henry of Langenstein, tried to convert him, but Nicholas was ultimately burned at the stake.[66] Both sources that tell of this agree that Nicholas brought two more of his disciples, apostolically named James and John, with him to Vienna, but another record, unaccountably overlooked, though published in 1900, reveals that at least one of them escaped.

The source is a fragment from an inquisitorial protocol taken at Basel about 1405 in connection with a campaign there against beguines.[67] A domestic servant who was examined told of how his master had hired a certain James to dig a well some two years earlier. The job took about six weeks and the servant became acquainted with James well enough to learn that he was the disciple of Nicholas who had been in Vienna.[68] He added that the name James, as one might have guessed, was just an alias, and that the man's dialect revealed that he came from the Lower Rhine. This shows how peripatetic the fraternity was: Nicholas of Basel was burned at Vienna; Martin of Mainz was once a monk on Lake Constance, but was burned at Cologne; other disciples were burned at Heidelberg; and James was born on the Lower Rhine, but was present with Nicholas in Vienna and was last seen in Basel.

Outside of this, the protocol fram Basel gives a completely different impression of Nicholas' circle than the other evidence. Though the sources that speak of Nicholas directly claim that he wore a habit like a beghard, James definitely did not wear one: the servant insisted twice (he examiners were persistent) that he only saw James in secular dress. The same witness also said with assurance that James never took the oath of secrecy that beghards supposedly were accustomed to swear. As for antinomianism, James' only violation of the moral law

---

66. J. Nider, *Formicarius*, ed. G. Colvener (Douai, 1602), Lib. III, cap. 2, p. 192 (reprinted by Schmidt, p. 69), confirmed by a marginal notation in MS Mainz 247 published by Haupt, "Beiträge," 510.

67. Ed. M. Straganz, "Zum Begharden und Beghinenstreite in Basel zu Beginn des 15. Jahrhunderts," *Alemannia*, XXVII (1900), 20–28.

68. *Ibid.*, 26: ". . . qui Jacobus sibi loquenti retulit, quod ipse Jacobus olim fuit discipulus cuiusdam Beghardi nomine Nicolaus de Basilea et habuit quendam alium discipulum ipsius Nicolai, nomine Johannes, et quod ipse Nicolaus de Basilea Beghardus eorum dicti Jacobi et Johannis magister fuerit et sit Wyenne crematus seu combustus."

that emerges from the detailed protocol was that he played with dice for small sums! Thus, either he had changed his manner of life or else Nicholas of Basel's teachings were not so effective or entirely what they were reported to have been by Martin of Mainz.

In addition to this negative evidence the value of the testimony lies in the servant's description of the close relations between James and his master, a member of one of the leading families of Basel. Even after James had finished digging the well he was welcomed in the house and ate at the family table (a fact which the servant seems to have resented). The master and mistress knew that he had been a disciple of the executed Nicholas of Basel, but this did not limit their hospitality, although they kept James' presence a secret from their son, their maid, and the servant's wife. Apparently they were impressed with James' holiness and took him on as a private spiritual director. They must have been aware that they were defying their local clergy, but it is inconceivable that a prominent family like this would have given shelter to the follower of a known blasphemer and preacher of fornication and murder. Rather, the wandering Nicholas of Basel, who reportedly believed that Christ acted in his person[69] and named his disciples James and John, was probably a deluded but charismatic seeker of the extra-hierarchical but literally Christ-like life.

The protocol which contains the information about James was drawn up during a great persecution of beguines in Basel that also spread to other cities. These unfortunate women were the incidental victims of a dispute between Dominicans and Franciscans, among other local rivalries.[70] Their persecutor was the Dominican standard-bearer John Mulberg who had risen from an insignificant family to become one of the most influential preachers of his day. In 1400 he began to attack the beguines and was immediately answered by Rudolf Buchsmann, lector of the Franciscan cloister in the city, who defended the apostolic life of the accused.[71] The dispute continued and boiled over in the summer of 1405 when Mulberg preached against the beguines before the entire assembled clergy of Basel.[72] It is noteworthy

69. Nider, p. 192.

70. On the local aspects of the dispute beyond the scope of this study, R. Wackernagel, *Geschichte der Stadt Basel* (Basel, 1907–24), II, 2, 804–809.

71. *Positio pro defensione beginarum* in MS Basel A. IX. 21, fol. 91; see also Christian Wurstisen, *Baszler Chronick* (Basel, 1580), p. 201.

72. Mulberg, *Materia contra beghardos, beginas, lolhardos, et swestriones*, MS

that he complained of disciplinary infractions and questioned the legality of lay poverty and mendicancy rather than accusing the beguines of spreading mystical or antinomian heresies. Nonetheless, his ally, the Bishop of Basel, expelled all beguines from the city and placed their allies, the Franciscans, under interdict.

Sometime during the course of these events the Bishop ordered an inquisition to be held against the beguines and all those suspected of being their accomplices. At least twenty-four witnesses were called and we have the testimony, sometimes fragmentary, of seven of them.[73] Three were female Franciscan tertiaries, a fact which shows the real target of Mulberg's campaign (tertiaries and beguines were frequently indistinguishable) and explains the deep involvement of the Friars Minor. One of these swore that she knew nothing about any deviance from the faith in the diocese of Basel and a second could tell only of the visits to her house of a certain "beghard" who preached "good words about God and the martyrdom of Christ."

The third told a story concerning pastoral discipline which is incidentally more informative about the extent of beguinal heresy than piles of polemics. This woman, along with several others, insisted on obeying her parish priest and was therefore called before a convocation of tertiaries meeting in the Franciscan convent. There, Rudolf Buchsmann, the lector who had opposed Mulberg, allegedly bullied her, saying that her parish priest was her devil and that God alone was the judge of her soul. To that the mistress of all the tertiaries in Basel insultingly added: "You must be one of those who follows the articles," meaning the errors of *Ad nostrum*. But the witness replied that she did not even know what the articles were.[74] This is a vivid illustration of the fact that the later disputes concerning beguines were

---

cit., fol. 91v–109v. Another version which includes complete texts of documents that Mulberg referred to is described by Haupt, "Beiträge," 511–31. See also Justinger (as above, n. 39), p. 193: "der hat geprediet wider die beghart und beginen und wider ir müssiggan und wider die starken betler."

73. Published by Straganz (as above, n. 67).

74. *Ibid.*, 24–25: "Soror vero Nesa de Arberg alias matzerin, magistra sororum tercie regule in civitate Basiliensi existentium, versus loquentem insultando incenso animo prorupit in hec verba: 'Ego teneo te talem, quod tu sis una illarum, que in se tenet articulos,' notando octo articulos a jure reprobatos wlgariter: 'Ich halte dich, daz du der eine siest, die die artickl an ir hat.' Loquens vero eidem responderit dicens: 'Quomodo potestis me pro tati habere? nescio tamen, qui sint illi articuli.'"

organizational and that the Clementine errors were by this time merely a club with which to threaten one's enemies.

The other testimony shows the extent to which the inquisition was directed against lay piety. The wife of a citizen of Basel was charged with having washed the feet of beguines, but she denied this and said that the only time she even saw the ritual of foot-washing was in Church on Holy Thursday. The wife of the citizen who patronized Nicholas of Basel's disciple was charged with having been flagellated by her maid, but the same servant whose testimony we have already examined swore that he never saw or heard of such a thing. He did say that the family was visited by a beghard who spoke "good words about God," but they did nothing with him in secret. Finally, a witness told of a man who gave up his wife and children to assume the habit of a beghard. Even if all these charges were true the evidence would only tell us about the degree of ascetic religiosity among the patriciate of Basel in the waning Middle Ages.

Other incidents connected with Mulberg's campaign confirm the view that mystical heresy was not at issue. Mulberg obtained the support of the University of Heidelberg, but that the experts there were concerned with the problem of mendicancy alone is indicated by a surviving *questio* written by the theologian Nicholas Magni de Jawor that attacks beghards and beguines only for their life of absolute poverty.[75] We have seen that the town council of Strassburg was concerned only with the legal status of beguines[76] and in Bern the arrival of fugitives from Basel prompted the councilors to consult a commission of learned clergy in Lausanne about the same question. They followed this with a ruling that the women give up their hoods and wear veils instead, but according to a chronicler even this injunction was not long observed.[77]

More serious were events in Mainz, where in 1406 there was a persecution of beguines and "lollards" undoubtedly initiated under Mulberg's impetus. The chronicler, whose report is all we have, tells

---

75. The University's support of Mulberg in *UB der Universität Heidelberg*, ed. E. Winkelmann (Heidelberg, 1886), II, 19, #158 (see also #157). A. Franz, *Der Magister Nikolaus Magni de Jawor* (Freiburg, 1898), discusses Nicholas' *De mendicantibus* pp. 107–114 and edits the text pp. 206–16.

76. Above, p. 104.

77. Justinger, pp. 193–94, who records these events for the year 1404.

about a youth who was born in Rothenburg and supposedly was one of seventy disciples of the devil.[78] He had been deceived by an old "lollard" who heard his confessions and those of other so-called lollards and beguines. This arrogation of sacramental functions was apparently the major crime at stake. The youth was released after doing public penance and attaching a cross to his clothing, but a local beguine as well as several that had fled from Strassburg were imprisoned. Meanwhile the dispute about beguines continued in Basel until the final liquidation of all beguinages in 1411, but Mulberg himself died in retirement because he tenaciously supported the wrong pope.

7. THE "MEN OF INTELLIGENCE"

No case dealt with in this book is more famous than that of the *homines intelligentiae* or "Men of Intelligence." Not only has it been discussed by all who are interested in the heresy of the Free Spirit, but it is always cited as an example of popular Joachism in the later Middle Ages, a source of radical "Picardism" in the Hussite Revolution, and even as a skeleton key for understanding the cryptic triptychs of Hieronymus Bosch.[79] But the case is far less sensational than is commonly supposed.

There are only two primary sources concerning the "Men of Intelligence" and the first is very unreliable. This is a hagiographic chronicle of Groenendael which reports that Henry Selle, the fourth provost of that abbey, was appointed in 1410 to extirpate heresy in Brussels by the noted theologian Pierre d'Ailly, then Bishop of Cambrai.[80] The chronicle goes on to assert that the heretics tried to assassinate Henry from ambush and that a mocking song was sung about him in the streets, but it must be remembered that these details were written some fifty years after the fact in a work of hagiography. Moddern scholars still write that the heretics of Brussels descended lineally from Bloemardinne, a woman who lived in the first half of the four-

---

78. *Chronicon Moguntinum*, ed. C. Hegel, SRG, XX, 82.

79. E.g. respectively, H. Grundmann, *Studien über Joachim von Fiore* (Leipzig and Berlin, 1927), p. 183; H. Kaminsky, *A History of the Hussite Revolution* (Berkeley and Los Angeles, 1967), pp. 358–59; and W. Fraenger, *The Millennium of Hieronymus Bosch* (Chicago, 1951), *passim*.

80. Jan de Joncheere, *Virologium Viridis Vallis*, recapitulated in the seventeenth century by Jan van Hoybergen, and reprinted in Fredericq, I, 266–67, #248.

teenth century, but it was demonstrated as long ago as 1904 that there is no textual evidence for such a hypothesis.[81] Indeed, all that we know about Bloemardinne shows that she was not a sectary in any conventional sense.

The other source, a notarial act, is by its nature far more informative and reliable, though it still leaves many gaps in our knowledge.[82] This document, sealed in 1411 at the episcopal court of Cambrai, describes the trial and recantation of a Carmelite of Brussels by the name of William of Hildernissen.[83] Essentially it records three lists of charges made by hostile witnesses and William's responses to them. The first and most famous list describes the beliefs and practices of a sect supposedly known as the "Men of Intelligence" and their leader, an illiterate sexagenarian layman named Aegidius Cantor. The latter believed that he was illuminated by the Holy Spirit and was the saviour of mankind. In addition to attacking the dispensation of the Church, he and his followers allegedly preached shocking sexual license. A passage that has attracted the attention of many, including Aldous Huxley, refers to Aegidius' "special method of intercourse, *not against nature*, practiced by Adam in paradise."[84] A certain old woman of the

81. Léonard Willems Az, "De ketter Willem van Hildernissem en diens verhouding tot Bloemaerdinne," *Mélanges Paul Fredericq* (Brussels, 1904), pp. 259–66. On Bloemardinne, see further below, pp. 190–92.

82. An unidentified Parisian MS was the basis of a seventeenth-century edition by Baluze, reprinted by Fredericq, I, 267–79, # 249. A far superior version, hitherto unused, is MS Wolfenb., Helmst., 279, fol. 264r–269v, from what appears to be part of an inquisitorial handbook compiled in the first half of the fifteenth century. The MS was in Nürnberg before Flacius Illyricus obtained it for his own collection in the sixteenth century. I note a few of the significant variants from Fredericq below.

83. The Wolfenbüttel MS gives this spelling of the name throughout.

84. The italics are mine. It is hard to guess what this technique involved. William Hepworth Dixon, *Spiritual Wives* (London and Philadelphia, 1868), pp. 109–13, said that the heretics of the Free Spirit "invented the seraphic kiss; the kiss of love, of innocence and peace," but as a proper Victorian he never defined what he meant, though he declared that "hundreds of them perished in the flames, for no higher crime than that of having offered to each other a seraphic kiss." Fraenger, p. 129, followed by Huxley, *Tomorrow and Tomorrow and Tomorrow* (New York, 1956), pp. 289–301, more explicitly thought that it was *coitus interruptus*, but that was also regarded as a sin against nature. According to John T. Noonan, Jr., *Contraception: A History of Its Treatment by the Catholic Theologians and Canonists* (Cambridge, Mass., 1965), p. 224: "In the theological development of the thirteenth century, anal intercourse, oral intercourse, coitus

sect said openly that intercourse is a natural act like eating and drinking and can be indulged in without sin outside of marriage, and another
accepted this teaching by making no distinction between her husband
and other men. Moved by the Holy Spirit, Aegidius himself went
entirely naked carrying a plate of meat on his head to a pauper. The
stress on the Spirit also influenced the sect's view of history: now is the
time of Elias, or third age of the Holy Spirit, coming after that of the
Father and the Son. In this age Holy Scripture will be overcome[85] and
the opposite of Catholic views on poverty, continence, and obedience
must be taught.

Up to now scholars have accepted the veracity of these charges,
but there are good reasons for calling them into question. First of
all, Aegidius Cantor was dead by the time of the trial and was thus one
of a number of supposedly outrageous heresiarchs who was allowed
to spread his teachings (in his case, also to run around naked) until
his death. If his doctrines and conduct were so shocking, why did the
authorities not act sooner? Perhaps at other times they were too slug-
gish, but the turn of the fifteenth century was, as we have seen, an age
of widespread persecutions. Secondly, the notarial document never
clearly identifies its sources of information and even refers to "conjecture" when listing the heretics' refusal to observe fasts.[86] But William of Hildernissen, who was named by the hostile witnesses as the
co-leader of the sect, denied that he had ever heard of many tenets on
the first list, and swore that he never taught any of them, though he
did recant a number of other errors. This signal fact has never been
mentioned by any of the numerous historians on the qui vive for
libertine heresy.

---

interruptus, and departure from the assumed norm of position in intercourse
were all analyzed as instances of the marital sin against nature." The question is,
what is left? Perhaps Aegidius was trying to perfect techniques based on St.
Augustine's speculations about intercourse in Eden (*City of God*, XIV, 24, 26),
where Adam supposedly was able to raise his reproductive member by his will
without lust (like raising his hand) and inseminate Eve without rupturing her
hymen. (This fertile suggestion was made to me by Professor Howard Kaminsky.)

85. MS *cit.*, fol. 266r, reads *"removabuntur"* for Fredericq's *"reconciliabuntur."*

86. A clause significantly deleted in the Fredericq version, but appearing as an
extra item after Fredericq's #4 (p. 271) in MS *cit.*, fol. 265v: "Item ex verisimilibus
conjecturis credendum est quod bene comederent carnes feriis sextis et in
quadragesima."

William maintained that his alleged leadership of the sectaries was a simple falsehood and added that he preached against them after he had learned their errors. The only time that he was at one of their conventicles within the last ten years was three years before the trial when he went to investigate a rumor that had been spread about Aegidius; had he known that he would find a congregation of women he never would have entered. Aegidius never told him about the sect's sexual doctrines but William urged all who confessed to him to desist from illicit acts of *conjugal* intercourse (emphasis mine).[87] He was willing to believe some of the other rumors about Aegidius (a dead man) such as the statement that the latter went naked, but he resolutely denied having heard the teachings about the third age from Aegidius or anybody else.

William did confess to another list of errors of a considerably different nature.[88] In opposition to the self-proclaimed savior Aegidius, William taught that all merit and eternal life come through Christ's passion rather than human will or acts, and that Christ had the power to save Jews, pagans, and even devils. Since God makes sin as well as good works,[89] not the sinner, nor the priest hearing confession, but Christ alone can remit sin. Accordingly, a number of William's errors involved criticism of the clergy. How far these presuppositions led to consistent rejection of Christian dogma and the moral law is hard to determine, no doubt because even the second list was compiled not by William himself, but by hostile witnesses who claimed to have heard him preach such errors in sermons and private discussions. Thus, while he allegedly said that the present law will now cease, he did not reject the Bible but called for its understanding through the Holy Spirit.

The list includes two examples of antinomianism, but they are disparate and mild. William recanted his statement that there is no guilt in dressing extravagantly, but the authorities agreed that this

87. MS *cit.*, fol. 268r, reads *"monere"* for Fredericq's *"movere"* (p. 276).

88. In addition to the two MSS described above (n. 82), Werner, *Nachrichten* (as above, n. 51), pp. 277–79, edits a portion of a MS from Olmütz that contains only this list of errors, and Kaminsky (as above, n. 79), p. 358, notes another copy of the list in the Metropolitan Chapter at Prague (MS C 40, fol. 294v).

89. MS Wolfenb., Helmst., 279, fol. 266v, adds an extra phrase after Fredericq, 273, tenet #3, *"esse,"* thus: "per hoc dant (MS= dans) intelligere quod deus eque facit peccata sicut bona opera, revoco etc."

tenet was not so much false as "ill sounding" because extravagance in dress is the cause and occasion for sin rather than being sinful in itself. Somewhat more serious was the statement that a fallen woman has the same merit as a virgin if she does not have to care for children or a husband, but this might have been motivated by a spirit of charity for prostitutes.[90] That William did not otherwise support immorality is indicated by his insistence that he spoke against unnatural marital intercourse in the confessional.

Despite all this, William was a Free Spirit to the extent that he spoke the language of radical mysticism. He believed that "the exterior man cannot stain the interior man" and that "the interior man will not be damned." He was convinced that he himself had once been illuminated by God so that he briefly had the joy of eternal life and afterwards understood Scripture differently and better than others. This led him to teach that a time will come in the near future when the Holy Spirit will illuminate the human intellect more clearly than ever before, even more than in the time of the apostles, who only had the "husk" of understanding. Then the present law will cease and be replaced by that of the Holy Spirit and "spiritual liberty" (*"libertas spiritualis"*).[91] In addition to all this, he taught that God is as much in stones, human members, and hell as in the sacrament of the altar, one of the few instances of a thorough pantheism since the trial of the Amaurians, whose beliefs William might have read about.

He also abjured a final list of errors, apparently for the sake of good form: Pierre d'Ailly admitted that these were only based on rumor, but he insisted that William disavow them anyway. This is the most scandalous list. It recapitulates many errors from *Ad nostrum*, such as the tenet that man can become so united to God in this life that he cannot sin at all by "exterior acts," and adds such embellishments as the claim that it is good to sin often. But it is pointless to discuss these errors since even the authorities had doubts about their authenticity.

Even putting them aside, one can see why witnesses associated William with Aegidius Cantor. Both men believed that they had

90. Fredericq's tenet #18 (p. 274) only makes sense in the reading of MS *cit.*, fol. 267r: ". . . si non haberet curam circa prolem vel virum . . . ."

91. *Ibid.*, fol. 266v has the following variant after Fredericq, 274, tenet #10, *"revelanda"*: "erit lex spiritualis libertatis et quod in brevi erit illa lex spiritus sancti et tunc etc."

reached a supernatural state which inspired them to teach a new dispensation. Though we know too little for certain to say more about Aegidius, the thought of William of Hildernissen fits into a familiar pattern. Many of his ideas were apparently his own, but he must have learned much of his mystical terminology from tracts of the Pseudo-Eckhart tradition. In particular, his hope for the illumination and autonomy of the "interior man," still recognizing the omnipotence of God, was typical of the literature that we will examine later as the most accessible locus of the Free-Spirit heresy.

The end of William's story helps place the episode of his trial in perspective. The Bishop of Cambrai sentenced him to public confession followed by the choice of imprisonment for three years in an episcopal castle or confinement in a Carmelite convent outside of the diocese for as long as the Bishop pleased. We do not know which of these punishments William chose, but we do know that in 1422 he was made lector of the Carmelite cloister of Tirlemont in the diocese of Cambrai.[92] Apparently he had ceased to be dangerous.

Nothing more is heard of the heresy at Brussels.[93] The notarial act makes no reference at all to beghards or beguines and though it does mention several female followers of Aegidius it does not indicate if any of them were brought to trial. If some were, it is improbable that any were stubborn enough to be executed; such events were usually recorded in chronicles and the silence of all contemporary narrative sources is striking. For this reason the theory that the *homines intelligentiae* continued to flourish secretly for another century to influence the iconography of Bosch seems preposterous.

Attempts at neat chronology are most often artificial, but an argument can be made that the concerted campaign against beguines, beghards, and antinomian heretics was abandoned at the Council of Constance, exactly a century after John XXII had promulgated the persecuting decrees of the previous ecumenical Council of Vienne. When Matthew Grabon, a Dominican of Wismar, presented articles maintaining that all semi-religious associations ought to be abolished,

---

92. Willems Az (as above, n. 81), pp. 260–61.
93. The German Hussite John Drändorf preached to "beghards" in Brabant in 1424—see Hermann Heimpel, *Drei Inquisitions-Verfahren aus dem Jahre 1425* (Göttingen, 1969), pp. 99–100—but whether these were in any way Free Spirits, let alone "Men of Intelligence" is impossible to tell.

he was sharply attacked by Pierre d'Ailly and Jean Gerson, and forced to abjure. D'Ailly, as we have seen, and Gerson, as we will see, were not lax on deviations from the faith, but neither was willing to assume that beguinal organizations were ipso facto heretical.[94] Thereafter the popes of the fifteenth century consistently favored beguines[95] and did not trouble to order new Inquisitions against antinomian heretics, perhaps because they were too busy with the Hussites and then with witches.

This chapter has shown that the relaxation came too late rather than too soon. The evidence that we have examined indicates that in over half a century of determined and often bloody persecutions Inquisitors could find no antinomian heresy in beguinages and the cases of doctrinal error that they did discover were, aside from Waldensianism, scattered and few. There certainly were no contacts between Hermann Kuchener, Constantine of Erfurt, Berthold of Rohrbach, and John Hartmann, or between Conrad Kannler, William of Lübeck, Nicholas of Basel, and William of Hildernissen. Most of these men were less radical than has been supposed and most were not beghards but eccentrics who represented no threatening mass movement. At first sight they may look alike because they were called the same names by their enemies and because they were examined on the basis of the same set of questions, but had they all been invited to a conference together it is doubtful that they would have emerged with a unified platform. What they did have in common was their conviction of their own perfection and a mystical vocabulary which in many cases seems to have derived from the influence of Meister Eckhart.

94. The pertinent documents are reprinted in Fredericq, II, 216–25, #133–36.
95. Kurze, 68.

Chapter Seven

THE FIFTEENTH CENTURY

In the fifteenth century, just as well as in the fourteenth, there were deviant mystics who were convinced of their own perfection. But since there was no longer a concerted inquisitorial search for them there are few surviving records and by the second half of the century their tracks begin to disappear. The historian's work is further complicated by the growth of inexact terminology. The words "beghard" and "lollard" were still occasionally used to denote mystical or antinomian heretics, but they had a bewildering range of other meanings including wandering mendicants, semi-religious hermits, and, most confusingly, heretics of any stripe. Up to now the disparate evidence from the fifteenth century has never been assembled and the few texts that have been examined have not been analyzed carefully enough in light of this problem in nomenclature.[1]

1. THE POLEMICS OF GERSON

Most fifteenth-century opponents of "beghards" objected primarily to experiments in apostolic conduct, but this was not true of the most influential thinker of the first part of the century, the French theologian Jean Gerson who was in full sympathy with the *devotio moderna* and helped to protect the status of beguines and Brethren

---

1. An important exception is the scrupulous work of Kurze, to which I am much endebted, but this is unfortunately confined to uses of the word "lollard."

of the Common Life at the Council of Constance.[2] Gerson's concern was with the speculative errors ascribed to the beghards which he attacked in at least fifteen of his works written throughout the course of his life. The only question is how far his polemics were based on direct experience and how far they were merely formal, and this can best be answered by proceeding chronologically.

Though several scholars have cited Gerson's numerous attacks, none have noticed that the earliest examples imply that antinomian heresy was not an immediate threat. In one of his first published sermons, delivered most likely in 1393, he includes among the qualities of a good teacher the necessity of preaching against lax morals so that students do not fall into the error of the beghards and *turlupins* who taught, like the ancient cynics, that there was no shame in anything natural.[3] Here Gerson not only refers to the beghards in the past tense, but also suggests that the duty of preaching morality against their example was a conventionalized one. More famous is his first attack against Ruysbroeck as an associate of beghards, most recently dated to March 1402, in which he talks of Ruysbroeck as having been *"proximus eorum tempori,"* as if they were a thing of the past.[4] Most explicitly, in his treatise against the *Roman de la Rose*, published two months later, he attacks the alleged immorality of that work by comparing it to the "former error of the *turlupins*," and again in a tract of 1402–1403 he refers to antinomian beghards and *turlupins* in the past tense.[5]

Gerson first becomes specific about the sources of his information in his *De distinctione verarum revelationum a falsis* of 1401. There, in talking of false mysticism, he refers to an "incredibly subtle book" of "Maria of Valenciennes," who must have been Marguerite Porete, and also tells of having heard from an unnamed Carthusian about an

---

2. James L. Connolly, *John Gerson, Reformer and Mystic* (Louvain, 1928), pp. 74–75, 187–88, and above p. 163, n. 94.

3. *In festo S. Ludovico regis*, ed. P. Glorieux, *Jean Gerson, Oeuvres complètes* (Paris, 1960–), V, 163. I follow Glorieux' tentative dating.

4. *Oeuvres*, II, 60. I follow the dating of Glorieux, p. xiv. A. Combes, *Essai sur la critique de Ruysbroeck par Gerson* (Paris, 1945–59), I, 567–68, dates this work to between December 1398 and March 1399.

5. E. Langlois (ed.), "Le traité de Gerson contre le Roman de la Rose," *Romania*, XLV (1918), 45: "Cest erreur aussi estoit jadiz l'erreur des Turlupins. . . ." *De mystica theologia*, ed. A. Combes (Lucca, n.d. [1958]), p. 20.

unnamed "great man" who taught the highly qualified antinomian doctrine that mortal sin does not always impede charity.[6] It is impossible to elicit any precise chronology from the latter remark, but it has already been pointed out that it concerns the remembrance of hearsay from an earlier date.[7] Since this is the only information that Gerson has to offer, it seems clear that up until this period of his life, when he was already a well-travelled forty, and was in a position of great importance, he had never himself met a heretical beghard or "*turlupin.*"

A turning point is marked by his second letter against Ruysbroeck written in 1408.[8] There he tells of having met and spoken with a woman who was regarded by many as a prophetess and worker of miracles who said and ordered to be written that her spirit had been annihilated in the contemplation of God. He does not identify this woman further and it is noteworthy that he refrains from accusing her of antinomianism or even calling her a beguine even though he refers to male and female beghards in his next paragraph. That reference is again in the past tense, as is another mention of *turlupins* in a work of 1414.[9]

It was only after he assumed the role of arbiter of orthodoxy at the Council of Constance that Gerson first mentioned the beghards in the present tense. In a Pentecostal sermon delivered at the Council in 1416, only two weeks after the burning of Jerome of Prague, he attacked the madness of beghards who say that they have reached such liberty of the spirit through contemplation that they no longer are subject to divine precepts.[10] That this switch to the present may have been a homiletic rhetorical device meant to emphasize the im-

6. *Oeuvres*, III, 51–52. The judgment that Maria of Valenciennes was really Marguerite Porete is that of Guarnieri, 453–54, 461–62, who sees a passage from Gerson's *Aliqua notanda super doctrina Hubertini* as an explicit citation from *The Mirror of Simple Souls*.

7. Combes, *Essai*, II, 312, n. 1.

8. *Oeuvres*, II, 102. Leff, p. 357, sees the mention of the prophetess as "clearly an allusion to Bloemardinne of Brussels," but this woman died decades before Gerson was so much as a glint in his father's eye (see below, pp. 190–92).

9. *Considérations sur saint Joseph*, cited by P. Beuzart, *Les hérésies pendant le Moyen Age et la Réforme dans la région de Douai, d'Arras et au Pays de l'Alleu* (Le Puy, 1912), p. 51.

10. *Oeuvres*, V, 533.

mediacy of heresy in general is suggested by the fact that he included beghards and Waldensians in his contemporary tract on Utraquism, going so far as to say that their errors were growing daily because of their translations of Scripture.[11] Gerson nowhere else said that beghards translated the Bible but probably added this to his tract in order to cast guilt on the Hussites by association. In any event, in the *Treatise on the Marriage between Christ and the Church* of 1417 and shortly afterwards in *The Consolation of Theology* of 1418 Gerson reverted to his habit of describing beghards and *turlupins* in the past tense.[12]

Toward the end of his life he again maintained that "the followers of the *turlupins* exist even today." These he charged with being "Epicureans under the tunic of Christ" who gained the confidence of "little women" by simulating devotion and thus making them the playthings of their passions. Is this just a cliché derived from St. Paul's Second Epistle to Timothy or did Gerson have any real grounds for warning of the threat of antinomianism? All he presents as evidence is an accompanying passage about a woman who was accused of saying that she was one of five messengers sent to redeem souls in hell and of claiming that she could read men's sins on their foreheads. She was apprehended about 1423: after the application of torture she confessed to these errors and was imprisoned at Bourg-en-Bresse, not far from Gerson's retreat at Lyons.[13] There is no indication that she was an antinomian or even a beguine though her story does recall that of her contemporary, Joan of Arc, who was only *shown* the instruments of torture.

In another late work Gerson spoke of "the error of the law or the spirit of liberty" of male and female beghards who say that the perfect soul loses its will in God and can indulge in carnal affections without sin. Under such pretexts they lead simple people to promise obedience to them and commit unmentionable perversities. Similarly,

11. Cited by H. Kaminsky, *A History of the Hussite Revolution* (Berkeley and Los Angeles, 1967), pp. 124–25, with the reply of Jakoubek of Střibo.

12. Passages quoted by Connolly (as cited above, n. 42), pp. 122, n. 2, and 248, n. 1.

13. Passages of the *De examinatione doctrinarum* cited by Beuzart, p. 51, and Connolly, p. 240. See also Glorieux in *Oeuvres*, I, 135 and A. Jundt, *Histoire du panthéisme populaire au moyen âge* (Paris, 1875), p. 111.

in a final reference, he claimed that beghards and *"Fraticelli"* had fallen into the most abominable carnality.[14] Gerson wrote these bitter passages in retirement when he was preoccupied with describing the mystical experience and was anxious to distinguish himself from false mystics. But there is no reason to believe that he knew about them in his old age from anything more than texts or hearsay.

Reviewing his writings we see that the only heretical mystic Gerson seems to have met was the "prophetess" who thought that her spirit was annihilated in Divinity. But he mentions her only in a brief passage and refrains from calling her a beguine or charging her with immorality. Otherwise he refers to false mystics most frequently in the past tense: if he had any direct knowledge of the "Men of Intelligence" investigated by his friend d'Ailly he never says so. For these reasons his repetitive polemics tell us more about the orthodox state of mind at the turn of the fifteenth century than they do about the extent of antinomian mysticism.[15]

2. THE ERA OF THE COUNCIL OF BASEL

Entirely different from Gerson were fifteenth-century reformers who were bothered by the practice of lay mendicancy. An anonymous proposal prepared for the Council of Basel early in 1433 demanded measures against lollards and beguines for taking alms and refusing to work even though they were healthy enough to do so, and versions of the *Reformation of Kaiser Sigismund* attacked lollards as wandering idlers, terming it a deadly sin to give anything to them or to beguines.[16] We do not have the full minutes of the Council of Basel itself, but an unpublished manuscript refers to an interchange between

14. Passages of *Aliqua notanda super doctrina Hubertini* (*De libris caute legendis*), cited by Combes, I, 837–38 and *De susceptione humanitatis Christi*, cited by Beuzart, p. 52.

15. Excluding the writings of Gerson, there is no evidence at all for the existence of such heresy in fifteenth-century France. Beuzart, p. 47, proves on the basis of an archival document (which he edits pp. 476–79) that heretics arrested at Arras in 1420 were Waldensians and, pp. 58–60, shows that even though heretics examined at Lille in 1465 were called *turlupins*, they preached a Waldensian morality which included an attack on adultery.

16. The former in *Anonyme Denkschrift über die Reform der Kirche*, in *Handakten des Konzilspräsidenten Cesarini*, ed. H. Dannenbauer, *Concilium Basiliense: Studien und Quellen zur Geschichte des Concils von Basel* (Basel, 1896–1935), VIII, 1, 109; the latter cited by Kurze, 69.

the president of the early phase, Cesarini, and an Abbot of Speyer about whether all or only some beguines had been excommunicated; no legislation appears to have resulted.[17]

After the final break with Eugenius IV the conciliar rump had more reason to press the issue because the abhorred Pope had supported beguines in a bull of 1431. Coincidentally, in July of 1439 a Master of Arts and Medicine named James brought to the attention of the Council the fact that Eugenius had also approved of *The Mirror of Simple Souls* in a case at Venice.[18] James cited thirty errors from that work to show that the Pope was a patron of heresy (canonical grounds for deposition), but since no one knew that the *Mirror* had been written by a beguine the prelates of Basel did not follow their predecessors of Vienne in associating beghards and beguines with heretical mysticism.

This step, however, was taken by the prestigious theologian, John Wenck, who felt particularly bitter toward the papalists because he was the only Professor at Heidelberg who actively supported the party of Basel. The earliest evidence of Wenck's position on beguines comes from a controversy he had at Heidelberg with an unidentified doctor in the beginning of July 1441.[19] The latter had set forth a thesis concerning church reform which included the proposition that beguines should be considered as part of the ecclesiastical hierarchy. To this Wenck answered that holy Scripture treats Church reform sufficiently but nowhere mentions beguines. In a long rejoinder the doctor illustrated their piety with the contention that during times of plague, when sons flee from their fathers, beguines remain long nights to attend the ill and exhort them in the faith. He also cited the bulls of Gregory XI and Eugenius IV in the beguines' favor, in the latter case revealing his own position in the current schism.[20] After another

17. Defense of beguines by an unknown doctor of Heidelberg in 1441 (see below, n. 19) in MS Vat. Pal. 600, fol. 219r: "Respondit dominus Julianus: credo quod . . . sustinemus multas tales personas."

18. John of Segovia, *Historia generalis synodi Basiliensis*, cited by Guarnieri, 474–75.

19. This is contained in MS Vat. Pal. 600 and is described by R. Haubst, *Studien zu Nikolaus von Kues und Johannes Wenck* (Münster, 1955), pp. 58–61. It should be added that Wenck was a student of the anti-beguinal writer Nicholas Magni, on whom see above, p. 156.

20. MS *cit.*, fol. 219r: ". . . in pestilentiis dum filius a patre fugit . . . assistunt infectis diu noctu . . . hortantur egros in catholica fide ne in agone resiliant. Et

series of interchanges, Wenck used his University office to silence his opponent.

At about the same time, Wenck began to collect and annotate materials in preparation for a public campaign against beghards. These works survive together with Wenck's notes and marginalia; they include Felix Hemmerlin's *Contra validos mendicantes* (to be discussed below), extracts from the "heresies of the new spirit" (the Nördlingen list), and a description of life in "lollard" houses which told of total obedience to "Marthas" instead of to parish priests.[21] Most valuable to the emerging polemicist was a tract of unknown date and authorship which attributed pantheistic and mystical errors to the beghards and saw these best expressed in a book called *De simplici anima* (clearly *The Mirror of Simple Souls*) that was owned, according to the author, by the Carthusians of Strassburg.[22] At this point, Wenck, who copiously annotated this text, wrote in the margin "*ecce librum de simplici anima*" and called attention to the passage with a pointing hand. No doubt he had recognized the title that had been introduced against Pope Eugenius at Basel and realized how it could be used.[23]

By the spring of 1442 Wenck had acquired a reputation through sermons which have not survived as a bitter enemy of "the errors and frightful singularities of the Waldensians and insane beghards." This was the estimate of John of Gelnhausen, a former Abbot of Maulbronn, whose brother had retired to a self-built forest hermitage in the Austrian mountains. John believed that his brother's step had been taken under "lollard" influence and pleaded with him to join an approved order, but to no avail. Therefore, he sent his brother's defense of his retirement to Wenck with an appeal for help. The text

---

forte propter hoc et alia papa Eugenius et ante eum papa Gregorius . . . susceperunt huiusmodi personas sub apostolice sedis protectione."

21. MS *cit.*, fol. 249r–261r (Hemmerlin's text), and fol. 226r: "Hec sunt hereses de novo spiritu" (the Nördlingen list) and "Recipienda ad lolhardicam vitam." Both of the latter must have been taken from an inquisitor's handbook; on the Nördlingen list see above, p. 15.

22. Described by Haubst, pp. 56, 114–15. The work probably dates from the fifteenth century since the author cites the sermons of Jordan of Quedlinburg (MS *cit.*, fol. 230r).

23. MS *cit.*, fol. 228v. Haubst has not mentioned that Wenck's marginalia twice include the note "*Eckharde*" (fols. 228v, 232r) which shows that he was interested in "Eckhardisms" before his later controversy with Nicholas of Cusa.

in question shows how loosely the word "lollard" could be used. The Abbot's brother felt driven by God to become a hermit in order to free himself from his own desires and earthly concerns. His goal was to withdraw into his "inner man" and become so detached that he could imitate Christ and "die daily," not caring what learned men thought of him. It has already been noted that although this defense is redolent with Eckhartian terms it would not today seem evil or heretical. But Wenck found seventeen errors in it which he bitterly rejected for displaying insufferable pride and not paying enough heed to the Bible and the sacraments. Such is the age-old response to subjective religiosity.[24]

Most famous is Wenck's subsequent attack on Nicholas of Cusa as a crypto-beghard. Since his treatise against Nicholas' *Docta ignorantia* has been edited and described at length, it is only necessary to say that its burden lies in charging Nicholas with having fallen into the errors of Eckhart and the beghards who were condemned by John of Strassburg in 1317.[25] Far from being intimidated, Cusanus, in the *Apologia doctae ignorantiae* (1449), rejected Wenck's charges of pantheism but defended the teachings of Eckhart. Later, in his journey as legate through Germany in 1451–52, he self-confidently approved statutes of beguinal communities because "he did not regard them as dangerous."[26] Wenck's attack on Cusanus—the "Hercules of the Eugenians"—shows how far he was driven in his blind hatred of mysticism and his partisanship for the party of Basel; it places his whole campaign in perspective because we know that Nicholas of Cusa was not a member or follower of any heretical sect.

Another fifteenth-century enemy of "lollards," Felix Hemmerlin of Zürich, was also a strong conciliarist who wished to embarrass Eugenius IV. But, unlike the anti-mystical theologian Wenck, Hem-

---

24. The texts are in MS Mainz 190 and are recapitulated by G. Ritter, *Die Heidelberger Universität, I. Das Mittelalter* (Heidelberg, 1936), pp. 430–31, 433, and Haubst, pp. 113–17. I follow the latter's interpretation closely.

25. Ed. E. Vansteenberghe, *Le "De ignota litteratura" de Jean Wenck de Herrenberg contre Nicolas de Cuse* (Münster, 1910). See also Ritter, pp. 431–34, and Haubst, pp. 118–36. There is disagreement about the dating: Ritter, p. 503, dates it "nach 1448," Haubst, p. 118, at the latest one and one quarter years after March 1442.

26. Haubst, p. 118, citing E. Vansteenberghe, *Le cardinal Nicolas de Cuse* (Paris, 1920), p. 101.

merlin was primarily concerned with the problem of mendicancy. This was the exclusive subject of his first and most popular polemic against beghards, the *Contra validos mendicantes* of 1438.[27] This work is in the form of a dialogue between the author and a beghard who travels on a donkey loaded with bread and wine and cites not only Scripture, but Aristotle, Isidore, and canon law. The two debate whether any men can take alms, whether the benefices of priests are alms, and particularly, whether Christ himself took alms; naturally the beghard (who prefers to be called an anchorite since beghard was a term of abuse) is thoroughly routed at the end. *Contra validos mendicantes* was a great success. It was sold at the Council of Basel and, as we have seen, it was studied before 1442 by John Wenck. Later it was published in several editions, not only in Latin, but in a German translation originally done in 1464 by Nicholas von Wyle.[28] A woodcut done for the latter in the early sixteenth century (see frontispiece) shows that as late as that time beghards were dressing like friars.

At the outset of his first tract, Hemmerlin calls his opponent one of the "evil people" mentioned in the edict *Ad nostrum.* This shows that he was familiar with the original document that linked beghards with antinomian heresy, but he makes no further use of it in that work or in a sequel entitled *Contra anachoritas behardos beginasque silvestres*, in which he debates a senior member of a forest community whose inmates all wear habits and cowls.[29] But in a third tract, *Lollhardorum descriptio*,[30] he does bring up the subject of heresy by enumerating the following Swiss and south German "beghards" who were brought before inquisitors in his day: Burkhard and others of Zürich, who did penance and took the cross, but relapsed and were executed; "brother Karl" and his followers from Uri, who were burned for the same reason; Henry from Tierrenz near Constance and John of Ulm, who both did public penance; and a "great heresiarch" from Württemberg, who was convicted only with great dif-

---

27. In F. Hemmerlin, *Varie oblectationis opuscula et tractatus* (Basel, 1497), fol. a ɪv–b 3r. This is the same as *De beghardis sive Lollardis*, ᴍꜱ Clm 6603, fol. 277r–290r, that is listed by Leff, p. 352, as an anonymous treatise.

28. Adalbert von Keller (ed.), *Translationen von Niclas von Wyle* (Stuttgart, 1861), pp. 157–97. On the tract at the Council of Basel, B. Reber, *Felix Hemmerlin von Zürich* (Zürich, 1846), p. 130.

29. In Hemmerlin, *Varie oblectationis*, fol. b 3v–c ɪr.

30. *Ibid.*, fol. c ɪr–2v.

ficulty by theological experts. Unfortunately, Hemmerlin does not say what any of these men believed, but when he adds that many "beghards" came from Bohemia to infect the populace of Bern and Solothurn, it seems clear that he is talking of Hussites. Furthermore, at the end of his tirade he insists that no heresy was introduced in all of Upper Germany except by the beghards, lollards, and beguines. Since this was written at a time when Hussites and Waldensians were the major threats to orthodoxy, it is apparent that Hemmerlin used the terms "lollard" and "beghard," when he so desired, to mean heretic of any stripe.

That he was not punctilious in his usage is shown again in a final work, *Glosa bullarum per beghardos impetratarum*, in which he not only attacks Pope Eugenius IV for supporting beguines, but asserts that the Pope himself had been a beghard "in a hermitage near Padua."[31] This in fact is a reference to Eugenius' earlier career in the monastery of St. Giorgio d'Alga, but a conservative secular cleric like Hemmerlin could term austere hermits beghards just as well as Hussites when it suited his polemical purpose. Hemmerlin, then, was typical of those whose attacks on beghards and beguines had nothing to do with the problem of mystical heresy.

That real beguines were not carriers of such heresy in the fifteenth century can be shown by the patronage granted to them by Nicholas of Cusa and also by a defense written by John Spenlin, a theologian of Heidelberg who ironically had been a student of John Wenck.[32] The occasion for this was a campaign against beguines un-

31. *Ibid.*, fol. c 3r–3v. The date of composition is given here as 1449, but this must be a misprint for 1439. There would have been little reason for an attack on Eugenius IV when the Pope was already two years dead, whereas in 1439 partisans of the Council of Basel like Hemmerlin were looking for grounds to depose him. See further on this, Reber, pp. 125–26 and 140–42.

32. The defense is in Spenlin's *Speculum religiosorum*, MS Karlsruhe, Reichenau (Augiensia), CXLVII, fol. 155rb–157rb. The catalogue of the Reichenau MSS at Karlsruhe (ed. A. Holder [Leipzig, 1906]) does not identify the author of this work, but there are innumerable indications that he is Spenlin. On Wenck's recommendation of Spenlin for the degree of Doctor of Theology at Heidelberg in 1441, see Haubst (as cited above, n. 19), pp. 34, 61–64. The fact that Spenlin was not influenced by Wenck's views on beguines might be explained by the circumstance that he was no mere boy, but a mature man who had already gained the M.A. (Paris) and M.D. degrees and had been present at the court of Pope Alexander V as far back as 1410 (*Spec. relig.*, fol. 156va: "Quia praesens fui Bononie tempore Allexander papae existente curia ibidem.")

dertaken by Konrad Bömlin, a Provincial Minister of the Franciscans who belonged to the Conventual party in the organizational dispute that then racked the order. We do not have Bömlin's side of the story, but according to Spenlin the Minister was persecuting beguines at the same time that he was persecuting Franciscan Observants.[33] In response Spenlin wrote a long letter to Bömlin on August 1, 1447 in which he pointed out, among other things, that beguines had been defended not only by the prestigious Chancellor of Paris, Gerson, but also by three different popes: Gregory XI, Martin V, and the recently deceased Eugenius IV. Therefore he urged Bömlin to desist from his campaign. What happened then we do not know, but since the Minister died in 1449 his campaign could not have gone on much longer. Spenlin's letter makes clear that organizational disagreements rather than heresy were at issue and suggests that south German beguines (he probably used the term to include tertiaries) were allied with the stricter Franciscan Observants; this would show that their initial urge to the strict *vita apostolica* had not disappeared over the centuries.

The writings of Wenck and Hemmerlin display the range of meanings attached to the term beghard but contain no original information about heretics other than Hemmerlin's valueless list of names in his *Lollhardorum descriptio*. On the other hand, a third figure associated with the Council of Basel, the Dominican John Nider, described specific cases of heresy in his *Formicarius* of 1435. Nider had no anti-papal animus, but he could not have been initially unprejudiced toward beghards and beguines because he had been an admiring associate of the persecutor John Mulberg. Thus, it is not surprising that in an oft-cited passage he pilloried secular and religious persons of both sexes in Swabia who taught that they could lie at their pleasure and kill even the most innocent, including their father or mother.[34] But, even though Nider was very well-informed and was occasionally an inquisitor himself, he only tried to substantiate his

---

33. Paul-Gerhard Völker, *Die deutschen Schriften des Franziskaners Konrad Bömlin* (Munich, 1964–), I, 143–44, tries to dismiss the assertion of the chronicler Tschamser that Bömlin was an active persecutor of the Observants, but Spenlin's writings (unknown to Völker) bear out Tschamser.

34. *Formicarius*, ed. G. Colvener (Douai, 1602), Lib. III, cap. 5, p. 214.

charges with the account of one case and that, as we have seen, was entirely lacking in circumstantial details.[35]

His other stories have no sexual piquancy, but do have the sort of details that convince. One is about a certain "beghard" named Burgin who lived in the diocese of Constance at the time of the Council of Pisa.[36] Though Burgin was a layman he became a hermit and led an austere life of prayer and contemplation. But, according to Nider, he was ensnared by an evil spirit disguised as an angel of light, who led him to write a rule for a new order and take on disciples "as if he were St. Anthony or Pachomius." Even though this rule was unusually severe, Burgin was arrested with his followers for violating the ban against new orders and was burned when he refused to recant. Unfortunately for him, the times did not call for a new St. Anthony.

Clearly Burgin was not a Free Spirit, but Nider's most detailed report gives the best and most reliable impression of the nature of that heresy in the first half of the fifteenth century.[37] In 1434 Nider was in Regensburg with the Archdeacon of Barcelona, John of Palomar, on a mission for the Council of Basel. There they were invited to participate in the trial of a woman who had spent her life wandering from town to town until she was imprisoned in Regensburg for having said some "incautious" things about the faith. According to Nider, she was not insane, but she insisted that she had divine revelations. She refused to obey the pope, saying that she was more blessed than the Apostles, and she added that she could not sin.

Though her examiners tried to convert her with Scripture, she defiantly maintained that they were more in error than she and that she would willingly undergo the ordeal of fire to show the truth of her words. Instead, John of Palomar advised torture ("only as much as her sex could stand") and whispered to Nider and another Dominican that they should appear to disapprove of this measure so that the woman should later have confidence in them. This was done and the scheme was successful. After "her limbs were sufficiently hu-

35. See above, pp. 11–13.
36. *Formicarius*, Lib. III, cap. 2, pp. 191–92. It is unnecessary to recount the tale that Nider tells of the "*Fraticellus* and semi-beghard" of Bern because the man was not suspected of heresy but was hanged as a thief (Lib. III, cap. 1, pp. 181–82).
37. *Ibid.*, Lib. III, cap. 7, pp. 226–28.

miliated," the Dominicans visited her and persuaded her that even excellent learned men had been misled by false revelations and that the female sex was especially weak. By then she had had enough: she made a full confession to Nider of all her sins since youth and agreed to recant and do penance.

Here, then, is a firsthand account of a genuine wandering heretic who so believed in her own perfection that she backed down only after torture. But she definitely was not a practicing antinomian: Nider reported that she was not even suspected of incontinence and was a virgin; since he had heard her full confession in an hour when she could hardly have been on guard, there is reason to take his word for this. She also was not a member of any sect: she claimed to have been enlightened only by the "spirit of God" and even while tortured denied that she ever had had any teachers, disciples, or coreligionaries. To this Nider added that he thought she spoke the truth.

One more pertinent case is related in a chronicle of Constance according to which in 1434, the same year as the trial at Regensburg, a schoolteacher of Ulm named master Werner recanted thirteen or fourteen "evil articles" that had been taught him by a beghard named Ulrich.[38] The first was that a perfect man may sin promiscuously with all, including nuns sworn to chastity; since he was perfect, such acts would not be sinful, although they would be so for the nuns. Supposedly Werner acted on this belief one Saturday by visiting a house of prostitution (*"gemain frowenhus"*) even though he was married, and he maintained that his conduct was as natural and sinless as eating and drinking. On the other hand, he allegedly said that women should indulge in sexual relations only for the sake of procreation: if he met even the Virgin Mary walking on earth he would tell her to surrender herself for the sake of "fruit." Needless to say, he also considered himself to be so perfect that he had no need to fast or pray. Instructed by masters of Scripture he admitted his errors and agreed to do penance by wearing a yellow cross for a year.

It is a pity that we have no more reliable evidence concerning this case. The chronicler, resident in Constance, did not reveal the sources of his information for events in Ulm and there is no way of knowing if he exaggerated. But even if his account is taken at face

38. *Konstanzer Chronik von 307 bis 1466*, ed. F. J. Mone, *Quellensammlung der badischen Landesgeschichte* (Karlsruhe, 1848), I, 336.

value it is not clear how Werner was induced to confess—by this late date the possibility of torture cannot be excluded. It appears that he was successful in shifting the blame to the "beghard" who was no longer present, but it is still striking that the punishment for shocking heresies and the actual crime of adultery was so mild. Werner might well have taught antinomianism and a sexual ethic marked by a masculine double standard, but a fair evaluation of his case cannot be made without more information.

3. HANS BECKER

After the disappearance of the mysterious Ulrich, references to heretical beghards or beguines become very scarce. Beguines under Franciscan supervision in Freiburg, Switzerland, were known as "Sisters of the Free Spirit," but were never persecuted for heresy during their entire existence from 1360 to 1504 or 1509.[39] In 1457 the Archbishop of Mainz supposedly ordered the town council of Frankfurt to proceed against a "lollard brother named Bosehans," but the nineteenth-century historian who reported this order did not even give his source, and though Matthew of Kemnat, writing about 1475, mentioned heretical "beghards" and "lollards," he said nothing about them except for the localities in which they were found.[40] Since these were mostly areas infected by the Hussites, it is likely that he really had them in mind. For example, he mentioned "lollards" at Eger, but we know enough about the heretics found there in 1466 to say that they were Hussite chiliasts.[41]

This leaves us with only one case for the second half of the fifteenth century, but it is one of the most instructive to be treated in this book. Johannes Becker, called "Henne" (i.e. Hans), was examined over a period of two months in Mainz by a commission headed by the Papal Inquisitor Heinrich Kalteisen (i.e. "cold-iron") and burned in October 1458 as an obdurate heretic. Kalteisen, a Dominican

39. R. Pfister, *Kirchengeschichte der Schweiz* (Zürich, 1964–), I, 321.

40. G. L. Kriegk, *Deutsches Bürgerthum im Mittelalter* (Frankfurt, 1868), pp. 129, 537; Matthew of Kemnat, *Chronik Friedrich I. des Siegreichen*, ed. C. Hofmann, *Quellen zur bayerischen und deutschen Geschichte* (Munich, 1862), II, 109, 111.

41. O. Schiff, "Die Wirsberger. Ein Beitrag zur Geschichte der revolutionären Apokalyptik im 15. Jahrhundert," *Historische Vierteljahrschrift*, XXVI (1931), 776–86.

who had earlier been a friend of John Nider, issued a report of Becker's examination to the Archbishop of Mainz which he organized topically rather than adhering to the actual order of the confession. Thus, it is further removed from verbatim testimony than a protocol, but it is still the only inquisitorial document that records the thought of a mystical heretic after the confession of William of Hildernissen in 1411.[42]

The report begins with Becker's account of his conversion: sixteen years earlier in 1442, on the last day of the feast of Pentecost, he was praying in a church at Mainz when the Holy Spirit descended with a terrible noise, seizing him so that he felt a great pain within. After that time the Spirit often carried him away to the degree that he could do nothing without its guidance and he believed that no man before or after him was or could be so illuminated. This experience changed the course of his life. While formerly he had obeyed the Church he could no longer do so because he was governed "by the Spirit in his interior man" (*"per spiritum in interiori homine"*). For the last sixteen years he had neither confessed, nor communicated, nor observed the fasts of the Church, and during the elevation of the host in the Cathedral of Mainz and other churches the Holy Spirit compelled him to stick out his tongue.

Much of Becker's talk about the dispensation of the Spirit sounds like a crude Joachism. He rejected the authority of the New Testament with the words of Paul that "the letter killeth but the spirit giveth life." Taking this saying literally (an irony he apparently did not consider) he regarded the New Testament as a dead letter and accounted the Spirit within himself as the "eternal testament." Like-

---

42. The text was first edited from a Vatican ms by G. Ritter, "Zur Geschichte des häretischen Pantheismus in Deutschland im 15. Jahrhundert," ZfK, XLIII (1924), 153–58. Later, F. Hermann, "Die letzte Ketzerverbrennung in Mainz," *Beiträge zur Kunst und Geschichte des Mainzer Lebensraumes: Festschrift für Ernst Neeb* (Mainz, 1936), pp. 105–10, called attention to another copy surviving in the papers of Kalteisen at Coblentz. A critical edition based on these two mss is in Grundmann, "Ketzerverhöre," 566–74. Hermann also summarizes the negotiation recorded in an archival document at Würzburg between the town council and the Archbishop of Mainz concerning the place of imprisonment and Eva G. Neumann, *Rheinisches Beginen-und Begardenwesen* (Meisenheim/Glan, 1960), pp. 159–60, refers to a ms at Darmstadt which also deals with the legal technicalities of the case.

wise, for the past sixteen years he did not revere Christ's humanity or his passion because he believed that man is reborn not through Christ, but through the Holy Spirit and that he himself had reached a state superior to that of the human Christ.

Unlike many other inquisitorial victims, Becker knew that he was by common understanding a heretic. He spoke of two Churches: one here below and another that was "risen." If the first considered members of the second, like himself, to be heretical, he could not agree, for in his view it was members of the entire inferior Church, commonly called Christianity, who were damned. To this he added that Jews and pagans were not necessarily unbelievers because the only baptism that mattered was that of the Spirit. No torture was necessary for the examination of one so convinced and after his confession he refused to recant, though he did admit that he sometimes prayed more during a day of confinement than he had for the previous eight years.

Was Becker a heretic of the Free Spirit? The answer depends upon how one defines this term. Unlike the beghards described by the Bishop of Strassburg in 1317 he believed that the attainment of a supernatural state comes through Divine Grace, not nature, but we have already seen that this was the position of Conrad Kannler and we will see it restated in several Free-Spirit tracts.[43] Similarly, defiant as he was, Becker does not seem to have preached immorality. He insisted that he could disobey the Church and all secular powers, but the only thing he said about morality was that sin for other men would not be such for him, providing it were impelled by the Spirit within. This, of course, is purely conditional and it is noteworthy that the report goes no further since Kalteisen used *Ad nostrum* as the basis for Becker's condemnation. The only Free Spirit we have seen so far who can reliably be said to have stressed the importance of immoral acts was John Hartmann and we will see that the best sources, the writings of Free Spirits, have a different position on this subject.

Though the documents call him a beghard or a lollard, Becker was not literally one of these because he was not a wanderer or a beggar:

43. Grundmann, "Ketzerverhöre," 571: "quod homo potest effici per graciam illud, quod est deus per naturam." Leff, p. 385, mistranslates this in the same way he does the similar statement of Kannler (see above, p. 143, n. 42).

he was born in a village near Aachen, but had been in Mainz for at least sixteen years and he seems to have made his living as an artisan.[44] More important, he did not belong to any sect. He spoke of a solitary supernatural conversion and never mentioned any accomplices. But we have now seen that many Free Spirits, especially the later ones, were not beghards or members of any organization, rather they were individuals who turned toward radical mysticism out of a conversion experience or from reading mystical literature.

Becker was influenced by both. Kalteisen, in a covering letter to the Archbishop, was astute enough to see that the heretic could not have made up all his errors unless he had been led to them by the knowledge of books.[45] He did not specify what they were, but they must have included some of the Pseudo-Eckhart writings that we will examine in another chapter. Becker was so literate that he himself wrote a book that was unfortunately burned with him.[46] Had Kalteisen preserved this it no doubt would have revealed its indebtedness to the Pseudo-Eckhartian tradition and shown that, although Becker was isolated in space and time, he was the last of the known medieval Free Spirits.

While the doomed man was in custody awaiting his trial another proceeding was taking place which illustrates how stereotyped the whole controversy about beghards and beguines had become. It was the custom at German universities to break the monotony of official ceremonies by staging a mock lecture of grotesque erudition for the purposes of entertainment. In Heidelberg in the late summer of 1458 an unnamed master, perhaps prompted by Becker's arrest, comically held forth about beghards: his talk consisted of a pastiche from earlier polemicists—Conrad of Megenberg, John Wasmod of Homburg, and Felix Hemmerlin—as well as anecdotes about Eulenspiegel-like tricksters and a satirical list of twenty-seven different varieties of such

44. A reference to Becker in the *Chronicon Moguntinum* is published in the edition of C. Hegel, SRG, XX, 89, as "Bruderhenn becker," but according to Hermann, p. 105, who examined the original MS, this should read *Benderhenn*. Hermann construes this as a reference to Becker's profession.

45. The letter is edited by Grundmann, "Ketzerverhöre," 574–75.

46. He might even have written more than one: Kalteisen parenthetically mentions a book of Becker's (Grundmann, "Ketzerverhöre," 569), but the *Chronicon Moguntinum*, 89, says that he was burned with all his *books*.

scoundrels.[47] That the scholars of Heidelberg were able to poke fun at themselves minimizes the daring of a passage in the anti-Scholastic *Letters of Obscure Men* in which one benighted logic-chopper beseeches another to compile the opinions of theological authorities on the question whether "the Lollards and Beguins in Cologne [are] seculars or religious? Have they taken vows? Can they wed?"[48] With this clear recognition of the subject as a joke we may end our chronological survey, having shown that there was no organized sect of the Free Spirit to have influenced the Reformation.[49]

47. Described by Ritter, "Pantheismus," 151–52, who edits a passage that he thought was written by Hemmerlin, but which really comes from Conrad of Megenberg's *Lacrima ecclesiae.*

48. Tr. Francis Griffin Stokes, *On the Eve of the Reformation* (New York; Harper "Torchbook" ed., 1964), p. 64.

49. Claus-Peter Clasen, "Medieval Heresies in the Reformation," *Church History*, XXXII (1963), 1–23, is only able to present parallels rather than concrete evidence of continuity between Free-Spirit heresy and Reformation sects; it may be added that Luther was so ill-informed about the "pestilentissimi Pighardorum errores" that he confused them with the teachings of the Czech Brethren (*Briefe*, Weimar ed., 2, 41–42, cited by F. G. Heymann, "The Impact of Martin Luther upon Bohemia," *Central European History*, I [1968], 113).

Chapter Eight

THE PREDICAMENT OF THE MYSTICS

We have seen in the previous chapters that the identification of Free-Spirit heretics is, in most cases, by no means easy. The use of the term "beghard" in a source is the least reliable of tests and even when there are inquisitorial records to guide us they sometimes reveal cases of mystics who just skirted the borders of heresy. Thus it is not surprising that the famous continental mystics who today are all accounted orthodox were often accused of heresy and were forced to dissociate themselves from theories they did not support by leading the attack on others. This chapter will return to the fourteenth century, the golden age of mysticism, to examine the relationships between orthodox mystics and Free Spirits from the point of view of the former.

1. MEISTER ECKHART

The case of Meister Eckhart is the most famous, but certainly the most complex. There are still many questions concerning the motives for his trial and his thought will always be difficult of access. The modern edition of his sermons is still unfinished, but even when it is completed his language will assuredly continue to seem paradoxical and purposely elusive. Clearly, this is not the place for an exposition of his theology. What can be shown here is that although Eckhart attacked unregulated mysticism, he was still often taken for a Free Spirit himself.

Long before his own trial Eckhart must have been aware that others had been condemned for espousing heretical mysticism. We have mentioned in our Introduction that a colleague of his at the Dominican convent at Paris, where he resided from 1311 to 1313, was Berengar of Landora, one of the theologians charged with examining *The Mirror of Simple Souls* in 1310 and who also participated in the Council of Vienne in the two succeeding years. It may be added that Josef Koch believed that Eckhart definitely knew *The Mirror of Simple Souls* (Koch, the most knowledgeable student of Eckhart's thought, planned to document his conviction before his recent death). From Paris Eckhart left for Strassburg and was there just at the time of John of Dürbheim's campaign against heretical beghards and beguines. There is no evidence to indicate whether he was directly involved in this affair, but he surely could not have been ignorant of it.

It is in this light that his own attacks on antinomianism are to be understood. In one sermon he criticizes those "people who say 'if I have God and God's love, I can do everything that I please.'" (Cf. St. Paul's "caritate habe, et fac quod vis.") For him, "so long as one wishes something that is against God and his commandments one does not have God's love. . . but the man who observes God's will and has God's love gladly does everything that God loves and shuns everything that is ungodly."[1] In another sermon he attacks the heresy of those who do not consider sin to be sin, who do not practice virtues or recognize the nobility of Christ, but speak of divine secrets which in truth are foreign to them.[2] Finally, he expresses similar sentiments in the *Liber positionum*, where he warns against believing that one can sin without regard for the consequences and urges the necessity of distinguishing between right and wrong.[3]

---

1. Ed. Franz Pfeiffer, *Deutsche Mystiker des vierzehnten Jahrhunderts* (Leipzig, 1845–57), II, sermon 74, 232. The passage is also reproduced by Guarnieri, 417, and the text of the entire sermon is translated by R. B. Blakney, *Meister Eckhart, A Modern Translation* (New York, 1941), pp. 192–96.

2. Ed. A. Jundt, *Histoire du panthéisme populaire au moyen âge* (Paris, 1875), sermon 6, pp. 254–55.

3. Ed. Pfeiffer, II, 664. If there is doubt concerning the attribution of the above two sermons, there is no question at all that Eckhart wrote the *Liber positionum*.

Just as he attacks antinomianism in these works, so he attacks autotheism in his *Book of Divine Consolation*. There he insists that man is naturally a creature of evil and infirmity whose only goodness is borrowed from God. In a following passage he clarifies this with the remark that "if I assume that the goodness that I have is given to me for my own and not merely borrowed, then I am saying that I am the master and am God's son from nature, when, in fact, I am not even God's son from grace."[4] This, then, is a pointed rebuke of the heresy that "man can become God by nature without distinction" that the Bishop of Strassburg explicitly attributed to beghards and beguines in 1317.

In view of Eckhart's stand on these matters it seems at first ironic that he was indicted for heresy by Henry of Virneburg—the same Archbishop of Cologne who was the first to condemn beghards for antinomianism in 1307—and that even after he conducted a vigorous defense he was posthumously condemned by Pope John XXII. But even Eckhart's most extreme admirers admit that his language was often subject to misunderstanding and that the Papacy, at least, proceeded against him in good faith.[5] There is no denying that of the twenty-eight articles in the bull of condemnation, *In agro Dominico*, the first twenty-six were extracted directly from his published writings, and examination shows that many were closely related to the alleged errors of the beghards.[6] Points four through six maintain that bad works as well as good manifest the glory of God and that vituperation, sin, and blasphemy are ways of praising God. Even more shocking is article fifteen, which says, as we have seen in the Introduction, that if a man is rightly disposed he should not regret commiting so many as a thousand mortal sins, while other articles recommend indifference to good works and even salvation (8, 16–19). There is also the pantheistic statement that "we are transformed totally into God and converted into Him in a similar manner as in the Sacrament the bread is converted into the Body of Christ," (10) followed by

4. Ed. J. Quint, *Eckhart: Die deutschen Werke* (Stuttgart, 1936–), V, 36–38.
5. E.g. Otto Karrer, "Eckhart," in H. J. Schultz (ed.), *Die Wahrheit der Ketzer* (Stuttgart, 1968), p. 76.
6. Text ed. H. Denifle, "Acten zum Processe Meister Eckeharts," ALKG, II, 636–40. There is an English translation in James M. Clark, *Meister Eckhart* (London, 1957), pp. 253–58.

the claims that all good men are equal to Christ (11, 12, 20–22) and that men can will whatever God wills (13, 14).

Needless to say, even though such articles may have been taken out of context, they gave Eckhart a bad reputation after he was no longer alive to defend himself. William of Ockham, for example, referred in 1337, to Eckhart's errors as not so much heretical as insane, a direct and probably conscious echo of the condemnation of Amaury of Bène by the Fourth Lateran Council.[7] Ockham, writing from Munich, did not know that John XXII had in fact judged most of the errors in question to be heretical because *In agro Dominico* was published only in the province of Cologne,[8] but others who became familiar with the bull directly or indirectly became even more abusive. The outstanding, if most extreme example was Jan van Leeuwen, "the good cook of Groenendael," who, though a devoted follower of Ruysbroeck, went so far as to say that Eckhart never gave a sermon that was true because he knew only as much doctrine as a mushroom. Though Jan seems to have been challenged in this, he stuck to his position in a later tract in which he insisted that Eckhart was "an enormous Antichrist" (*"een swaer antkerst"*) because he taught that we can become God's son without distinction (one of the articles of *In agro Dominico*).[9]

Jan also thought that Eckhart was the founder of a perverse heresy, i.e. that of the Free Spirit, that flourished in his own day. We will see in the next chapter that many Free Spirits did in fact consider themselves to have been Eckhart's disciples and many heretical tracts

7. *Tractatus contra Benedictum XII*, ed. H. S. Offler, *Guillelmi de Ockham opera politica*, III (Manchester, 1956), 161–62; also Ockham, *Dialogus de imperio et pontificia potestate* (Lyons, 1494; repr., 1962), part III, tr. II, lib. 2, cap 8 (fol. 251r).

8. J. Koch, "Zur Analogielehre Meister Eckharts," *Mélanges offerts à Etienne Gilson* (Toronto and Paris, 1959), p. 350 and *Idem*, "Meister Eckharts Weiterwirken im deutsch-niederländischen Raum im 14. und 15. Jahrhundert," *La mystique rhénane. Colloque de Strasbourg 16–19 mai 1961* (Paris, 1963), pp. 136–37.

9. The first attack is in Jan's *Boexken van Meester Eckaerts leere* written sometime before 1355 and the second in his *Van den tien gheboden* of 1358. These and other references to Eckhart are edited by C. G. N. de Vooys, "Meister Eckart en de Nederlandse Mystiek," *Nederlandsch archief voor kerkgeschiedenis*, n.s. III (1905), 182–94.

were preserved under his name. Consequently, for some the distinction between him and the heretical beghards became entirely forgotten: even the Dominican, Henry of Herford, wrote as early as the mid-fourteenth century that the bull, *In agro Dominico*, was "a condemnation of beghards" and he was followed in this by another Dominican, Hermann Korner, in the fifteenth century.[10] Thus, though Eckhart may not have had pantheist or antinomian intentions, many heretical beghards saw him as one of their own and many of his enemies concurred.

2. ECKHART'S ORTHODOX FOLLOWERS

The next generation of German mystics was most anxious to redress the balance by formulating a mystical theology free from the slightest taint of heresy, but even they were not immune from charges of straying from the faith.

Heinrich Suso's earliest work, *The Little Book of the Truth*, reflects most clearly the author's reaction to the trial of Eckhart, written as it was under the immediate impress of that event.[11] In Chapter Six he describes an apparition in which he encountered a subtle Free Spirit who called himself "the nameless wild man" (*"das namelos wilde"*). The latter claimed to come from nowhere, be nothing, and want nothing, referring to the doctrine of "annihilation in nothingness," and added that his wisdom allowed him complete liberty. The major interest of the chapter lies in the way this figure invokes the words and reputation of Meister Eckhart. He cites a certain *"hohe Meister"* who recognized no "distinctions" and spoke beautifully about the Christ-like man (apparent references to errors that appeared as articles 23, 24, 11, 12, and 22 in the bull, *In agro Dominico*).[12] Suso responded by quoting clearly orthodox passages from Eckhart's

---

10. Henry of Herford, *Liber de rebus memorabilioribus sive chronicon*, ed. A. Potthast (Göttingen, 1859), pp. 247–48; Hermann Korner, *Chronica novella*, ed. J. Schwalm (Göttingen, 1895), p. 244.

11. Ed. K. Bihlmeyer, *Suso: Deutsche Schriften* (Stuttgart, 1907), pp. 326–59. There is a translation by James M. Clark, *Little Book of Eternal Wisdom and Little Book of Truth* (London, 1953).

12. The identification of the *"hohe Meister"* as Eckhart is agreed upon by all scholars, e.g. most recently, Herma Piesch, "Seuses 'Büchlein der Wahrheit' und Meister Eckhart," *Heinrich Seuse, Studien zum 600. Todestag*, ed. E. M. Filthaut (Cologne, 1966), p. 93.

writings, probably with the intent of lecturing the papal curia as well as the heretical beghards. For example, he quotes Eckhart as saying: "Christ is the only-begotten Son, and we are not. He is the Son by nature. . . , but we men are not the natural Son. . . ." In the end the "wild man" respectfully capitulates.

This dialogue is not only a vivid illustration of how heretics cited the authority of Meister Eckhart, but it is also a fair summary of some of their own beliefs. The man who claims that he comes from nowhere and wants nothing because he has been annihilated has reached a goal of thorough passivity that is similarly described in the most authentic Free-Spirit tracts. But in a later work, *The Life*, Suso becomes more unfairly polemical.[13] Not only does he refer to heretics who say that the righteous need not fear or avoid sin, but he claims that they insist on the necessity of wading through every swamp of sin in order to arrive at perfect resignation. This is putting the cart before the horse because known Free Spirits believed that imperviousness to sin was a consequence rather than a presupposition of perfect resignation. Likewise, there is no evidence to support Suso's reference to heretics who said that God is a dangerous obstacle for those who wish to attain the highest good.[14]

Despite Suso's militance against heresy, which went so far as to prompt this apparently purposeful distortion, his language on occasion was not different from that of some Free Spirits. In the same *Life* he wrote that a man should so tame the forces of his soul that when he looks inward he beholds the Almighty, a statement that is almost the same as a passage in the heretical tract *Schwester Katrei*. There the sister who becomes one with God says that "I so tamed the powers of my soul that when I looked within me I saw God and all that God ever created."[15]

13. Ed. Bihlmeyer, pp. 7–195. There are two English translations: one from the modern German edition of N. Heller by Sister M. Ann Edward (Dubuque, Iowa, 1962), and another directly from Bihlmeyer's edition by James M. Clark, under the title, *The Life of the Servant*; the latter is superior, but is unfortunately abridged.

14. Chapters 46, 48, 51.

15. Cf. Suso's *Life*, ed. Bihlmeyer, p. 170 (cap. 49): "ein gelassenr mensch sŏlte alle siner sel krefte also gezemmen, wenn er in sich sehe, daz sich daz al da erzogti" to *Schwester Katrei*, ed. Pfeiffer (as cited above, n. 1), II, 468: "ich hête aller mîner sêle krefte gezemt. Wenne ich in mich sach, sô sach ich

That one of the most orthodox of mystics had something in common with heretics was recognized even in Suso's own time. As he tells us, he was charged to his face at a Dominican chapter meeting in the Netherlands with writing books that contained "false doctrine which polluted the land with heretical filth."[16] Suso's modern devotées have regarded this report as so fantastic that they cannot believe it,[17] but no intense mystic was immune from suspicion of heresy in the later Middle Ages, try though he might to polish his reputation. Suso and the "nameless wild man" might have had serious differences, but they both were children of Meister Eckhart, as people at that time well knew.

The same may be said about Johan Tauler, who continually attacked "false" and "disordered freedom" from his pulpit. According to him, those that followed false lights and their own natural inclinations were not only proud and immoral, but were condemned to eternal damnation. One should instead overcome one's lower urges and submit to the divine will.[18] Since Tauler specifically referred to "free spirits who glory in false freedom" there is no doubt that he was attacking heretics similar to the "sect of the Free Spirit" condemned in 1317 by the Bishop of Strasburg—the city in which Tauler himself was most active.

But when Tauler described the mystical experience he used the image of the complete miscibility of liquids—the "loss of all distinction" of a drop of water in a jug of wine—that was used by contemporary Free Spirits.[19] A century and a half later, Geiler von Kaysers-

---

got in mir und allez daz got ie geschouf. . . ." This similarity was first noted by H. S. Denifle, *Die deutschen Schriften des Seligen Heinrich Suso* (Munich, 1876–80), I, 251.

16. *Life*, cap. 23.

17. E.g. Karl Rieder in *Göttinger gelehrter Anzeiger* (1909), I, 497. Piesch (as cited above, n. 12), p. 132, tries to explain the incident away as a reaction to Suso's defense of Eckhart, but would this have happened at a *Dominican* chapter meeting?

18. *Predigten*, ed. F. Vetter, *Deutsche Texte des Mittelalters*, XI (Berlin, 1910), pp. 55, 99, 167, 218–19, 257–58.

19. *Ibid.*, p. 33: ". . . und kummet also verre daz der geist in diseme so versinket das er die underscheit so verlúret, er wurt also ein mit der süssekeit der gotheit daz sin wesen also mit dem göttelichen wesen durchgangen wurt daz er sich verlúret, rechte alse ein troppfe wassers in eime grossen vasse wines; also wurt der geist versunken in Got in götlicher einekeit, daz er do verlúst alle underscheit, . . ."

berg attacked the use of this image as heretical, adding with some embarrassment: "You can also find it in Tauler, but you must understand him nicely"![20] Tauler was never formally charged with heresy in his own lifetime, but in the sixteenth century Eck accused him of having fallen into the errors of *Ad nostrum*, and he did complain that when he warned false Christians of the perils of their life and how carefully they should prepare for death they jeered and called him a beghard, shouting "here is a new spirit who comes from those of the high spirit."[21] If even Tauler was treated this way, one must wonder how many others were abused as "beghards" who were in fact equally devout.

Directly under Tauler's influence was the banker, Rulman Merswin of Strassburg, who, as a layman writing on religious subjects in a city noted for being a center of heresy, had an even greater need than the Dominican mystics to establish a reputation for orthodoxy. One of his works, *The Little Book of the Banner*, is devoted entirely to castigating the *"valschen frigen menschen"* assembled under Lucifer's banner against the forces of Christ.[22] These were heretics who said that one must satisfy nature so that the spirit may be undisturbed. They also said that they no longer had to suffer and die and that those who must do so are "crude" (*"grob"*) men. When others opposed them with the Bible, they scoffed at subservience to mere "ink and parchment." These last two charges have the ring of authenticity since they coincide with information that we have from inquisitorial protocols,[23] but it is hard to know what to make of the rest because we have seen that Merswin was so hostile to Free Spirits that he made

20. Johannes Geiler von Kaysersberg, *Postill* (Strassburg, 1522), II, lxvii: "Du findest das ouch im Taweler; du must in aber hüpschlich verston." On the various uses of the images of miscibility see further my article, "The Image of Mixed Liquids in Late Medieval Mystical Thought," *Church History*, XL 1971.

21. J. Eck, *De purgatorio contra Lutherum hostesque ecclesiae* (Antwerp, 1545), fol. 109v–112r (Lib. III, cap. 13). Tauler's complaint is in *Predigten*, ed. Vetter, p. 138; James M. Clark, *The Great German Mystics. Eckhart, Tauler and Suso* (Oxford, 1949), p. 39, believes that this passage probably refers to an actual experience.

22. Ed. Jundt (as cited above, n. 2), pp. 211–14.

23. E.g. the use of the pejorative expression *"grossus"* by Albert of Brünn, John Hartmann, and the beguines of Mühlhausen, and the testimony of Albert (ed. Wattenbach, 536): "quia beghardus studuit suam doctrinam in libro Trinitatis, set sacerdos in pellibus vitulorum."

up a story about one of them out of whole cloth.[24] That his thought was really closely related to that of Free Spirits is shown by the fact that his *Book of the Nine Rocks* bears the same title as a Free-Spirit tract also written in Strassburg in the fourteenth century.[25]

Most similar in intent to the writings of Tauler and Merswin is the *Theologia Deutsch*. The unknown author of this tract states in his preface that he aimed to distinguish between the real "Friends of God" and the "false Free Spirits." He devotes an entire chapter to describing the latter, who he says are guided by a light that they think is God but is really Lucifer. They profess a state beyond conscience that makes them indifferent to works, words, and rules; specifically, one "Free Spirit" said that "were he to slay ten men, he should have as little remorse about it as if he had killed a dog."[26] Some scholars have thought that the purpose of the entire *Theologia Deutsch* was to combat the Free-Spirit heresy,[27] but this did not prevent it from being criticized as an apology for pantheism and later being placed on the papal *Index.*[28]

3. RUYSBROECK

Jan van Ruysbroeck's hatred of heresy was probably the most intense of all the fourteenth-century mystics, dominating as it did not only his writings but a significant episode of his life. This was his campaign against the memory of a woman called Bloemardinne, undertaken while he was still a secular cleric in Brussels before his retreat to Groenendael. Unfortunately, the only surviving account is by Ruysbroeck's biographer, Pomerius, who wrote three quarters of a century after the events he described. His story has been treated with scepticism, but there is good reason to believe that it contains a substantial kernel of truth.[29]

24. See above, pp. 11–13.

25. On the heretical *Book of the Nine Rocks* see below, pp. 209–10.

26. There are numerous editions of this work. I use *Theologia Germania*, ed. Joseph Bernhart, tr. S. Winkworth and W. R. Trask (London, 1950), pp. 112, 184–90.

27. E.g. J. Pasquier, *L'orthodoxie de la théologie germanique* (Paris, 1922), pp. 21, 25–26, 71.

28. On the later controversy concerning the orthodoxy of the *Theologia Deutsch*, J. Orcibal, *La rencontre du Carmel thérésien avec les mystiques du Nord* (Paris, 1959).

29. Pomerius, *De origine Monasterii Viridisvallis*, in *Analecta Bollandiana*,

According to Pomerius, Bloemardinne of Brussels was a woman of perverse doctrine who, sitting on a silver chair, taught and wrote much about "the spirit of freedom" and an erotic love which she called "seraphic." Far from being deemed a heretic during her lifetime she was so highly regarded that when she approached the altar to receive communion she was thought to have been flanked by two seraphim. Among the many who came under her influence was the Duchess of Brabant who received the silver chair on Bloemardinne's death as if it were a relic, while paralytics went to touch the mystic's dead body in the hope of cure. It was then that Ruysbroeck, having pity on such delusions, began to attack her writings.

Belgian archival scholarship has been able to identify the woman in question as Heylwig, a member of the patrician family of Bloemaert, a fact which explains her wealth and aristocratic connections. She is mentioned in échevinal acts as early as 1305 and is believed to have founded a hospice for elderly beguines before her death in 1335. As late as 1371 a notarial act refers to the founder of this beguinage with praise as "laudabilis persona et in Christo devota, domicella Heylwigis quodam dicta Bloemards, bone memorie."[30] If Bloemardinne was so revered decades after her death, it is not surprising that Pomerius refers to Ruysbroeck's campaign against her as an act of courage.

Considering these circumstances, it is hardly likely that her heresies were manifest. Even Pomerius admits that he himself "can affirm from personal experience that the writings of Bloemardinne, though excessively baleful, have such an aspect of truth and piety that no one could perceive in them any seed of heresy unless he receives help or special gifts from Him who teaches all truth." This sounds like

IV (1886), 286; reproduced and translated by McDonnell. pp. 493–94. P. O'Sheridan, "La doctrine vauvertine sur le communisme ecclésiastique," *Revue des sciences religieuses*, VIII (1928), 208–209, considers the whole story a fable, and Axters, II, 222–25, sees the incident as an insignificant neighborly quarrel blown into epic proportions by Pomerius.

30. Best on Bloemardinne's career is the article by J. van Mierlo in the *Dictionnaire d'histoire et de géographie ecclésiastiques*, IX (1937), 207–12, which conveniently summarizes his conclusions after decades of research on the subject. As a philologist as well as an ecclesiastical historian Mierlo was able to show that the female ending -inne was no longer current in Pomerius' time, so that the hagiographer must have written on the basis of some textual information. The praise of 1371 is cited by Axters, II, 225.

Gerson's reference to the "incredibly subtle book" of Marguerite Porete who might in fact have influenced Bloemardinne's carnal or seraphic mysticism.[31] The two could have known each other in Brabant in the early fourteenth century and that one died in the flames while the other lived to teach from a silver chair might have been an accident of birth or circumstance rather than any great difference in doctrine.

Doubters wonder whether Ruysbroeck really did attack Bloemardinne since he never mentions her by name in his writings, but a reliable authority, his disciple Jan van Schoonhoven, does testify that the master endeavored to extirpate the "sect of the Free Spirit" that was then flourishing in Brabant.[32] Ruysbroeck's presumed campaign against Bloemardinne took place just before his retirement from Brussels and it is possible that he made this decision partially because of the hostility he engendered.[33] In any event, there can be no question that he persistently attacked the errors of unregulated mysticism from his earliest works until his last.

His first book, *The Kingdom of Lovers*, has been characterized as "from beginning to end. . . a refutation of the false mystics. . ."[34] and his second, *The Adornment of the Spiritual Marriage*, written, so far as we know, just after his departure from Brussels, contains a description of mystical theories so explicit that it could have been based on the lost works of Bloemardinne.[35] At the end of the second book of *The Adornment* Ruysbroeck describes deviations from the faith based on the confusion of mere nature with the grace of God. Men can empty themselves by nature, but cannot in that way find

31. Gerson's remark is quoted above, p. 165; for Marguerite's comparison of the liberated soul to the seraphim see below, p. 203.

32. Text ed. A. Combes, *Essai sur la critique de Ruysbroeck par Gerson* (Paris, 1945–59), I, 729. Jan's answer also supports our conclusion of previous chapters that by his own time (i.e. the first decade of the fifteenth century) the heretical beghards were no longer a threat.

33. Van Mierlo, 210, whose interpretation I find more convincing than that of Axters.

34. A. Wautier d'Aygalliers, *Ruysbroeck the Admirable*, tr. F. Rothwell (London and New York, 1925), p. 83.

35. The work is translated as *The Spiritual Espousals* by Eric Colledge (London, 1952), whose dating is based on the latest Belgian scholarship. The attack on false mystics is in Book II, caps. 39–43, pp. 166–75.

God. Even many who do good works and are reputed to be holy are sometimes deceived by the devil into thinking that they have attained supernatural union when in fact they are untouched by God because of their spiritual pride. Worst of all are those who "through the natural rest which they feel and have in themselves in emptiness. . . maintain that they are free, and united with God without mean, and that they are advanced beyond all the exercises of Holy Church, and beyond the law, and beyond all the virtuous works which one can in any way practice."[36] They claim that they are so empty that they can no longer praise God and so perfect that they can never increase in virtue nor be conscience-stricken for indulging their bodily desires.

Because Ruysbroeck was not explicit on the last point and mentioned no particular immoral acts it has been objected that his diatribe was not a full description of the Free-Spirit heresy,[37] but, in my opinion, the reference to the indulgence in bodily desires is the only part that is unreliable because, as Guarnieri has noted, the passage in *The Adornment* otherwise reads like a condensation of *The Mirror of Simple Souls*.[38] Having combatted Bloemardinne, a woman who had a wide and influential following, Ruysbroeck was reflecting actual experience when he said that the false mystics believe themselves to be holy and some are so subtle that they can only be detected with the aid of divine enlightenment.[39]

Many similar attacks in his other works have been enumerated elsewhere in detail.[40] Here one need only mention passages from two of the last, *The Book of the Twelve Beguines* and *The Little Book of Enlightenment*, both written in a simpler language and for a wider public than *The Adornment of the Spiritual Marriage*. In *The Twelve Beguines* Ruysbroeck divides the errors of heretical mystics into four classes: against the Holy Spirit, the Father, the Son, and the Church. They offend each one of the persons of the Trinity because they consider themselves to be their equals or superiors by nature, and this, of

36. *Ibid.*, p. 170.
37. Combes, II, 305–307.
38. Guarnieri, 443–44.
39. Tr. Colledge, p. 173.
40. J. van Mierlo, "Ruusbroec's bestrijding van de ketterij," *Ons geestelijk erf*, VI (1932), 304—46.

course, is contrary to Scripture and the teachings of the Church, all of which they hold in contempt.[41]

The Little Book of Enlightenment has been called "the most openly anti-heretical" of all Ruysbroeck's works.[42] There he most clearly distinguishes his own position from that of autotheistic mystics when he writes: "behold, thus you must observe that we are united with God through means, both here in grace and also in glory. . . . And St. Paul undoubtedly understood this when he said that he desired to be released from his body and to be with Christ. But he did not say that he wished to be Christ Himself, or God, as now some faithless and perverted men do. . . ." After attacking indifference in a fashion similar to passages from *The Adornment* he concludes the whole work with a declaration of his own orthodoxy and a plea to his readers to hold "aloof from those men who are in their empty ignorance so deceived that crassly and foolishly they believe that out of their own natures they have found within themselves the indwelling of God, and who wish to be one with God without His grace and without the exercise of virtue, and in disobedience to God and to Holy Church."[43]

One would think that such strenuous protest would have freed Ruysbroeck from all suspicion himself, but such was not to be the case. A generation after his death the prestigious Gerson levelled an attack on *The Adornment of the Spiritual Marriage* which has recently inspired three thick volumes of commentary by the late A. Combes.[44] Even though Gerson recognized the passages we have discussed from the end of Book Two as a criticism of heretical beghards,

41. *Van den XII Beghinen,* in *Werken,* ed. L. Reypens and M. Schurmans (Malines and Amsterdam, 1932), IV, caps. 18–22.

42. Joyce Bazire and Eric Colledge, *The Chastising of God's Children and the Treatise of Perfection of the Sons of God* (Oxford, 1957), p. 55.

43. Passages translated by Colledge, *Espousals,* pp. 27–28, 40. Ruysbroeck's influence can be seen in Jan van Brederode's *Coninx Summe,* ed. D. C. Tinbergen (Leiden, 1907), pp. 193–94, 236, 245, 345–46, 568. This translation of the *Somme le Roi* done at the Carthusian monastery of Zelem between 1402 and 1409 once refers to lollards as hypocrites, but in two other passages says that many heretics may be found among them, and in a long digression attacks them specifically as "free spirits" who claim to have God's grace without love or works, concluding: "Dit sijn des duvels eighen beesten/ al heten si hem selven die vrye gheesten."

44. As cited above, n. 32.

he associated Ruysbroeck with similar errors and also claimed that he had renewed the "insanity" of Amaury of Bène.[45] That Gerson was not the only one who thought that he was a radical mystic is shown by the crowning irony that Ruysbroeck was taken in fifteenth-century England and sixteenth-century Italy to have been the author of *The Mirror of Simple Souls*.[46]

4. GROOTE AND THE BRETHREN OF THE COMMON LIFE

Gert Groote, less of a writer than Ruysbroeck, was far more active in public campaigns against presumed heresy. But if it was with very good reason that his earliest biographer called him "a hammer of heretics like a second Jerome,"[47] he and his followers were themselves no more free from suspicions of heterodoxy than the more speculative mystics before them.

We know of three different campaigns that Groote waged and the victims of all seem to have been as much on the borderlines of heresy as Bloemardinne of Brussels. The first case concerns a man who, like Bloemardinne and Aegidius Cantor, was already dead before

45. *Ibid.*, I, 668–69, 869, and II, 304–20.

46. Of course the English were not well-informed about Free-Spirit mysticism. In a fourteenth-century MS of John Baconthorp's Commentaries on the *Sentences* there is a reference to "the errors of the Berengarians in *Ad nostrum*" (MS British Museum, Royal 9 C. VII, fol. 85rb) which indicates that either Baconthorp or a scribe knew so little about beghards that he took them for followers of Berengar of Tours who lived three centuries earlier. In the later fourteenth century Walter Hilton and the author of *The Cloud of Unknowing* did attack unregulated mysticism, but did so in language that indicates formal imitation of continental models. Hilton's *Scale of Perfection*, Book II, chapter 26, considers false illuminations to be the work of the noonday fiend, the same diagnosis made by the German Augustinian Thomas of Strassburg in his *Commentaria in quattuor libros sententiarum* (Genoa, 1585), fol. 110va, and the attack in chapters 56 and 57 of *The Cloud* may have been based on Ruysbroeck (for evidence of *The Cloud's* reliance on Ruysbroeck's *Little Book of Enlightenment*, see Bazire, *Chastising*, p. 55). The clearest indication that there was no Free-Spirit movement in England comes from the English translation of Ruysbroeck's *Adornment* (ca. 1382), which recasts the attacks on false mystics to make them apply to followers of Wyclif (Bazire, pp. 35, 130–45, 277).

47. *Dictamen rigmicum*, ed. T. Brandsma, *Ons geestelijk erf*, XVI (1942), 34 line 117. A good summary of Groote's campaigns against heresy is T. P. van Zijl, *Gerard Groote, Ascetic and Reformer* (Washington, D. C., 1963), pp. 169–83.

Groote called his reputation into question. This was Matthew (or Meus) of Gouda who, according to a fifteenth-century biographer of Groote, taught his disciples twenty-two articles full of blasphemies concerning the humanity and divinity of Christ, the sacraments of the Church, and purgatory. Of these the only point that has come down is that he claimed to have had a better knowledge of truth than the Apostles and that he had more right to be called God than Christ did. But if Matthew really taught such heresies, why was he not apprehended during his lifetime? And if he had disciples, why did not Groote proceed against them instead of attacking the memory of a dead man? These questions cannot be answered, though they certainly evoke suspicion. All that is known for sure is that Groote's campaign forced the Bishop of Utrecht to exhume Matthew's body sometime between 1379 and 1384, publicly burn the remains, and scatter the ashes in the canals of Utrecht.[48]

All we know about a second presumed heretic, a surgeon or barber of Kampen named Gerbrand, is that Groote mentioned him in a letter of 1382 as an associate of "free spirits" and finally forced him to do penance.[49] Groote's letters are also our most valuable source concerning his third and best known victim, an Augustinian friar of Dordrecht named Bartholomew, who was active in Kampen and the surrounding region. Early in 1382 Groote wrote to his friends in that town warning them of heretical teachers. Though he did not mention any names, he must have meant Bartholomew and Gerbrand because he referred to both in a second letter written in May.[50] In particular, Groote was disturbed about three or four sermons Bartholomew had given in which he had allegedly mentioned and praised the "free spirits" by name. He said that the eremetical life was not perfect since Christ had never entered a monastery and that the good man need not do so either. To that he added that whatever God is by nature man can become by grace, that penance need only be done gradually, and that the life of the perfect man must be founded on "pure nothing." For

---

48. On Matthew, Petrus Horn, *Vita Magistri Gerardi Magni*, ed. W. J. Kühler, *Nederlandsch archief voor kerkgeschiedenis*, n. s. VI (1909), 344, 346, and Guilelmus Heda, *Historia episcoporum Ultraiectensium*, ed. Lap v. Waveren (Utrecht, 1643), p. 259.

49. Groote, *Epistolae*, ed. W. Mulder (Antwerp, 1933), p. 133, and Horn, 344, 346–47.

50. *Epistolae*, pp. 132–37.

these reasons he did not inculpate the magnates who spent their time in taverns, but joined them there.[51]

The most recent editor of Groote's letters could not believe that Bartholomew said man can become *by grace* whatever God is by nature and wished to replace this with the affirmation that man can become *by nature* whatever God is by nature because that error is commonly understood to be the essence of the Free-Spirit heresy. But Groote's text is clear and corresponds with the testimony of Conrad Kannler taken just the year before in another part of Europe, not to mention the case of Hans Becker and Free-Spirit writings still to be examined. Bartholomew did not attribute supernatural powers to man and his criticism of the monastic life could just as well have been made by Groote himself. His attitude toward penance does sound extreme, but it must be borne in mind that Groote did not hear his sermons with his own ears but learned of them through an informant.[52] Moreover, even Groote never went so far as to say that Bartholomew or Gerbrand were actual "free spirits," but only said that they were like them.

This circumspection was probably warranted. Though Groote pressured the episcopal court of Utrecht to bring the Augustinian to trial, the latter freely admitted that the tenets he was charged with were false, but denied that he had ever preached them and was dismissed. Unsatisfied, Groote demanded and won a second trial. This time Bartholomew brought along the town fathers of Kampen, but Groote travelled from Deventer to testify against him in person and won the case. Nonetheless, the citizens of Kampen remained refractory and the next year expelled Groote's party. The last we hear of the incident is in a letter of 1383 in which Groote laments the treatment of his leading supporter at Kampen, comparing him to the early martyrs.[53] Had the "hammer of heretics" lived beyond 1384 he perhaps would again have taken up his cudgels.

51. *Ibid.*, pp. 133–37. See also Horn, 345, who adds that Bartholomew said that Christ was a good fellow who drank wine and did not teach avoidance of fleshly delights.

52. *Epistolae*, p. 133: "Bartholomeus. . . fecit tres sermones vel quatuor, de quibus michi scriptum est. . . ."

53. *Ibid.*, pp. 200–203. Further details about the case are in *idem*, pp. 149–52; Johannes Busch, *Chronicon Windeshemense*, ed. K. Grube, *Geschichtsquellen der Provinz Sachsen*, XIX (Halle, 1886), 260–62; and Rudolph Dier de Muden,

This zealousness probably arose from Groote's sensitivity to being called a heretic himself. He had only been made a deacon in 1380 and in 1383 his calls for reform and communion with God encountered so much opposition that his license to preach was revoked. During his life he was insulted as a beghard or lollard and as late as 1504 he was referred to as the founder of a house of lollards by Johannes Schiphower.[54] Groote's followers among the Brethren of the Common Life suffered even more than he because they in fact resembled beghards and beguines in their semi-religious organization. When a rich citizen of Zwolle went to join the Brethren in Deventer, his friends were scandalized because they thought he was becoming a lollard and a contemporary source tells of how some Brethren riding in a cart were abused by workers in the streets who shouted "where are these lollards going? Let's throw these devils into the Yssel."[55]

Most exposed, as usual, were the women. Around 1393 the Inquisitor, Jacob of Soest, harassed the female communities of the Common Life in Utrecht and Rhenen, charging that they lived like nuns without authorization, prayed in the vernacular, and sometimes confessed to the overseers of their houses known as "Marthas."[56] On this occasion the women were successfully defended by Florens Radewijns, who had taken over Groote's mantle, but in 1397 the controversy about the orthodoxy of the Common Life movement broke out again and raged until a decision was made in favor of the Brethren in the following year by a commission of canon lawyers and theologians in Cologne.[57] Nonetheless, as we have seen, Eylard Schoenveld still

---

De magistro Gherardo Groote, domino Florencio et multis aliis devotis fratribus, ed. G. Dumbar, *Analecta seu vetera aliquot scripta inedita* (Deventer, 1719–22), I, 6.

54. D. A. Brinkerink, "De 'Vita venerabilis Joannis Brinckerinck'," *Nederlandsch archief voor kerkgeschiedenis,* n. s. I (1902), 326–27 (also in Fredericq, III, 46, #37), and J. Schiphower, *Chronica archicomitum Oldenburgensium,* cited by Kurze, 60, n. 48.

55. Busch, p. 115; Brinkerink, 350; Fredericq, III, 47, #37.

56. Fredericq, II, 153–56, #106.

57. *Ibid.,* II, 160–85, #109–14. A different MS reading of the last two documents is in MS Wolfenb., Helmst., 315, fol. 214v–217r. The case is described by C. Van der Wansem, *Het ontstaan en de geschiedenis der Broederschap van het Gemene Leven tot 1400* (Louvain, 1958), pp. 148–55, and in greater detail by W. Ribbeck, "Beiträge zur Geschichte der römischen Inquisition in Deutschland während des 14. und 15. Jahrhunderts," *Zeitschrift für vaterländische Geschichte und Alterthumskunde,* XLVI (1888), 129–56.

tried to proceed against the Brethren in 1400 and the matter was not finally resolved in their favor until the Council of Constance.[58]

Obviously the Brethren of the Common Life were attacked for their manner of living rather than for speculative mysticism. On the other hand, Groote's followers who became Augustinian canons at Windesheim escaped the opprobrium that faced the lay Brethren but were more preoccupied with problems of mystical theology. Thus the *Soliloquium* of Gerlac Peters, one of the more important writers of that community, has been thought to display the influence of Eckhart or Ruysbroeck. The same Peters wrote a tract called *De libertate spiritus*, now lost, and a perfect illustration of the contradictions we have been examining in this chapter is that it conceivably could be either a diatribe against false mysticism or a treatise on spiritual freedom in a neo-Eckhartian style.[59]

In conclusion it may be said that the predicament of the orthodox mystics lay in their desire to express a subjective religious experience and to keep clear of suspicions of heresy at the same time. They sought a way out of this dilemma by intense and sometimes exaggerated attacks on Free Spirits, which, because of their clearly ulterior motives, cannot be treated as reliable source material. But they could still not thoroughly clear their reputations because Free-Spirit thought was in fact embarrassingly related to their own. There were, of course, differences, but it is chastening to remember that even the admirable Ruysbroeck had to admit in a candid moment that some Free Spirits were impossible to detect without the aid of divine illumination.

58. See above, p. 163, n. 94, and p. 165, n. 2.
59. On Peters and his work, Axters, III, 144–46.

Chapter Nine

THE LITERATURE OF THE
FREE SPIRIT

Having heard what hostile parties had to say about Free Spirits, let us now let them speak for themselves, not through the filtered medium of trial records but in their own chosen words. For their literature survived, indeed proliferated, in the later Middle Ages, to the dismay of critics like John Nider who complained about German books "written in a subtle style . . . by beghards or heretics and falsely ascribed to certain honest and ancient doctors of theology."[1] One need not view this as the triumph of skulduggery; the literature we will examine, though daring, was drenched with love and awe of God and was therefore copied not clandestinely but in orthodox monasteries and nunneries. Its transmission through the efforts of numerous monks and nuns is evidence in itself that Free-Spirit thought was not a medieval aberration.

1. THE MIRROR OF SIMPLE SOULS

The first specimen, which, as we have already seen, was frequently copied and translated in monastic houses, is Marguerite Porete's *Mirror of Simple Souls*.[2] It would be foolhardy for a non-denominational

1. *Formicarius*, ed. G. Colvener (Douai, 1602), Lib. III, cap. 5, p. 216.
2. On the history of Marguerite Porete and the transmission of her work, see above pp. 71–77.

historian to issue an ultimate judgment on its orthodoxy, especially since the only manuscript in the original language that has been edited is late and corrupt. But we can try to describe the work as we know it without any *parti pris*.[3]

The most striking aspect of the tract at first glance is its ambitious scope; doubts have been expressed about the elegance of its style, but there is no questioning its bulk.[4] *The Mirror of Simple Souls* extends to 60,000 words (over 100 folio pages) purporting to be a dialogue between *Amour* and *Raison* concerning the conduct of a soul (*Ame*). This form is not constant: verses and *exempla* comment on the development of the dialogue and unheralded characters break in frequently when their advice is needed and then disappear. At no time is there any explicit citing of theological authorities or the Bible, but there are implicit echoes from orthodox mystical texts and Scripture which make it clear that Marguerite Porete was well educated. Indeed, a later chronicler reports that she actually translated the Bible, but there are no references to such in the trial documents and the statement may have been a mistake.[5] The dialogue, meant to be read aloud,[6]

3. Theological experts have so far had differing views about *The Mirror's* orthodoxy. We have seen how it was published by the Downside Benedictines with the *nihil obstat* and *imprimatur*, and even after the recognition of Marguerite's authorship the Dominican Axters, II, 174, remained convinced of its orthodoxy. Sister M. Doiron, "The Middle English Translation of Le Mirouer des Simples Ames," *Dr. L. Reypens-Album, Studiën en Tektsuitgaven van Ons geestelijk erf*, XVI (Antwerp, 1964), p. 134, believes that "misinterpretation of the treatise led the ecclesiastical authorities to question Margaret's orthodoxy," but Edmund Colledge, O. S. A. and R. Guarnieri, "The Glosses by 'M. N.' and Richard Methley to 'The Mirror of Simple Souls'," *Archivio Italiano per la storia della pietà*, V (1968), 381–82, write that "the *Mirror* is a work of heresy, written by a teacher of false doctrine skilled in concealing her unorthodoxy behind ambiguity and imprecision." The last view appears to me to be mistaken not necessarily in the contention that Marguerite was a heretic but in the conviction that she used purposely Aesopian language to confuse the authorities; this is not how I read her personality from the facts of her life.

4. The only literary historian who has dealt with *The Mirror* is Jean Dagens in *La mystique rhénane. Colloque de Strasbourg, 16–19 mai 1961* (Paris, 1963), pp. 281–89 and *idem*, "I mistici cattolici dal sec. xiv al 1650," *Grande antologia filosofico*, IX (1964), 2449: "Purtroppo l'autore dello Specchio non è un bravo scrittore: letterariamente l'opera è assai povera e mal costruita e le parti in versi mostrano una grande debolezza. . . ." Dagens has not made an exhaustive study and further work by a literary expert might be profitable.

5. Jean d'Outremeuse, *Chronique*, in Fredericq, II, 64–65, #39: "Margarite Porte, qui translatat la divine Escripture, en queile translation mult elle errat es

is poorly organized and repetitive, but it has an interesting form and an extensive mystical vocabulary.

The Mirror of Simple Souls postulates "seven states of grace" which lead up to the union of the soul with God. Right here the use of the term "grace" shows a less radical stance than that customarily attributed to Free-Spirit heretics, but for Marguerite it is only divine grace which guides the soul to the plane of perfection.[7] In the first four states the soul is still in "tres grant servage."[8] Initially it observes the Divine Commandments and secondly the special counsels which teach evangelical perfection as typified by Christ. In the third stage it gives up good works and destroys its will (that is, "the will of the spirit," which The Mirror claims is harder to destroy than "the will of the body," which was overcome in the first two states). Thereby it reaches the fourth stage—a level of contemplation in which it becomes free of "all outward labors and obedience" and rejoices in being so abandoned to love that it thinks God has no greater gift to offer on earth.

But it is only thereafter that the soul achieves the supernatural. In the fifth state it is lowered by Divine Goodness to the depths of humility and nothingness. While in the fourth it was young and proud, now it is old and without desires. In its abyss it sees and wants nothing, but then, in the sixth state of "clarification," God totally liberates and purifies it. The soul arrives at a state of "glorification," however, only in the seventh step, and that takes place when it leaves the body and achieves eternal glory and the perfection of paradise. It is important to stress the fact that for Marguerite the first six stages can take place

---

artycles de la foid." As Guarnieri, 412, has shown, Jean was dependent on Les grandes chroniques de la France (ed. J. Viard [Paris, 1934], VIII, 273), which said that Marguerite had "trespassée et transcendée l'escriture devine," and perhaps misunderstood his source or used the verb to translate in the sense of trespass or transcend.

6. Thus ed. Guarnieri, 564: "a tous ceulx qui orront ce livre;" 566: "Entendez ces motz divinement, par amour, auditeurs de ce livre!" I disagree with Axters II, 170, and Guarnieri, 510, who argue that the work was written only for women; see 544: "or entendez, seigneurs amans."

7. Ed. Guarnieri, 521: "Ame de Dieu touchee, et denuee de peché ou premier estat de grace, est montee par divines graces ou septiesme estat de grace, ouquel estat l'Ame a le plain de sa parfection. . . ."

8. Ibid., 568.

"here below," but the seventh, perfection, can be attained in the future life alone.[9]

Despite Marguerite's assertion that there is as much difference between each one of these states as between a drop of water and the ocean, the distinction between some of them seems rather fine or even confusing to the modern reader. But the real purport of the book lies not in these distinctions, but in the description of the soul in the fifth and sixth states; and it is here that the work is most daring. Marguerite compares the "annihilated" or "liberated" soul to the angels. It has six wings like the seraphim and like the seraphim there are no intermediaries between its love and divine love.[10] The soul is also united to the Holy Trinity and wherever it looks God is to be found, though it can find God within itself without even looking.[11]

These and other similar passages approach autotheism, but Marguerite does draw a line between the six states to be had on earth and the perfection of paradise. Also, many of her images derive from the orthodox mystical tradition. It has already been shown how she borrowed ideas from William of St. Thierry's *Epistola ad fratres de Monte Dei* and in comparing the preliminary mystical states to the mixture of liquids or the union of fire with the materials it consumes she chose similes that had been used by St. Bernard in his *De diligendo Deo*.[12] In the latter case, however, the crucial difference is that Bernard was talking about heaven and Marguerite about a mystical state on earth. My own impression is that Marguerite's formulations did go

---

9. *Ibid.*, 609–613. N. Cohn, *The Pursuit of the Millennium*, 3rd ed. (New York, 1970), p. 184, is mistaken in referring to "the seventh and last stage of the ascent, where the soul rejoices permanently, while still on this earth, in the glory and blessedness which orthodox theology reserves for heaven."

10. Ed. Guarnieri, 524: "Ceste Ame, dit Amour, a six ales, aussi comme les Seraphins. Elle ne vieult plus chose qui viengne par moyen, c'est le propre estre des Seraphins: il n'y a nul moyen entre leur amour et l'amour divine."

11. *Ibid.*, 572: "Ceste Ame, dit Amour, est toute remise, fondue et tiree, joincte et unie a haulte Trinité," also pp. 549, 550, 574; 593: "trouve elle Dieu en elle, sans le querir."

12. Cf. *Ibid.*, 585: "nulle nature de feu n'atrait nulle matere en luy; car if fait de luy et de la matere une chose, non mye deux, mais une," and the union of rivers with St. Bernard, *De dil. Deo*, PL CLXXXII, 990–91. On the reliance on William of St. Thierry, see Sister Doiron's ed. of the Middle English version of *The Mirror* in *Archivio Italiano per la storia della pietà*, V (1968), 274.

beyond orthodoxy, but final judgment will have to be issued by theologians.

As for her views on conduct, it is true that the extravagant statements attributed to her in the procès-verbal of the Parisian theological examination appear in her book. In one of the earliest chapters the soul delivers a little poem beginning "virtues, I take leave of you forever," which then becomes an incessantly recurrent theme.[13] Later Marguerite writes that the soul does not wish the gifts or comforts of God because they interfere with the process of liberation, and we have already seen in Chapter III how she goes so far as to say that the soul "gives to nature, without remorse, all that it asks." But Marguerite explains that because of the soul's transformation, nature is so well ordered that it does not demand anything prohibited.[14]

If the soul takes leave of the virtues it is not to travel down a path of immorality: "She is so far from the work of virtues that she no longer understands their language, but all the works of virtues are enclosed within the soul and obey her without contradiction."[15] In another passage "Reason" is astonished at the paradox of the soul taking leave of the virtues and yet still being with them, and "Love" patiently answers that if the soul was once the servant it has now become the master, but without any conflict: the virtues are always with the liberated soul and in perfect obedience.[16] (This, of course, does not dispose of "Reason's" paradox, but Marguerite is never bothered by logical technicalities.) It is notable that Marguerite's opponents never accused her of immoral acts and there is no evidence in her work that she advocated libertinism in any way.

Rather than immorality, it is the position of passivity taken in *The Mirror* that is theologically most questionable. Because the soul is unified with God it has no independent needs or desires. It has become so free that it answers to no one and has absolutely no cares. It takes no account of honor or shame, of salvation or damnation. If anyone asked it if it wished to be in purgatory it would say no, but if asked if it wished to be certain of salvation it would also say no, and

13. Ed. Guarnieri, 525, 544, etc.
14. See above, Chapter III, Section 3, n. 41.
15. Ed. Guarnieri, 632: "Elle est si loing de l'oeuvre des Vertuz, qu'elle ne pourroit entendre leur langage. Mais les oeuvres des Vertuz sont toutes dedans telle Ame encloses, qui obeyssent sans contredit a elle. . . ."
16. *Ibid.*, p. 540.

even if it were asked if it wished to be in paradise it would say no.[17] This nay-saying has its most threatening aspects in its denial of all traditional intermediaries to salvation. The liberated soul need not concern itself with masses, sermons, fasts, or prayers, since God is already there without these just as well as with them. It "does not seek God by penance, nor by any sacrament of the Holy Church, nor by thoughts, words, or works." Especially the latter is ruled out entirely: the soul cares not for works of the body, works of the heart, or works of the spirit because it is saved by "faith without works."[18]

Thus there is a sharp distinction in *The Mirror* between the liberated souls and those still under the dispensation of the Church. At one point Marguerite introduces "Holy Church" as a character to be taught about the liberated souls and to admit that such souls are above it. Elsewhere she distinguishes more explicitly between "Holy Church the Little," which is governed by reason, and "Holy Church the Great," which is governed by divine love, in a passage that may well have influenced the theory of two Churches expressed by Hans Becker. For Marguerite the community of liberated souls comprises the real Holy Church and she even implies at one point that "Holy Church the Little" will not last long into the future.[19]

Still, it remains to be asked how far Marguerite was willing to tolerate the official Church at all. This is difficult to answer because the entire *Mirror* so exults in the soul's new dispensation that it con-

17. *Ibid.*, pp. 534, 583, 586, 525: "Ceste Ame, dit Amour, ne fait compte ne de honte ne de honneur, de pouvreté ne de richesse, d'aise ne de mesaise, d'amour ne hayne, d'enfer ne de paradis."; p. 527: "Qui demanderoit a telles franches Ames. . . se elles vouldroient estre en purgatoire, elles diroient que non; se elles vouldroient estre en ceste vie certifees de leur salut, elles diroient que non; ou s'elles vouldroient estre en paradis, elle[s] diroient que non." The entire passage expatiates on this state of indifference.

18. *Ibid.*, 536–37: "Ceste fille de Syon ne desire ne messes ne sermons, ne jeunes ne oraisons." "Pourquoy desireroit celle Ame ces choses devant nommees, puisque Dieu est aussi bien partout sans ce comme avec ce?" p. 586: "Ceste. . . ne quiert plus Dieu par penitance ne par sacrement nul de Saincte Eglise, ne par pensees ne par paroles ne par oeuvres. . ."; p. 529: "ceste Ame se saulve de foy sans oeuvres."

19. *Ibid.*, 555, 571: "telles Ames, dit Amour, sont proprement appellees Saincte Eglise, car elles soustiennent et enseignent et nourrissent toute Saincte Eglise"; "Et vraiement petite est elle [Saincte Eglise la Petite], car gueres ne demourera, que elle vendra affin, dit ceste Ame, dont elle aura grant leesse." See also below, n. 21; for the similar views of Hans Becker, see above Chapter VII, Section 3.

stantly disparages the old. John Baconthorp, who was a student at Paris around the time that Marguerite was condemned, even described her work as "a little book against the clergy."[20] Yet Marguerite leaves open the possibility, however slightly or unwillingly, of gaining salvation by the accepted paths alone. At one point, for example, while attacking those who mortify the flesh in performing works of charity she parenthetically admits that they are blessed. Likewise, the virtues say that no one can perish who follows their teachings and "Holy Church the Little" defends itself by saying that while love dwells in the liberated souls and not in itself, the Church never opposes love, but indeed commands and praises it in "the gloss of our scriptures."[21]

It also must be remembered that the early stages in the soul's journey toward perfection are the traditional ones of obedience to the Commandments of Scripture and imitation of the model set by Christ. Marguerite emphasizes this when she has "Love" explain that just as a servant can earn and learn so much from his master that he becomes richer and wiser and, eventually, master himself, so the soul can profit from her servitude to the virtues to the extent that she can become master over them.[22] It is best to be liberated, but Marguerite never suggests that this can be attained without first undergoing servitude.

Finally, it must be pointed out that *The Mirror* was meant only for an esoteric audience of those who had "understanding." This did not mean education or reason; indeed, quite the opposite: the book

20. Cited in John Bale, *Scriptorum illustrium maioris Brytannie* (Basel, 1557), 367: "Beguuina quaedam, quae libellum quendam adversus clerum ediderat, prope Parisium combusta fuit, cum quodam converso, qui a fide (ut dicunt) apostatasset." On Baconthorp's years at Paris, see B. M. Xiberta, "De Magistro Iohanne Baconthorpe," *Analecta ordinis carmelitarum*, VI (1927), 11.

21. Ed. Guarnieri, 563: "Les ungs sont qui du tout mortiffient le corps, en faisant o[e]uvres de charité. . . . Telles gens, dit Amour, sont beneurez, mais ilz perissent en leurs oeuvres, pour la souffisance qu'ilz ont en leur estre." (It is possible that the text here is corrupt because the Middle English translation (ed. Doiron, as cited above n. 12), 296, reads "this peple, seith love, ben blynded. . . ." But see also 564: "nous [les Vertuz] ne povons entendre que nul puisse perir qui du tout fait l'enseignement de nous, par l'ardeur de desir qui vray sentiment donne de Jhesucrist"; and 555: "Nous voulons dire, dit Saincte Eglise, que telles Ames sont en vie dessus nous, car Amour demoure en elles et Raison demoure en nous; mais ce n'est mie contre nous, dit Saincte Eglise la Petite, mais aincoys la commandons et louons de cela parmy la glose de noz escriptures."

22. *Ibid.*, 540–41.

was designed to enlighten those who had already taken leave of reason and had nothing to say to those who still lived rationally within "Holy Church the Little."[23] Presumably, Marguerite did not wish to disturb those who were satisfied with the ways of the Church and was anxious only to reach those who wanted to go beyond them. Her original ecclesiastical censors thought she was right in this: Friar John of Quaregnon wrote that Marguerite's book was inspired by the Holy Ghost, but hoped that few would see it because even "alle the clerkes of the world" would not understand it unless they had "highe goostli felynges." Similarly, Godfrey of Fountaines thought that many should not read it because "thei myghten leve her owen werkynge and folowe this clepynge, to the whiche thei schulden nevere come; and so thei myghten deceyve hemsilf, for it is ymaad of a spirit so strong and so kuttynge, that ther ben but fewe suche or noone."[24] This insistence on the esoteric nature of the work was not unusual in mystical literature: the prologue to the orthodox *Cloud of Unknowing*, for example, begs "with all the strength and power that love can bring to bear" that the book be read only by a strictly limited audience of contemplatives.

Certainly Marguerite herself was aware that *The Mirror* was controversial. Toward the end she enumerated beguines, priests, clerks, Preachers, Augustinians, Carmelites, and Friars Minor as those who have accused her of error.[25] This long list does not leave much out; the fact that even beguines were included is probably to be explained by the predominance of orthodox beguinal communities in the areas where Marguerite was active. Because of such opposition she tried to clarify difficult concepts by constant rephrasing and use of fresh imagery, but she still knew that her work contained many ambiguous passages ("*doubles mots*") that were difficult to understand.

23. *Ibid.*, 578: "ces exemples souffisent assez, a ceulx qui ont entendement . . . pour aultres gens n'est escript ce livre."; 563: "dame Amour, . . . dit Raison, dictes le nous, non mie seulement pour moy, ne pour ceulx qui j'ay nourriz, mais aussi pour ceulx qui ont prins congé de moy, a qui ce [liv]re pourte[ra], [se D]ieu plaist, lumiere;" 572: "A qui parlez vous? dit Raison. A tous ceulx, dit elle, qui de vostre conseil vivent, qui sont si bestes et siasnes que il m'esconvient pour la rudesse d'eulx celer et non parler mon langage. . . . Je di, dit l' Ame, qu'il m'esconvient pour leur rudesse taire et celer mon langage, lequel j'ay aprins es secrez de la court secrete du doulx pays."
24. Ed. Doiron (as above n. 12), 249–50.
25. Ed. Guarnieri, 618–19.

She was anxious to explain these as best she could, but she warned that "simple minds might misunderstand them at their peril."[26] More work needs to be done before it can be decided whether the men who condemned Marguerite in 1310 were such simple minds. Provisionally it may be said that *The Mirror* describes a completer union between the soul and God this side of paradise than would have been accepted by most orthodox mystics and it talks of a state of complete passivity that goes beyond and then ignores the spiritual ministrations of the Church. But it postulates grace rather than nature as the motive force propelling the soul toward God and it avoids the antinomian or libertine conclusions traditionally associated with the heresy of the Free Spirit. Marguerite was probably a heretic, but had she been submissive and content to enter a cloister like Mechthild of Magdeburg, with whom she is compared, she probably would have attracted little notice. Her active life, her pertinacity, and the political situation surrounding her arrest certainly contributed to her death.

2. THE PSEUDO-ECKHART LITERATURE

Most other extant Free-Spirit writings survived under the name of Meister Eckhart. This phenomenon was noted as early as the fourteenth century by Gerard Zerbolt of Zutphen who warned that there were certain spurious books in the German vernacular that were called "sermons of Eckhart" or had other titles associated with his name. Many of these works, according to Gerard, spoke of "pure abstraction" and "freedom of the spirit" and should not be read by laymen because of their novelties.[27] Rather than looking upon this as a conspiracy on the part of devious heretics to propagate their errors under a false label, one can see that the master himself bore considerable responsibility. In Strassburg and Cologne he preached to audiences of lay-people and beguines who lacked rigorous theological training

---

26. *Ibid.*, 533, 537.

27. Text ed. A. Hyma, "The 'De libris teutonicalibus' by Gerard Zerbolt of Zutphen," *Nederlandsch archief voor kerkgeschiedenis*, n. s. XVII. (1922–24), 62. J. Koch, "Meister Eckharts Weiterwirken im deutsch-niederländischen Raum im 14. und 15. Jahrhundert," *La mystique rhénane* (as cited above, n. 4), p. 151, mistakenly refers to a shorter version of this passage in a Viennese manuscript as an anonymous *questio*, but this was in fact written by Gerard himself as part of his *Super modo vivendi* (see Hyma, 42–43, who cites three different editions).

and his obscure language was certainly open to misinterpretation. He was warned during his life that in preaching about subtle things to "coarse common folk" he was casting pearls to swine, but this does not seem to have inhibited him. Indeed, he once almost boastfully remarked that "if anyone has understood this sermon, I wish him well."[28] The result was that he left behind him radically mystical disciples who circulated writings that appealed to his authority.

Suso, as we have seen in the previous chapter, tried to differentiate his master's teachings from those of these "wild men,"[29] but in some cases the latter were merely repeating what Eckhart had actually said. The most striking example of this is the heretical *Book of the Nine Rocks (De novem rupibus spiritualibus)*. This work, not to be confused with Rulman Merswin's tract of the same name, is now lost, but it was seen in the eighteenth century by Mosheim, who published extracts from it.[30] Far from being original heresies or even perversions of Eckhart's thought, these were all German translations or paraphrases of the master's writings as itemized in the bull *In agro Dominico*. The extracts contain no reference to "nine rocks," but Mosheim explains that these represented the grades by which a man desirous of God was supposed to reach his goal and one can guess that they might have borne a similarity to Marguerite Porete's seven states of grace. Mosheim's description is confirmed by the mid-fourteenth-century report of Jordan of Quedlinburg that certain heretics taught that "the good man is the only-begotten son of God."[31] This is error twenty-one of *In agro Dominico*, but Mosheim also lists it independently as a tenet found in *The Book of the Nine Rocks*.

---

28. From sermon, "Nolite timere eos," tr. R. B. Blakney, *Meister Eckhart, A Modern Translation* (New York, 1941), p. 226; for the warning about preaching to "common folk," *idem*, pp. 253–56.

29. Above, pp. 186–87.

30. J. L. Mosheim, *Institutionum historiae ecclesiasticae antiquae et recentioris* (Helmstedt, 1755), pp. 551–55 (notes n, p, and s). The errors are from *In agro Dominico* (ed. Denifle, ALKG, II, 638), 21, 26–28, 22, 12–15 (in that order). I cannot accept the interpretation of P. Strauch, "Zur Gottesfreund-Frage: I. Das Neunfelsenbuch," *Zeitschrift für deutsche Philologie*, XXXIV (1902), 286, that the errors listed by Mosheim were not from *The Book of the Nine Rocks*; in footnote s Mosheim explicitly lists that as his source and the last error in footnote p (where he is not so specific) is part of the first error (*In agro Dominico*, 13) of footnote s.

31. *Opus Postillarum* (Strassburg, 1483), fol. 95ra and *Opus Jor*, MS Göttingen,

It used to be thought that this book was written in Strassburg before 1317 because it seemed that John of Dürbheim referred to it in his condemnation of beghards of that year. The rediscovery of the only manuscript copy of his condemnation, however, shows that the words *"in nona rupe"* were written *in the margin* after a tenet listing the beghards' claim to "immutability."[32] The three words were probably not in the original text, but must have been interpolated later by the marginaliast who recognized the doctrine of "immutability" as something he knew to be in the heretical book. The only other dating we have comes from another part of the same manuscript which concerns the procedures taken against the beguines of Strassburg in 1374. As we have seen, a list of questions prepared in that year assumed that a German book called *de novem rupibus* or *bůch von den nùn feilsen* was circulated in beguinages.[33] Thus it may be concluded that this book was written after the condemnation of Meister Eckhart by someone in Strassburg who might have remembered the master himself and who definitely used the text of *In agro Dominico* as a source of instruction. In this light it might not be correct to call the work a "Pseudo-Eckhartian" writing since it was made up, at least in part, of sentences taken verbatim from the publications of the master.

As for Gerard Zerbolt's reference to spurious sermons of Eckhart, it is hard to know which of the many extant sermons ascribed to Eckhart should be classified as spurious. All our texts were copied by hearers, none of whom were stenographers, and many sermons reflect different emphases that sometimes resulted from the proclivities of the copyists. Some veer in the direction of heresy, but so, of course, do passages in Eckhart's authentic writings. Thus it will probably never be known which sermons, if any, are entirely spurious, though several certainly seem to represent Eckhart as he was understood by his most heterodox devotées.

Outstanding among these are sermons seventeen, eighteen, and thirty-seven from Pfeiffer's nineteenth-century collection, none of which have been admitted by the experts into the true Eckhartian corpus.[34] In sermon seventeen the speaker declares that "the eternal

---

Lüneburg 38, fol. 49va. On Jordan's attitude toward Eckhart himself, see Koch, "Eckharts Weiterwirken," pp. 146–47.

32. ms Wolfenb., Helmst., fol. 107rb.

33. See above, Chapter IV, Section 2, n. 43.

34. James M. Clark, *Meister Eckhart* (London, 1957), pp. 113–16, sets forth

Word itself, and no less, is born within the soul unceasingly . . . the soul has, if she wills, the Father, the Son, and the Holy Spirit; she mingles into the unity where nakedness is revealed in nakedness."[35] This autotheism is reiterated in sermon eighteen, written almost certainly by the same author. There the speaker quotes St. Paul's reference to a man who was "caught up to the third heaven" (II *Corin.* XII, 2) and insists that this must have happened to that man while his soul was *still in his body.* While in the previous sermon he spoke of the role of the will in the mystical union, here he clarifies this by explaining that the decision is ultimately God's: "God arranges to reach a longing soul when He is near to her."[36]

The fullest statement of the possibility of union between man and God is in sermon thirty-seven. The speaker boldly affirms: "That person who has renounced all visible creatures and in whom God performs His will completely . . . is both God and man . . . . His body is so completely penetrated with Divine light and with the soul essence which is of God that he can properly be called a Divine man. For this reason, my children, be kind to these men, for they are strangers and aliens in the world. Those who wish to come to God have only to model their lives after these men. . . . Those who are on the way to the same God and have not yet arrived will do well to become acquainted with these people. . . ."[37] Later in the same sermon it is argued that these men have a special dispensation whereby they are raised up to God by food and drink; while others are fasting and keeping vigils, they may be eating or sleeping. This is the nearest approach to antinomianism in the entire Pseudo-Eckhart literature, but even this is

---

the criteria used for judging authenticity and presents a list of the sermons generally agreed to be *echt.*

35. Ed. Franz Pfeiffer, *Deutsche Mystiker des vierzehnten Jahrhunderts* (Leipzig, 1845–57), II, 77: "daz êwige wort sich selber gebirt in die sêle, sich selber, und niut minre sunder underlâz. . . . Nû hât diu sêle, ob si wil, den vater und den sun und den heiligen geist: dâ fliuzet si in die einikeit und dâ wirt ir geoffenbâret blôz in blôz."

36. *Ibid.,* 78: "got vermac daz wol, daz er sich etwenne, einer begerender sêle erziuhet, sô er ir doch vil nâhe ist." Both St. Augustine and St. Thomas maintain that Paul did not know whether he was in the body when his soul was caught up to the third heaven. See St. Thomas, *Truth,* tr. James V. McGlynn (Chicago, 1953), quest. 13. art. 5, pp. 204–205.

37. *Ibid.,* 127–28. I use the translation of Rufus M. Jones, *Studies in Mystical Religion* (London, 1909), p. 223.

immediately mitigated by the statement that the perfect have in fact "no need of anything at all." Nor do natural acts lead to divine union. For the speaker, "all that Christ had from nature, the divine man has received from grace."[38]

The conduct of the perfect is discussed further in two Eckhartian tracts that are representative of the Free-Spirit outlook. The shorter of the two, *On the Poverty of the Spirit*, declares that the poor in spirit are "God with God by grace" and explains that when the soul has achieved intuition of the Spirit internally she follows externally "the model of Jesus Christ in voluntary poverty." Thus, the Godlike man will still in his daily acts imitate Christ.[39] The author of *On the Nobility of the Soul* has the same views.[40] By loving God one may become God with God, but this mystical union may only be achieved through grace. Moreover, whoever wants to come to God must be endowed with righteousness. He must follow a life of voluntary poverty and abandon all earthly things. The tract then goes on to speak of freedom of the spirit as consisting of total abandonment of the self. He who is free must find in himself no sin and "he who is most free forgets himself entirely and flows with everything he is into the groundless abyss of his origin." As the author says explicitly, "this happens to all the willing poor who have sunk into the valley of humility."[41] Thus, the Pseudo-Eckhartian tradition demanded the same

38. Pfeiffer, 127–28: "Sie bedürfent nihtes niht" and "er hât allez erkrieget von gnâden, daz Kristus hete von nâtûre."

39. *Ibid.*, Tract X: *Von Armuot des Geistes*, 493: "sie sint von gnâden got mit gote"; 494–95: "Wan als verre si mit dem innern menschen ist komen in die *Beginarum regni Alimanie et errorum eorundem* (= John Andreae, extract Jêsû Kristi in willige armuot." C. de B. Evans, *Meister Eckhart* (London, 1924–31), I, 348, translates the title of this work as *Spiritual Poverty*, but it is necessary to adhere to the literal word order to distinguish it from *The Book of Spiritual Poverty (von geistlicher Armut)* discussed in the last section of this chapter.

40. On the MSS of this work see A. Spamer, "Zur Überlieferung der Pfeiffer'schen Eckeharttexte," *Beiträge zur Geschichte der deutschen Sprache und Literatur*, XXXIV (1909), 371. What seems to be the original MS dates from 1323 and the MSS that have attributions ascribe the tract to Eckhart.

41. Pfeiffer, Tract II: *Von der Edelkeit der Sêle*. 392: "Seht, dar umbe sô minnet got, sô werdet ir got mit gote"; 384: "an der blôzen eigenschaft dâ hât der wille eine obenheit, dâ stêt der wille in sîner hoehsten edelkeit und enpfâhet von dem obersten guote, daz got selber ist. Waz enpfâhet er? Er enpfâhet gnâde unde daz oberste guot selber in der gnâde."; 392–93: "Wer gote widergelt wil geben, der sol haben eine tugent, diu heizet gerehtekeit. . . . Nû merket zweierhande vrîheit an den gewilligen armen. Zem êrsten mâle begebent sie vriunt

abnegation in the search for divinity that was called for in *The Mirror of Simple Souls.*

3. *DE ONBEKENDE LEEK* AND *SCHWESTER KATREI*

Eckhart's impact on certain lay devotional circles was so great that he began to play a role in their devotional dialogues. One might compare him in this regard to Plato's and Xenophon's Socrates if it were not for the fact that in these dialogues Eckhart is not the commanding figure but ends up being instructed by his interlocutor. The various Eckhartian dialogues represent different tendencies, but the two that we will discuss are among the clearest original expressions of Free-Spirit thought.

The first, a Dutch tract called *Meester Eggaert en de onbekende leek* (Meister Eckhart and the unknown layman), has been consistently overlooked in works about the heresy of the Free Spirit even though large portions of it were published early in this century.[42] The anonymous author might have known or at least seen Eckhart because the tract was written about 1336 in the diocese of Utrecht and it mentions events in Cologne.[43] But the dialogue is certainly a fiction: it belongs to a genre that aimed at displaying the inspired layman's ability to talk of theology with the most learned masters that reached its fullest expression in Nicholas of Cusa's *Idiota.* Though Cusanus lived a century later it should be remembered that he studied with the Brethren of the Common Life in Holland and thereby absorbed a tradition that began with the "*onbekende leek.*"

De Vooys, the scholar who uncovered the dialogue, called the author, with some warrant, a "Christian Democrat of the fourteenth century." His message is that "grace and the good spiritual life make

---

unde guot und êre der werlte unde werfent sich in daz tal der dêmüetikeit. . . . Zem andern mâle merket von der vrîheit des geistes. Der sol alsô vrî sîn, daz er sich in dekeiner schulde vinde, . . . Er sol aller vrîest sîn, alsô daz er vergezze sîn selbesheit unde vlieze mit alle dem, daz er ist, in daz gruntlôse abgründe sînes urspringes. Daz gehoeret allen gewilligen armen zuo, die sich habent gesenket in daz tal der dêmüetikeit."

42. C. G. N. de Vooys, "De dialoog van Meester Eggaert en de onbekende leek," *Nederlandsch archief voor kerkgeschiedenis*, n. s. VII (1910), 166–226. See also de Vooys' comments on the same tract in his *Letterkundige studieën, verzamelde opstellen* (Groningen, 1910), pp. 1–64. The only surviving copy, MS Brussels, Bibl. royale 888–90, fol. 205v–285v, dates from the sixteenth century.

43. The best attempt at dating is that of Axters, II, 452.

men holy and blessed and great before the eyes of God, but not the knowledge of letters or the wearing of a habit."[44] He insists that the spirit is above the letter and that even Abraham, Isaac, and Jacob, as well as the apostles, were not learned. For that reason he claims that the clergy should not be held in awe because of their learning and he attacks the abuses of the entire hierarchy, including the Papacy. He also criticizes the cult of Mary and the saints, as would later Erasmus, another student of the Brethren at Deventer.

On the positive side, he expresses the doctrine of "pure love" and the possibility of illumination through direct prayer to God. But he minimizes neither the role of grace nor the necessity for humility and the pursuit of the *vita apostolica*. In the latter context he refers to the good penitential life of wandering beghards and "sisters" who insist on talking about religious matters to the ignorant. He laments their persecution by the Papacy and the clergy and tells of having heard a Dominican preacher at Rijnsburg (South Holland) call the "sisters" and beghards of Cologne and other towns heretics. According to him, the Dominican should have spoken instead about godly love and heavenly wisdom; he admits that individual "sisters" and beghards occasionally speak carelessly about God "beyond the letter" but maintains that all the orders have their weaker vessels. Far from being hypocrites, most beghards speak "for heaven's sake" and should not be abused.[45]

44. Ed. de Vooys, 199: "Die lettere ende dat abijt dat en maect den mensche niet groot voer den oghen Gods. . . mer die gracie Gods ende dat goede gheestelike leven dat maect den mensche heilig ende salich ende groot voer den oghen Gods."

45. *Ibid.*, 191–92: "Meester, wat segdi tot desen onghestadeghen baggaerden ende tot desen susteren, die nu loepen achter lande wt haer goetwillicheit ende om haer broot, ende doen grote penitencie onbesceidelik. Ende als si dan werden verlicht van hemelscher wijsheit ende van godliker bekinnesse, ende si dan yet te veel willen spreken voer die onbekende, dies niet en willen verstaen, ende soe werden si vervolcht ende ghescandalisiert ende ghedoemt vander paepscap ende vanden abiten, om dat sy som weder keeren totter werelt ende bi wilen comen te valle. Al daer om soe werden die goede ghescandalisiert, die God vercoren heeft, ende die leven na haer overster reden van harrer sielen."; 196–97: "Meester, ic hoorde enen inwendeghen broeder preken van uwer oerden tot Reynsburch onder tconvent, dat die susteren ende die baggaerden ketters ende ongheloevich waren. Ende dat docte my onredeliken wesen ghepredict. . . . Het hadde hem bat betaemt datmen hem hadde gheprect hoe sy met al haer begheerten edeliken [redeliken?] Gode souden minnen om hem selven, ende hoe sy souden smaken ende ghevoelen gheestelike blijscap in haerre sielen, ende hoe sy souden werden verlicht van hemelscher wijsheit ende

This forthright defense shows that the author, if not a beghard himself, was well-disposed in their favor. His lack of deference for ecclesiastical authority and his mystical doctrine were certainly of a Free-Spirit complexion: at one point he even talks of the state of freedom from conscience and spotlessness from sin.[46] But he was hardly a heretic: Paul O'Sheridan has written that his tract is irreproachable from the point of view of Catholic doctrine and the Jesuit Axters maintains that it does not have the slightest trace of dangerous illuminism.[47] What the work does display is the close relationship between lay piety and mysticism in the first half of the fourteenth century. It also is an excellent indication that Gert Groote's ideas did not mature in a vacuum.

The Dutch tract has Meister Eckhart listening attentively to the *"onbekende leek"* and the master plays a similar role in the far more famous tract known as *Schwester Katrei*.[48] The latter is really a conglomeration of German texts, including in some versions complete sermons attributed to Eckhart. It is noteworthy that among these are Pfeiffer's sermons seventeen, eighteen, and thirty-seven, which all, as we have just seen, represent Free-Spirit tendencies.[49] Even putting

---

van godliker bekinnesse, . . . dat hadde betaemeliker gheweest dan dat hi predicte van den susteren ende van den baggaerden, die tot Colen ende in anderen steden gaen wt haerre goetwillicheit om haer broot. In menighen abijt soe vint men ghebreclicheit. Ende daer omme soe sijn die goede te quader niet. Al comet een suster te valle, oft een bagghaert, oft al spreken sy bi wilen onbehoedeliken van Gode oft van hemelschen saken, boven der letter, daer omme en sijn sy niet all quaet noch gheveyst noch ypocriten."

46. *Ibid.*, 197: ". . . hoe men soude vry worden van consciënciën ende onberispt van sonden."

47. P. O'Sheridan, "La doctrine vauvertine sur le communisme ecclésiastique," *Revue des sciences religieuses*, VIII (1928), 209, and Axters, II, 451.

48. Ed. Pfeiffer, Tract VI: *Daz ist Swester Katrei Meister Ekehartes Tohter von Strâzburc.*" A shorter, probably earlier version is edited by A. Birlinger, "Ein wunder nützes disputieren von einem ersamen bihter und siner bihtohter," *Alemannia*, III (1875), 15–45. (There is a great need for a modern critical edition.) The translation by C. de B. Evans (as cited above, n. 39), I, 312–34, though very literal, is terribly stilted—the Pseudo-Eckhartian literature is as difficult to translate as the authentic work of the master.

49. The author of sermon seventeen may have been the author of part of *Schwester Katrei*: cf. Pfeiffer, II, 455, lines 24–26 with *idem*, 77–78, lines 39–1. I owe this observation to marginalia made by W. Scherer, a nineteenth-century professor of German literature at Berlin, in his copy of Pfeiffer now in the library of Case Western Reserve University.

these aside, one must agree with the accepted view that the work is substantially of Free-Spirit origin. Despite that, *Schwester Katrei* passed muster in orthodox circles, surviving, like *The Mirror of Simple Souls*, in a large number of manuscripts that were copied in monasteries and nunneries.[50] A nun of the fifteenth century, for example, included the work in a spiritual anthology of otherwise blameless texts.

Schwester Katrei was also translated from the original Alemannic into Latin and other Germanic dialects as geographically disparate as Bavarian and Netherlandish. The Latin translation was the work of one Oswald of Brentzahusen, a Benedictine monk from Swabia who also translated the *Schwabenspiegel* in 1356. His version has not survived, but it was translated back into German in the fifteenth century and two manuscripts of this contain Oswald's prologue which explains that he undertook the translation because the work contained "some subtle sayings" (*"etlich subtil sprüch"*) which in his view were not suitable for simple lay people to read. He also toned down one of the most shocking passages, but his fundamental sympathy for the work is indicated by his favorable references to Eckhart (whom he took to be the author) and the very circumstance that he bothered to expend his energies on it at all.[51]

The fact that Oswald flourished in the mid-fourteenth century helps greatly with dating. Since one fourteenth-century manuscript says that the heroine of the dialogue came from Strassburg, the work was probably written in that city. One terminus is Eckhart's sojourn there in the second decade of the century and the other is about a generation later both because of Oswald of Brentzahusen's life span and a reference that has never been noticed. In 1337 William of Ockham wrote in his tract against Benedict XII that Eckhart had many male and female followers in Germany among whom was one unlearned person (*"idiota"*) who publicly preached that the soul viewing

---

50. Otto Simon, *Überlieferung und Handschriftsverhältnis des Traktates "Schwester Katrei"* (Halle, 1906). This enormously useful dissertation was meant as a preparatory work to precede a commentary and critical edition, but unfortunately neither, to my knowledge, ever appeared. Further MSS, unknown to Simon, are listed by Spamer (as above n. 40), 345–46, n. 1, and W. Dolch, *Die Verbreitung oberländischer Mystikerwerke im Niederländischen* (Weida, 1909), p. 44.

51. On Oswald and his prologue, Simon, pp. 62–63.

the divine essence is fully absorbed just as a drop of water thrown into the sea.[52] This *idiota* could have been the author of part of *Schwester Katrei* which uses the image of a drop of wine thrown into the sea,[53] but even if not, Ockham's remark shows that the ideas found in *Schwester Katrei* were expounded by men and women in Germany shortly after Eckhart's death.

The tract tells the story of the relationship between Sister Catherine, a beguine, and her confessor, Meister Eckhart.[54] In the first scene she is fully under his guidance: he urges her to obey the Ten Commandments and conquer her sins and she obeys. But then she begins to wonder whether she has found the surest way to eternal blessedness. In a second meeting she berates him for his compromising attitude in saying that one can only do one's best in following Christ and that one cannot become one with God. From now on she resolves to follow the promptings of the Holy Spirit which bid her to make a complete break with creatures. When the confessor answers that such perfection comes only with God's help, she assures him that God comes to the aid of those that surrender themselves to Him.

Thereupon she follows an uncompromisingly apostolic life in the attempt to become the most scorned and insignificant of creatures in Christ. Once she returns to her confessor to say that she still has all the virtues to cultivate and that she has never fully developed even one of them. Though she has forsaken all her relatives and surrendered all possessions and comforts she still has not surrendered herself. The confessor marvels that she can endure all the scorn she has provoked, but she says that she has been insensitive to it and that she has found more of God in such bitterness than she ever had formerly in "all the sweetness that ever happened in creatures." Thus saying, she departs for further persecution and exile.

The climax of the work occurs on her return from "foreign

52. *Tractatus contra Benedictum XII*, ed. H. S. Offler, *Guillelmi de Ockham opera politica*, *III* (Manchester, 1956), 161–62. The dating is by J. Koch, "Zur Analogielehre Meister Eckharts," *Mélanges offerts à Etienne Gilson* (Toronto and Paris, 1959), p. 350, n. 51.

53. Pfeiffer, II, 467, lines 7–8. For the use of a similar image by Tauler, see above, p. 188, and on the entire subject my article cited p. 189, n. 20.

54. In my exposition I have tried to rely on those sections of the work that are common to all the MSS on the assumption, still uncertain, that this is the best way of approximating its original state.

lands." She is now so transformed that her confessor no longer recognizes her and after receiving her confession he tells his brothers that he has just heard an angelic creature: one who, if still human, has powers of soul that rise to the angels in heaven. While the brethren cry "praise God," he seeks out his daughter in church. She has now reached a level where she can transcend all obstacles to union with God, but she cannot yet attain a stable rest in such a state of perfection. The confessor urges her to rid herself of all desire; when she does so she sinks into nothingness and God draws her into a divine light so illuminating that she thinks that she has become one with Him. She keeps struggling in this ecstatic condition in which "heaven and earth have become too narrow" for her until she finally announces to her confessor in oft-quoted words: "Sir, rejoice with me, I have become God."

The sensational nature of that ejaculation has obscured for many the significance of the events that then transpire. Instead of launching into unrestrained self-indulgence, the sister obeys her confessor's order to retire into solitude and retreats into a corner of the church. There she lies for three days (not a random number) in a trance so complete that bystanders would have buried her if her confessor had not intervened. On the third day she awakens and afterwards undertakes to instruct him in the secrets of her illumination. In the conclusion their roles are thus reversed.

Interpolated into this latter section in all the extant manuscripts is a short passage commonly referred to as the "ten points." There is sufficient evidence to show that this was written earlier and independently of the tract, perhaps in Latin and almost certainly by an orthodox party.[55] The "ten points" are those which lead to eternal truth: they include a searching for pain and endurance, resignation to poverty and self-sacrifice, endurance of insult and shame, and complete receptiveness to anything God wishes to work through the individual. These points were all typical of orthodox mystical asceticism, but they coincided so well with the spirit of Sister Catherine's teach-

55. Ed. Pfeiffer, 467–68, lines 30–15, and Birlinger, 24–25, lines 19–25. On the separate composition of the "ten points," Simon pp. 18–19. See also Dolch, p. 44, who lists eight MSS not discussed by Simon in which they appear alone; in one of the latter they appear in Netherlandish among a collection of sermons and pious sayings and a "goede leereghe van broeder gert" (Groote?) (MS BN Néerl. 40).

ings that the author could not resist interjecting them and no subsequent compiler saw need to take them out.

It is also only in the last section that the tract explicitly broaches the problem of antinomianism. The confessor expects the sister, now that she has become deified, to lead a life of freedom: to dress, eat, drink, and sleep, as she wishes. Norman Cohn has cited this passage out of context without mentioning the sister's answer which could almost have been written to confute him.[56] Despite having reached a supernatural state she says that she wants to be nothing but a poor and wretched mortal until her death. Far from breaking with the moral law, she insists that she will not deviate from the model of Jesus Christ; since He exercised his energies until His death, so will she. She does concede that she does not mortify herself as much as before, but her outer faculties are still fully concerned with the life, humanity, and teachings of Christ, and her goal is to help all men away from sin.

Thus, as in *The Mirror of Simple Souls,* there are no strikingly anarchic consequences stemming from unification with God. Though the sister at first goes into a three-day trance, she appears afterwards to be less passive than the "simple soul" in her willingness to instruct her confessor and her desire to keep others from sin. Also as in *The Mirror* there is no preference for nature over grace in the path to deification. In fact the author explicitly exults "praised and honored be the name of our Lord Jesus Christ, that he has revealed to us how we might receive in grace what He Himself is by nature."[57]

In what respects, then, does the tract diverge from orthodox mysticism? The most obvious answer is that it teaches the possibility of total unification with God on earth. The sister's exultant proclamation that she has "become God" was cautiously recast by Oswald of Brentzahusen to read "I have become one with God" and has recently been condemned as "blasphemous nonsense."[58] Some mystical nuns said similar things without being accused of heresy in their time or ours: Beatrice of Nazareth, for instance, wrote that the soul can reach a state wherein it "no longer can perceive difference between itself

56. Cohn (as cited above, n. 9), p. 178.

57. Pfeiffer, 465: "Gelobet unde geêret sî der name unsers herren Jêsû Kristî, daz er uns geoffenbâret hât, daz wir erkriegen mügen in gnâde daz er selber ist von nâtûre." Also Birlinger (as cited above, n. 48), 24: "ich han erkrieget in gnaden, das Kristus in nature ist."

58. Clark (as cited above, n. 34), p. 124; on Oswald's version, Simon, p. 78.

and God." But *Schwester Katrei's* proclamation was unqualified and justifies Ruysbroeck's complaint that some heretics wished to become God Himself.[59] Furthermore, not only is her union complete, but it is enduring, whereas in the orthodox tradition the mystical experience is never more than a fleeting glimpse of what can only be continuous in the future life. The orthodox glossator of *The Mirror of Simple Souls* says: "as for that tyme of unyoun, ful litel tyme it is,"[60] but in *Schwester Katrei* the confessor asks the sister after she comes out of her trance whether she is permanently confirmed in "the naked divinity" and she answers "yes."

Schwester Katrei also exhibits some of the anticlericalism that was expressed more virulently in *Meester Eggaert en de onbekende leek*. Not that the author was categorically opposed to the ministry of the Church. The confessor is a Dominican—not "clearly a Brother of the Free Spirit," as Cohn mistakenly asserts[61]—and his most important conversations with the sister, as well as her state of trance, take place within a church building. Even on her return from "foreign lands," she confesses to him, but their relationship is intensely ambivalent. First she is obedient, then truculent, then, after she has gone her own way, again obedient, and finally, after her deification, vastly superior. This can partially be explained by the author's essentially reformist feeling that the clergy is not living up to the apostolic ideal. For example, the sister regrets that priests do not only preach the gospels and the confessor says "Saint Dominic sold his book and everything he had and gave to the poor for the sake of God, but we do not do that nor other good deeds, but remain what we are and say that we are great priests, though we do not live accordingly."[62]

Such laments were a commonplace of medieval literature. More radical was the implication that the layman could reach God without priests or sacramental intermediaries. When the sister approaches the peak of her mystical experience, she tells her confessor "wonderful things of pure godly truth" that he thinks are unknown to all except

---

59. See above, Chapter VIII, Section 3. Beatrice of Nazareth is quoted by Eric Colledge, *Mediaeval Netherlands Religious Literature* (Leiden, London, and New York, 1965), p. 8.

60. Ed. Doiron, *Archivio Italiano per la storia della pietà*, V (1968), 251.

61. As cited above, n. 9, p. 175.

62. Pfeiffer, 457, lines 21–22 and 473, lines 4–9.

learned clergymen.[63] In another passage he asserts that "no one can resist one who is touched by God: not all the saints in heaven nor all the Dominicans and Franciscans on earth."[64] This is the sort of radical religious individualism that motivated a number of heretics we have met in earlier chapters and could not be assimilated by the medieval Church. It is most pronounced in the latter portion of *Schwester Katrei* when the sister becomes far wiser than the priest as a result of her illumination, but it must be stressed that she never makes a complete break with him. Indeed, in the crucial moments before her ecstasy she willingly accepts his advice and even begs for his prayers.

Schwester Katrei dramatizes conclusions not only of an extreme Eckhartian mysticism but also of the earlier *Frauenbewegung* that impelled women to become beguines and seek the *vita apostolica*. Catherine rises from adherence to the Commandments and virtues through an uncompromisingly ascetic and apostolic life to total abnegation and from there to a state of godliness, but all this is accomplished by divine guidance and the gift of grace. After she becomes one with God she continues to live in the world without violating evangelic teachings and resolves to help others on the way she has taken. Whatever we may think of this program, there is no denying its spiritual motivation or the fact that it gave much solace during the turbulence of the fourteenth century.

4. THE RHINELAND *LIBELLI* AND *THE BOOK OF SPIRITUAL POVERTY*

There are two more sources which must be examined to complete our review of the evidence and confirm some important points. A manuscript dating from 1450, discovered and edited by Wilhelm Preger, is headed: "A tract containing *determinationes* of master Henry von Kamp against certain erroneous articles contained in two *libelli* found in the possession of a beghard hermit near the Rhine" and neatly lists the erroneous articles under six headings.[65] Some scholars consider

---

63. *Ibid.*, 464, lines 30–34.
64. *Ibid.*, 457, lines 31–33.
65. W. Preger, "Beiträge zur Geschichte der religiösen Bewegung in der zweiten Hälfte des vierzehnten Jahrhunderts," Abh. bay., XXI, 1 (1894), 62–63. The text is reprinted in Guarnieri, 463, and M. d'Asbeck, *La mystique de Ruysbroeck l'Admirable* (Paris, 1930), pp. 30–31.

this to represent "authentic" Free-Spirit beliefs,[66] but this is by no means so certain. Because the articles were extracted by the hostile Henry (an Albertist professor of theology at Paris, Cologne, and Louvain in the first half of the fifteenth century), it is conceivable that they are as distorted as some of the hostile lists we have looked at earlier. Even if not, the heading does not say that the beghard wrote the two books, nor does it give any further indication of provenance or date (though it is usually guessed that they were of the fourteenth century). Most important is the fact that two works were at issue but the list of errors is a mélange which makes no attempt to distinguish between them. Thus, far from having internal consistency, the errors are often contradictory.

So far as can be told, one of the *libelli* must in fact have been written by an Averroist. How else are we to interpret such statements that have nothing to do with the Free-Spirit heresy as "man was not created but has existed eternally and lives eternally" (III, 3), or the use of such terms as "*intellectus agentis*" (IV, 8), which are found predominantly in Latin Averroist philosophy? On the other hand, there are sentences which are more relevant for us though even they are not always consistent. One expresses pantheism in saying that "the essence of God is the essence of all things" (I, 4), but this is qualified by the more limited statement that "the divine essence is my essence" (I, 3) and the assertion that "the perfect man is God" (I, 7). With the latter we are back in the realm of *Schwester Katrei*: individuals can become God, but not all of them, let alone all creatures, actually do.

The equally crucial problem of grace versus nature is more confused, owing to the brevity of the sentences and to the fact that they were taken from two different sources. It is impossible to evaluate such a cryptic tenet as "grace is nature, but not entirely" (IV, 1), although this seems to involve some sort of compromise which is maintained in the sentences that "God is not able to beatify man by grace unless he first does so by nature" (VI, 2) and that "the grace of God is able to be given to natural man" (IV, 7). But Gordon Leff is wrong in saying that the mystic union is conceived "through nature, not grace"[67] because the most explicit sentence states clearly that "the perfect man earns all by grace that Christ has by nature" (V, 5), a

66. E.g. d'Asbeck, p. 30.
67. Leff, p. 401, n. 3.

quotation that could have been taken out of the Pseudo-Eckhart literature.

The extracts are most heretical in their agreement with the doctrine of *Schwester Katrei* about the absolute nature of the mystical union: "man is able to have as maximum a union as Christ had with His Father" (V, 3) and "one is well able to say of the perfect man that he is God and man" (V, 4). The question then follows whether such a man is free of moral restraints. The nearest approach to antinomianism is made in the tenet that "no good work made in mortal sin is dead" (IV, 4), but this is ambiguous; perhaps it means that acts traditionally regarded as mortal sins are really good works (i.e. antinomianism), but it could just as well mean that a sinner's good works are never without merit. The statement that "he who worships one virtue more than another does not have God working in him" (IV, 3) implies that all should be pursued equally and is reminiscent of "Sister Catherine's" saying that she still had all the virtues to cultivate. Finally, anything but antinomian is the tenet that "the man touched by the virtues of justice and piety remains immutable in them" (V, 7). Thus, Henry von Kamp's list, though often unclear, appears to fit into the mystical tradition that we have been discussing.

What it does not mention at all is the cult of voluntary poverty, the theme of *The Book of Spiritual Poverty*.[68] This work was thought to have been written by Tauler until the later nineteenth century when Denifle demolished that theory of attribution. Since then there has been no agreement other than in dating it to the mid-fourteenth century. Denifle thought that it was written by a Franciscan because it stressed the doctrine of poverty, A. Ritschl argued on purely speculative grounds that it was a composite work, and modern scholars have returned to the theory of Dominican authorship "by a close disciple or perhaps some friend of Tauler."[69]

To this diversity of opinion must be added the hypothesis that the work was written by a beghard or a beguine. It has never been noticed that it refers to "poor people who live in *Sammenungen* and

68. The best edition is ed. H. S. Denifle, *Das Buch von geistlicher Armuth* (Munich, 1877). It is translated as *The Book of the Poor in Spirit* by C. F. Kelley (New York, n. d. [1954]).

69. A. Chiquot in *Dictionnaire de spiritualité* quoted by Kelley, p. 48, who agrees. Ritschl's position is stated in his "Untersuchung des Buches Von geistlicher Armut," ZfK, IV (1881), 337–59.

swear obedience to each other."[70] This term was used explicitly in Strassburg, the probable home of the author, as well as elsewhere, to refer to beguinal communities.[71] Moreover, the major theme of the work, the call for both external and internal poverty, was more the preoccupation of fourteenth-century beghards and beguines than it was of the mendicant orders. Many friars would have agreed with the author of *The Book of Spiritual Poverty* that "in order to become holy one must be rid of all earthly things,"[72] but few, if any, would have applied the doctrine of poverty, as did the author of the tract, not only to material goods but also to the life of the spirit. For him, as with Free Spirits, "if a man wants to come to God he must be free of all works and let God alone work" and "no one can be completely sheltered in God unless he is stripped of all creatures."[73] It is not for us to say whether this is heresy, especially since the work, like *The Mirror of Simple Souls*, was translated and published under the auspices of the Downside Benedictines with the nihil obstat and imprimatur, but Denifle is certainly right in arguing that a mystic like Tauler never taught the necessity of a total abandonment of earthly works and things.

The Book of Spiritual Poverty contains other Free-Spirit themes. The pure in heart remain "immovable": in such a state they have divine virtue "in essence" and can dismiss external virtues without sin. Such people also owe no one obedience but God and have overcome sin. Like the beghards condemned at Cologne in 1307, the author cites in this context the words of St. Paul that "the law is not made for the just"[74] and while he is careful to reject absolute identification of the

70. Ed. Denifle, p. 11. The theory that the work has Free-Spirit tendencies has already been put forth by Guarnieri, 391.

71. On the three "*reiche Samenungen*" of beguines in Strassburg, McDonnell, pp. 203–204, 532, and literature therein cited. McDonnell, p. 203, n. 123, also quotes a reference to a "*samenunge von begin*" in Nürnberg, and R. Pfister, *Kirchengeschichte der Schweiz* (Zürich, 1964–), I, 324, refers to "*die Samnung*" of beguines in Solothurn.

72. Denifle, p. 46: ". . . wilt du heilig sin, so můst du irdenscher dinge ledig sin."

73. *Ibid.*, p. 101: "sol der mensche zů got komen, so můs er ledig sin alles werckes und got allein lassen würken;" p. 112: "nieman mag sich zů grunde in got verbergen danne der, der von allen creaturen entlösset ist."

74. *Ibid.*, p. 87: "Und also beweget er die tugent und blibet er doch umbewegelich, und da von ist die tugent gottes tugent glich. Und wa soliche men-

soul with God, he verges on autotheism when he expresses the Eckhartian doctrine that the soul gives birth to the Eternal Word and is
a child of God. Though he clarifies this by saying "not a child by
nature. . . , but a child by grace,"[75] the same qualification, as we have
seen, would have been accepted by many alleged heretics.

What has impeded scholars from stressing these points is the fact
that the author, like the orthodox mystics, also included a section in
which he criticized "disordered freedom." Here he (or she?) attacked
those who are seduced by a "natural light" into believing that they
possess all the truth and think that they have no need of virtues and
good works. These, he says explicitly, are called "free spirits."[76] This
sally, however, proves little. The author of *The Book of Spiritual
Poverty* might have been influenced by radically mystical doctrines
and still have been so convinced of his own orthodoxy that he felt bold
enough to attack others. He thought, as did his contemporaries, that
the *real* Free Spirits were antinomians inspired by the devil and he was
sure that he was not such a one. But others who must be considered
Free Spirits did not think that they were heretics either.

5. CONCLUSIONS

Gerard Zerbolt of Zutphen, in attacking the Pseudo-Eckhartian works
that he knew to be written by Free Spirits, made an observation that
modern scholarship would do well to note. According to him, the
origin of the evil among the Free Spirits stemmed from their cult of
poverty and mendicancy.[77] This identifies the heresy correctly as an

---

schen sint die die tugent habent in wesen, die mügent die tugent lassen in dem
zůval ane gebresten und in rehter gelassenheit irs eigen willen."; p. 12: "ein
reht arm mensche is nieman nüt schuldig denne got;" p. 11: "der gerehte arm
mensche het alle sünde gelan und alle tugent gewunnen." The quotation from
St. Paul is also on this page.

75. *Ibid.*, p. 70: "So die sele dar zů komet, daz sich daz ewige wort in ir
gebirt und sie sich mit dem selben wort wider in got gebirt, so ist sie ein sun
gottes, nit ein natürliche sun, alz daz wurt in der gotheit, mer: ein gnedelicher
sun. . . ." Denifle, p. lii, seems correct in saying that the author of the book was
influenced by Eckhart even though he attacked that master when he rejected
at the outset the possibility of man becoming "God with God" (p. 3).

76. *Ibid.*, p. 19.

77. Ed. Hyma (as cited above, n. 27), 62, corrected by M. A. Lücker, *Meister
Eckhart und die devotio moderna* (Leiden, 1950), p. 57, n. 2: "Unde zyzania
et pessimum semen ipsorum librorum spiritum ortum est quidem de perfeccione
paupertatis et recommendacione mendicitatis."

outgrowth of the *vita apostolica* movement: Free Spirits believed that the attainment of spiritual perfection was an arduous process that began with the uncompromising pursuit of apostolic ideals. In the same tone as *The Book of Spiritual Poverty*, Marguerite Porete wrote of "seven states of grace" that began first with the Commandments and then with the evangelical precepts (i.e. the Old and New Testaments respectively), while "Sister Catherine" likewise obeyed the Commandments and then imitated the life of Christ so fully that she became the most despised and rejected of creatures. That this was not mere literature is shown by the testimony of the beguine of Schweidnitz who said that her community followed the Ten Commandments and the Gospels. As we have seen often enough, what this meant in practice was not only poverty and mendicancy but the frequent application of gruesome self-tortures. The road to blessedness in the Free-Spirit version was paved with rougher materials than good intentions.

But the *vita apostolica* was not conceived as an end in itself. Free Spirits believed that after purgation by external methods one should divest oneself of all internal will and desire to reach a state of total indifference that led to union with God. This view was based on assumptions opposite to those of modern self-glorifying superman theories. The prerequisite for deification was total abnegation and conviction of one's total worthlessness: for example, in *The Mirror of Simple Souls* the fifth state of grace, which is the first state of supernatural attainment, begins with the soul's realization that she is nothing and God is everything.[78]

That man can become deified by his own decision is a fundamental misconception of the Free-Spirit position that stems only from hostile sources. *The Mirror of Simple Souls* and the Pseudo-Eckhart literature agree that only God's miraculous intervention can bring about a state of perfection on earth. As Free-Spirit tracts say over and over again, man becomes God through grace, not nature. It is true that this conflicts with the formula of the Strassburg condemnation of 1317 and an aspersion in Ruysbroeck's polemical *Little Book of Enlightenment*, but bona fide texts should be preferred to these hostile sources, especially when they are confirmed in this point by Groote's

---

78. Ed. Guarnieri, 611: "Le quint estat est que l'Ame regarde que Dieu est, qui est, dont toute chose est, et elle n'est mie. . ."

letter describing Bartholomew of Dordrecht and the official trial records of the heretics Conrad Kannler and Hans Becker.

If Free Spirits went beyond the traditional apostolic ideal in seeking internal abnegation and union with God, they were still in step with the orthodox mystics. In fact, the two groups were so closely related that it is somewhat artificial to draw a line between them: works that are called Free-Spirit today may well be called orthodox tomorrow and vice versa. Still, Eckhart and his orthodox followers were not imagining things when they complained of a mysticism more radical than theirs. The evidence of this chapter makes it clear that they misconstrued the Free-Spirit position concerning the conduct of the perfect after deification, but Free Spirits did skirt orthodoxy on three points: their autotheism, or belief in the possibility of total identification with God on earth; their view that this identification could be lasting rather than momentary; and their frank circumvention of sacramental intermediaries in the mystical way. Such, allowing for individual discrepancies, was essentially the heresy of the Free Spirit as transmitted in the most authentic sources.

Chapter Ten

THE PLACE OF THE HERESY OF THE FREE SPIRIT IN SOCIAL AND CULTURAL HISTORY

Mason W. Gross, in his inaugural address as President of Rutgers University in 1959, said: "I can think of no words in the English language which are more beautiful than the words 'a free spirit.' Few of us can ever achieve this freedom fully, but without envy or regret, we can recognize it as the shining star which best symbolizes the profoundest aspirations of mankind."[1] This oratorical effusion did not refer to the heresy of the Free Spirit, but it is typical of an enthusiasm for those words which has led many historians to regard the medieval movement as a forerunner of modernity. To take just a few examples, an historian of atheism saw the heretics of the Free Spirit as prototypes of the irreligious Jacobins of 1793,[2] an historian of the Enlightenment saw them as *"Sturmgeister der Aufklärung,"*[3] and,

1. Quoted in *The Bulletin of the American Association of University Professors,* LII (1966), 212–13.

2. F. Mauthner, *Der Atheismus und seine Geschichte im Abendland* (Stuttgart and Berlin, 1920–23), I, 302: "Wenn man die zerstreuten Äusserungen der Brüder und Schwestern vom freien Geiste. . . liest, glaubt man, die aufreizende Rede eines Religionsvernichters von 1793 zu vernehmen."

3. H. Reuter, *Geschichte der religiösen Aufklärung im Mittelalter* (Berlin, 1875–77), II, 241.

most recently, there has been a rash of journalistic attempts to compare them to rebellious university students and hippies,[4] an argument that is helped by the fact that an ephemeral rock band of the late 1960s was called "the Free Spirits." It remains to assess these modern evaluations.

1. WHO WERE THE FREE SPIRITS?

The first step in analyzing the historical role of the Free Spirits is to determine who they were. The difficulty here, beyond the obvious lack of statistical evidence, is the fact that they did not comprise a sect or homogeneous organization. It is true that there seems to have been a network of communications between like-minded beghards and beguines as far distant as the Rhineland and Silesia in the first half of the fourteenth century, but even that did not ensure uniformity of belief or organization: the beghards of Metz and the beguines of Schweidnitz were examined within two years of each other but their differences were almost as great as their similarities. Furthermore, there were always unaffiliated individuals who taught Free-Spirit doctrines but who had no direct contacts with one another. Indeed, by the waning fourteenth century and throughout the fifteenth century, these were the only Free Spirits we know of. To call them all beghards and beguines, especially when some, like Martin of Mainz and William of Hildernissen, were actually in orders, is to perpetuate a mistake inspired by the undiscriminating language of the bull *Ad nostrum*.

Considering this situation, one of the few generalizations that can be made without hesitancy is that a disproportionate number of the heretics were women. From the female heretics in the Ries to the woman who confessed to John Nider at Regensburg, females were particularly attracted to doctrines of spiritual perfection. Many were beguines in a cloistered milieu, but others were lay city dwellers who became infatuated with heresiarchs like Aegidius Cantor or William of Lübeck. A few, like Marguerite Porete and Bloemardinne of Brussels, did not rely on men at all but were entirely independent and self-

4. I have not kept record of these Sunday-supplement pieces, most of which rely heavily on the work of Norman Cohn; typical of their line of argument is N. Adler, "The Antinomian Personality: The Hippie Character Type," *Psychiatry*, XXXI (1968), 325–38, an article called to my attention by Professor Natalie Zemon Davis.

impelled. It is impossible to make a head count of Free-Spirit heretics, but one has the feeling that if one could, the women would outnumber the men.[5]

This should not be surprising. Putting aside the male prejudice that females are particularly susceptible to religious enthusiasm (for Rabelais there was little difference between those *"molle à la fesse"* and *"folle à la messe"*), there were genuine sociological reasons for the attachment of women to the *vita apostolica* and psychological reasons for their leaning toward mysticism in the later Middle Ages. Because of the higher male death rate and the large number of unmarried clerics there was a surplus female population.[6] To make matters worse, there was a scarcity of legitimate female vocations and comparatively few women could gain entrance into nunneries. The beguinal life was thus a perfect avenue for the unmarried to obtain occupation and a modicum of communal security. Many, as we have seen, wanted no more than that, but it is easy enough to understand why a good number of women, some of whom were not beguines, turned to radical mysticism. The medieval relegation of women to an inferior status was as severe as their material problems. Women could not become priests, but Free-Spirit doctrine offered them something better than that: full union with divinity. A tract like *Schwester Katrei*, in which a woman rises to a position of distinct superiority to her learned male confessor, surely must have given a goal and sense of identification to numerous others.[7]

As for social class, the old belief that Free Spirits were poor laborers is supported only by insulting remarks of two polemicists. The Spaniard Alvarus Pelagius asserted that the heretics were easily recruited from the ranks of swineherds, masons, coal-miners, and smiths

5. W. Zippel, *Die Mystiker und die deutsche Gesellschaft des 13. und 14. Jahrhunderts* (Düren, 1935), p. 4, describes thirty-five mystics who lived between 1250 and 1350, of whom twenty-one were female.   ,

6. S. Thrupp, "Plague Effects in Medieval Europe," *Comparative Studies in Society and History*, VIII (1966), 476, notes that there is still no good study of sex ratios in medieval Europe, yet the few figures cited by R. Mols, *Introduction à la démographie historique* (Louvain, 1954–56), II, 185–87, show a clear predominance of women among adults in towns.

7. Women played a large role in other medieval heresies. For the view that heretical doctrines of the high Middle Ages satisfied female yearnings for emancipation, see Gottfried Koch, *Frauenfrage und Ketzertum im Mittelalter* (Berlin, 1962).

because such laborers desired to live lives of ease, but this can be dismissed not only on the grounds that it is a patent calumny, but also because Alvarus had no firsthand knowledge of conditions north of the Alps.[8] Conrad of Megenberg, on the other hand, was a German, but we have seen that his immediate knowledge was still scant.[9] He offered no support for his claim that most heretical beghards were "strong-bodied mechanics" and since his real aim was to discredit mendicancy, it may be taken as an example of the age-old argument that "sturdy beggars" ought to be made to work. Conrad also said that the Free Spirits were "*viri rusticani,*" a designation that also appeared in a reference to beghards in conciliar legislation of 1310.[10] But the medieval use of the term "rustic" should not be misunderstood. Most often it meant not country-dweller but one who was unlearned.[11] That Conrad meant the latter is indicated by his own elucidation that the heretics were "entirely ignorant of letters," but that statement shows just how unfair or ill-informed he was.

Far from being rural, the heresy we have studied was found in urban centers—Strassburg, Mainz, Cologne, Erfurt, Brussels—and middle-sized towns. Some of the heretics might have left the country within their own lifetimes, but the slender evidence we have suggests that those who may have done so were the well-to-do rather than shepherds and rustics. We are best informed about sedentary beguines. Bishop John of Dürbheim wrote that "good beguines" came from all classes: "aliquas clari, aliquas nobilis, alias mediocris, et alias humilis status. . . ,"[12] but in actuality few beguines were of humble origin. For example, a recent archival study of beguines in Mainz concludes that many came from the landed aristocracy and many more from the urban patriciate, but of 120 whose class could be determined, only

8. Alvarus Pelagius, *De planctu ecclesiae* (Lyons, 1517), II, arts. 51 and 52. A passage not included in the edition of 1517 is in MS Wolfenb., Hemst., 122, fol. 385r–392v, there entitled *Errores baghardorum cum reprobacionibus eorundem secundum fratrem Alvarum, iuris peritissim, Ordinis minorum Hispanum.* Leff, pp. 328–29, cites this from the edition of Ulm, 1479.

9. See above, pp. 55–57.

10. The council of Trier treated above, pp. 67–68.

11. On the term *rusticus*, Grundmann RB, pp. 29–30. J. Trithemius, *Annales Hirsaugienses* (St. Gall, 1690), II, 231, uses *indoctus* and *rusticus* as interchangeable terms.

12. S. Baluzius, *Vitae paparum Avenionensium,* ed. G. Mollat (Paris 1914–27), III, 354.

seven (or 5.83%) came from families of artisans.[13] The picture is similar for other cities like Cologne.[14]

These conclusions refer to beguinages that were probably orthodox, but though we cannot cite statistics about Free-Spirit heretics the evidence suggests that they too came preponderantly from the ranks of the prosperous. The best example is that of John of Brünn who gave up his wealth and travelled from Moravia to the Rhineland in order to embark upon a life of evangelical poverty. Bloemardinne of Brussels came from a leading patrician family and the Augustinian, Bartholomew of Dordrecht, won the friendship of "magnates" in Kampen who loyally defended him against Gert Groote's attacks. James, the disciple of Nicholas of Basel, worked as a well-digger in hiding from the Inquisition, but ate at the table of patricians to the resentment of their servants; and Hans Becker could have been an artisan, but since we know that he wrote a book, we know that he or his family had means to pay for an education.

There are even indications that some members of the aristocracy were attracted to the Free-Spirit heresy. Jan van Leeuwen spoke explicitly of Free-Spirit "*hoeftheren*" who talked of "high, subtle things,"[15] and one of Bloemardinne's disciples was Marie of Evreux, the Duchess of Brabant. "Sister Catherine" was a fictional personage, but the fourteenth-century prologue of Oswald of Brentzahusen characteristically spoke of her as noble: "quedam iuvenis puella, nobilis et delicata. . . edel und zart."[16] This corresponds to a distinct aristocratic prejudice in the tract *Schwester Katrei* itself. In one passage the sister says that "Christ was the most noble man who was ever born" because he descended from seventy-two princely families and then she goes on to assert that "one tests people by nobility. . . ."[17]

13. Eva G. Neumann, *Rheinisches Beginen-und Begardenwesen* (Meisenheim/Glan, 1960), pp. 105–107.

14. J. Asen, "Die Beginen in Köln," *Annalen des historischen Vereins für den Niederrhein*, CXI (1927), 92–93.

15. Ed. C. G. N. de Vooys, "Meister Eckart en de nederlandse mystiek," *Nederlandsch archief voor kerkgeschiedenis*, n. s. III (1905), 193: "Ende oec al noch soe hebben dese vrie onvrie gheeste hoeftheren onder hen, die hen van hoghen subtilen dinghen onderwenden te sprekene."

16. Ed. O. Simon, *Überlieferung und Handschriftsverhältnis des Traktates "Schwester Katrei"* (Halle, 1906), p. 66.

17. Ed. F. Pfeiffer, *Deutsche Mystiker des vierzehnten Jahrhunderts* (Leipzig, 1845–57), II, 456: "Ich weiz wol, daz Kristus der edelste mensche ist, der ie

Marguerite Porete expressed similar sentiments so frequently that she might well have come from an aristocratic background. The entire *Mirror*, as others have noticed, is a sterling example of the marriage between mysticism and the courtly literary tradition. Specifically, according to Marguerite, the annihilated soul was so free that it did not have to answer anyone who was not of its lineage, just as a gentleman need not deign to answer a *villain*. Nor was the author's contempt confined to serfs: merchants were also rightly called *villains* because "no gentleman meddles in trade." Such people were excluded from "the court of love's secrets like a *villain* is kept out of gentlemen's court in judgment of peers."[18]

The very literateness of the Free-Spirit movement was a token of comfortable social status in an age when literary composition was a near monopoly of the well-off. A startling number of our heretics were authors, many of those who were not could still read, and almost all seem to have had a well-developed theological vocabulary. Of course, they were not trained Latinists and this is what the hostile sources meant when they called them unlearned "idiots." For example, the Inquisitor Kalteisen referred to Hans Becker as "*laycus indoctus*" even though the latter could read and write books in German.[19] Thus, conceding the lack of statistics, it may still be concluded that the majority of Free Spirits should not be compared to ignorant rabble.

2. MOTIVATION

It follows from all this that the primary motivation for turning to the life and ideas of the Free Spirit was not that of material or social benefit, but the religious and emotional search for perfection. Free Spirits hoped to achieve this through imitating the apostolic life and reaching union with God, two goals that dominated the spirituality of the high and later Middle Ages. Indeed in the high Middle Ages the term "Free

---

geborn wart: er was von zwein and sibenzic fürsten geslehte. . . . Man prüevet die liute nâch adele: sô sie ie edeler sint, sô sie ie zarter sint."

18. Ed. Guarnieri, 586: "Elle ne respont a nully, se elle ne veult, se il n'est de son lignage; car ung gentilhomme ne daigneroit responde a ung vilain, se il l'appelloit ou requeroit de champ de bataille. . . ." 570: ". . . de gens marchans, qui sont au monde appellez villains, car villains sont ilz, car ja gentilz hons ne ce scet mesler de marchandise, . . . comme seroit ung villain de la court d'ung gentil homme en jugement de pers. . . ."

19. This was noticed by Grundmann, "Ketzerverhöre," 555.

Spirit" was by no means one of opprobrium. Joachim of Fiore characterized his third age as one of liberty of the spirit and a commentator glossed this by saying "liberty of the spirit is the apostolic life which has been renewed through Saint Francis,"[20] a clear indication that the term was then closely associated with the ideals of the mendicant movement.

Another high-medieval use of the term shows its relationship to mysticism. This, ironically, comes from a sermon of Albertus Magnus, one of the earliest opponents of Free-Spirit heresy. Preaching in Augsburg in 1257 or 1263, Albert defined liberty of the spirit as the ability to turn one's spirit toward all that one wishes without being impeded by the flesh; in this way, according to him, the free spirit could be next to the saints, next to the angels, and even next to God.[21] The key words, of course, are *next to*; Albert did not characterize such liberty as the ability to become *one* with God, but while he was preaching at Augsburg there were men and women in the nearby Ries who were saying just such things and Albert would later have to deal with them. By the fourteenth century, liberty of the spirit was no longer a slogan for Franciscan mendicancy or the ideal of becoming close to God, but was the designation of a heresy that had become anathema to the mendicant orders and most orthodox theologians.

What caused this shift? Simply stated it came about because the orthodox were becoming more conservative and many idealists more radical. After the later thirteenth century the cult of poverty was being placed more and more in question, the mendicant orders as a whole were being put on the defensive, and there was a growing dis-

---

20. Quoted by Marjorie Reeves, *The Influence of Prophecy in the later Middle Ages* (Oxford, 1969), p. 177: "Nota quod libertas Spiritus est vita apostolica que in beato Francisco renovata est."

21. Ed. J. B. Schneyer, "Alberts des Grossen Augsburger Prediktzyklus über den hl. Augustinus," RTAM, XXXVI (1969), 128: "Non enim est aliquis liber in spiritu, nisi possit vertere spiritum ad omne, quod vult, ut non impediatur a carne, ut sit quando vult juxta sanctos quando vult juxta angelos et quando vult juxta Deum." See also 130: "Sequitur de libertate spiritus, qui tunc liber est, quando libere ad Deum ingreditur. Quando auris audit rumores, oculus videt laeta etc. totum remanet ante ostium et solus spiritus intrat ad Dominum." This sermon was definitely not delivered in reference to the heresy of the Free Spirit which Albert then probably knew nothing about; rather it was a theoretical discussion of four kinds of freedom—of the will, of the soul, of the spirit and of judgment. Unfortunately in the surviving version the last three sections are greatly abbreviated.

taste among ecclesiastics, both secular and regular, for lay pursuit of the apostolic life. On the other hand, the laity who sought a life of perfection were alienated by the flagging esprit of the orders and official lack of patience for bold experiments in lay piety.

More than that, the calamities of the fourteenth century underscored dissatisfaction with established ways. The fourteenth century was a time of trauma in northern Europe, or, as I have called it elsewhere, an age of adversity. In the first half of the century, even before the onset of the Black Death, the economy was reeling from falling agricultural yields, climatic disasters, the worst of which was the terrible flood of 1314–1315, internecine wars, high taxes, shortage of bullion, and the contraction of trade routes, especially those to the East.[22] There can be no doubt that men knew they were living in bad times. For example, the author of *Meester Eggaert en de onbekende leek* wrote about 1336 that the year 1300 brought after it a period of decline and multiple catastrophes because thirteen was an unlucky number.[23] The economic crisis of this period put great pressures on the well-to-do, and it is understandable that some reacted by turning away from the world and inward.

Political turbulence must also have encouraged this tendency. In Germany there were eight years of intermittent war from 1314 to 1322 between the Emperor Ludwig of Bavaria and the Habsburgs and thereafter until Ludwig's death in 1347 a continual struggle with the Papacy and France that resulted in prolonged anarchy. Many Germans wished to rally around the Emperor, but the princes who for a while supported him shifted their allegiances and only Ludwig's death in 1347 saved the country from years more of civil war. While the Emperor was unable to rule effectively, Pope John XXII's sodden hostility to him and the divisive role played by the German clergy encouraged widespread anticlericalism. A song of that period, for example, told of a coming messianic Emperor who would destroy all monasteries, humble the priesthood, and make the previously idle clergy labor in the fields.[24]

22. An excellent summary of the economic troubles of the later Middle Ages can now be found in Harry A. Miskimin, *The Economy of Early Renaissance Europe, 1300–1460* (Englewood Cliffs, N. J., 1969).

23. Quoted by Axters, II, 430.

24. Quoted and discussed by G. Schultheiss, *Die deutsche Volkssage vom Fortleben und der Wiederkehr Kaiser Friedrichs II* (Berlin, 1911), pp. 53–59.

It is astonishing to note that John XXII knew very well what he was doing. In a letter of 1323 to the Archbishop of Cologne he predicted that the results of his interdict on all churches and localities that remained loyal to the Emperor would be that "corpses would lie unburied in piles for so long that their stink would infect the healthy; the innocent would have to go without the sacraments for so long that irreverence would grow; heresy would thrive and so would distress of soul. . . ."[25] None of this seemed to worry Christ's vicar, but even one of his Cardinals was moved in 1334 to implore him to become more flexible with the words, "Holy Father, believe me, this rigor may be lawful, but it is not expedient."[26] It would be absurd to place sole blame on Pope John XXII for the growth of the heresy of the Free Spirit; the heresy existed before his time and in areas that were not affected by his interdicts. Rather, the turbulence of the age combined with a growing dissatisfaction with the clergy and sacramental system made some men cast about for different spiritual and emotional shelters than the ones which had served them before. The heresy of the Free Spirit offered a new hope for godliness and was most satisfying to certain personalities in its extreme demands.

3. "THE PURSUIT OF THE MILLENNIUM" OR "BEYOND GOOD AND EVIL"?

But it was not a revolutionary force. One scholar has argued that a millenarian doctrine of social reform originated in Free-Spirit circles on the basis of a report by the chronicler John of Winterthur that in 1348 people from all classes believed that Frederick II would return to force monks, nuns, and "secular sisters" to marry, persecute the clergy so terribly that they would have to hide by covering their tonsures with dung, return everything that had been stolen from the unprotected, and marry the rich to the poor. The slender argument that this rumor was spread by Free Spirits is built on the facts that John told about antinomian heresy in Swabia in 1347 and undoubtedly

---

25. Quoted by K. Czok, "Zur Volksbewegung in den deutschen Städten des 14. Jahrhunderts," *Städtische Volksbewegungen im 14. Jahrhundert,* ed. E. Engelmann (Berlin, 1960), p. 166.

26. Quoted by G. Barraclough, *The Medieval Papacy* (New York, 1968), p. 147.

meant beguines by the term "secular sisters." But such women would hardly have circulated a prediction that they would be forced to marry and the chronicler, who was never loath to malign heretics, made no connection between Free Spirits and the expectation of a returning Frederick.[27]

As for the Joachite three-age theory of progressive betterment for the world, only a few Free Spirits, excluding the Amaurians, seem to have appropriated such views and they were confused or inexplicit about them. Conrad Kannler spoke of a third age, but unlike Joachim he thought that it would come after the last judgment. The rumor that Aegidius Cantor said that the third age had already come was rejected by William of Hildernissen. William himself did say that the present law would cease, as did Hans Becker, but neither spoke specifically about three ages.

The most radical view of history was stated by Kannler, who was otherwise so theologically cautious that it is hard to know whether to call him a Free Spirit. Not only did he think that he stood on the threshold of a new and better age, but he thought that it was his calling to help bring it about. Still, there is no indication that he foresaw any social reorganization in the third age and he had no notion of aiding it along with a sword. He conceived of his role only as that of a preacher and worker of miracles because he saw himself as just an instrument of God. The few others who thought that history was at a turning point were vaguer. Neither William of Hildernissen nor Hans Becker seem to have had clearly articulated views of history other than expecting a new dispensation and if Marguerite Porete hinted that "Holy Church the Little" would soon meet its end, she never indicated exactly when or how this would transpire, nor whether humans would have any role in helping the process. Most important,

27. Johannes Vitoduranus, *Chronica*, ed. F. Baethgen, MGH SS, new series, III, 280. The argument that the expectation originated among Free Spirits was made by P. Hosp, "Ketzertum und deutsche Kaisersage beim Minoriten Johann von Winterthur," *Franziskanische Studien*, III (1916), 161–68, and is refuted by B. Töpfer, *Das kommende Reich des Friedens* (Berlin, 1964), pp. 180–81. Töpfer, p. 277, n. 88, points to the difference between the Free-Spirit goal of perfection for the individual and chiliastic expectations of a changing world order though he cautiously maintains that there was an "elective affinity" between the two.

these cases were the exceptions, not the rule. The majority of Free Spirits were not interested in historical theories at all and it is incorrect to conceive of the entire movement as millenarian.

Conceding that most Free Spirits had no revolutionary historical program, some Marxists have seen the heresy as a doctrine of economic meliorism. Karl Kautsky, for example, looking for "forerunners of modern socialism," found that "if this pantheistic teaching is stripped of its mystical clothing, it represents a type of communist anarchism which must have had a great force of attraction for the mishandled and trampled proletariat."[28] This interpretation, however, is no longer prevalent. The fullest Marxist study of the heresy insists that Free Spirits were "plebians" who opposed the feudal order, but admits that they had reactionary, escapist traits and lacked practical goals.[29] It is also no longer controversial to say that "there was no trace of communism in the doctrines of . . . the Brethren of the Free Spirit."[30]

Very few heretics studied in this book openly commiserated with the poor. One tenet out of ninety-seven gathered in the Swabian Ries in the thirteenth century says that serfs or serving maids could appropriate the property of their masters, but this was never taken up by later Free Spirits. In fact, the only other reference of this sort that I can find in all the trial documents, polemics, and original literature are two vague passages in the Strassburg inquisitorial list of 1317 and the confession of William of Hildernissen. The former says that spiritual perfection frees one from servitude, but then it gives the example of

28. *Vorläufer des neueren Sozialismus: I. Kommunistische Bewegungen im Mittelalter*, 3rd ed. (Berlin, 1947), p. 235. Also Hermann Ley, *Studie zur Geschichte des Materialismus im Mittelalter* (Berlin, 1957), p. 220: "Sie verbanden damit die Hoffnung der Armen auf eine Besserung der Lebenslage," *et passim*.

29. Erbstösser, p. 129: "Ihr Gedankengebäude war mehr ein Sprung in die Vergessenheit als in die geistige Freiheit. Man kann ihr 'System' als Durchgangsstufe des ideologischen Wachwerdens der plebejischen Schichten betrachten, das notgedrungen neben extremster Gesellschaftskritik und Opposition gegen die Feudalordnung reaktionäre Züge trug und eine praktische Zielsetzung weitgehend vermissen lässt." Also p. 60: "Nicht Kampf gegen die materielle Not, sondern Idealisierung war der Ausweg. Die freigeistige Ideologie als Ganzes war nicht geeignet, die Menschen zum Kampf aufzurufen. . . ."

30. M. Beer, *Social Struggles in the Middle Ages*, tr. Stenning (New York, 1957), p. 204. The only exceptions I can find in the sources is the report of John of Dürbheim, *UB der Stadt Strassburg*, ed. W. Wiegand (Strassburg, 1879–1900), II, 311, that the Free Spirits of 1317 believed that "omnia esse communia," and the report that the beghards of Metz owned nothing (see above, p. 49).

dissolution of bonds to a king that could well have applied to men high on the feudal ladder. Moreover, in a spirit entirely opposed to sympathy with the downtrodden, the same document includes an insistence that Free Spirits should take alms even if that means *depriving the truly poor*.[31] William of Hildernissen does say that a fallen woman has the same merit as a virgin and this could indicate genuine social concern though it is not entirely clear whether he was really talking about prostitutes.

More frequent were justifications of theft, but these were made not on the Robin Hood principle of helping the poor, but only as shocking examples of individual freedom. It is also here that we are faced with the problem of the reliability of our sources. Theft is defended in articles from the Ries and Strassburg, but we do not know how these were compiled and we do know that John of Brünn, who justified murder in defence of theft, was the equivalent of a modern paid informer. The confession of John Hartmann raises none of these difficulties, but it does show the effect of leading questions: his statements that he could steal a golden chalice and kill even the Emperor if he stood in his way were answers to questions astutely posed by an Inquisitor who was an imperial chaplain and needed the Emperor's support for his activities. No doubt Hartmann loved to shock and he was so successful in this that his testimony has been cited constantly by historians intent on displaying Free-Spirit depravity, but there is every reason to believe that he was an atypical eccentric and even he seems to have had a basic contempt for worldly things as indicated by his declaration that his illumination was worth more than all the money in the coffers of Erfurt.

The entire problem of Free-Spirit antinomianism is rooted in the problem of the sources and may never be resolved to everyone's satisfaction. But two conclusions seem inescapable. First, no Free Spirit— not even the radical Hartmann—was ever to my knowledge charged with theft or murder and most charges of fornication were unofficial, imaginative, or vague. Second, all the best sources agree that Free Spirits were highly ascetic in their *pursuit* of perfection and that both

31. Ed. C. Schmidt, "Actenstücke besonders zur Geschichte der Waldenser," *Zeitschrift für die historischen Theologie,* XXII (1852), 248: "dicunt quod quamvis sint sani et fortes non debent laborare corporaliter, quamvis per receptionem elemosinarum veri pauperes defraudentur."

bodily and spiritual abnegation were absolute prerequisites for deification. Considering the long period of excessive austerities that was part of the Free-Spirit program, it is impossible to believe that anyone embarked upon it in light-headed hopes of material gratification.

The question that remains is what sort of liberties a Free Spirit might have indulged in *after* his deification. The answer seems to be everything, at least in theory, but what a heretic actually did after he thought he had become one with God is harder to say. Hostile parties imagined the worst and witnesses like Hartmann or even Conrad Kannler encouraged them by agreeing that the free in spirit *could* do this and *might* do that. But these are conditionals, not statements of facts. The younger beguines of Schweidnitz did say that the elders fornicated and consumed the best beer and butter, but we will never know how far these complaints stemmed from typical resentments of junior members for seniors in a tightly disciplined community. That leaves us with the authentic Free-Spirit literature which gives no evidence of calling for self-indulgence or libertine conduct. We have seen that Marguerite Porete's "simple soul" was first a servant of the virtues and then, after deification, their master, but Marguerite insisted that there was never any conflict between them and "Sister Catherine," after "becoming God," first sank into a trance and then relaxed her discipline but rejected the call to feast and wear fine clothes, preferring to remain humble unto death.

When it is recognized that Free Spirits aimed primarily at divine "annihilation" and trances it becomes clear that the best of the numerous modern analogies is between Free Spirits and hippies. If there is any justice in Norman Cohn's claim that the liberated Free Spirit "felt like some infinitely privileged aristocrat,"[32] it concerns an aristocracy of the spirit rather than of the flesh and if there is any social phenomenon to be observed, it is not of the poor seeking gold and silver, but of the prosperous abandoning material comforts for shreds and patches. Free Spirits, like the hippies, hoped to quicken the life of the "interior" rather than the "exterior" man and while some went preaching, others were sedentary and might have been entirely passive. It was probably not arbitrary that the German Augustinian Thomas of Strassburg charged that Free Spirits were deceived by the noonday

---

32. *The Pursuit of the Millennium*, 3rd ed. (New York, 1970), p. 178.

fiend—the traditional instigator of *acedia* or torpor[33]—for if some Free Spirits violated the moral law, it was probably in terms of idleness and indifference which could have seemed to others like sloth.

4. THE LAY SPIRIT AND THE DIGNITY OF MAN

Nonetheless, Free-Spirit thought had some progressive components. One was its stress on the powers of the laity and criticism of the late medieval Church. Over and over again Free Spirits argued for a direct relationship to God without sacramental mediation and insisted on their superiority to priests. A line, however thin, runs, for example from the *"onbekende leek"* through Groote to Cusanus and Erasmus. Though Free Spirits regarded poverty and bodily suffering as prerequisites for the divine life, some, like Marguerite Porete, also stressed faith over works. Such sentiments, implying the priesthood of all believers, amounted willy-nilly to social protest. In these respects the heretics of the Free Spirit resembled the Waldensians and were forerunners of the sixteenth-century Reformation.

It would, however, be mistaken to portray them as proto-Protestants in any other way because their views on the nature of man were entirely at odds with the Protestant tradition. Their most original contribution was their belief in man's potential for having the vision of God, indeed ultimate deification, *on earth.* This was a theological optimism so unheard of in the Middle Ages that the most fruitful comparison, startling though it may appear, is with Pico della Mirandola's *Oration on the Dignity of Man.* Needless to say, Free-Spirit writings contain none of Pico's pagan, Cabbalistic, or Hermetic apparatus, relying as they do merely on scraps from the Bible and borrowed Neoplatonism; nor do they ever refer to man as "chameleon." But Pico's claim that "if by charity we, with his devouring fire, burn for the Workman alone, we shall suddenly burst into flame in the likeness of a seraph" could just as well have been written by Marguerite Porete and all Free Spirits would gladly have accepted Pico's dictum that "he who is a seraph, that is, a lover, is in God; and more, God is in him, and God and he are one."[34]

33. Most exhaustive on this is R. Caillois, "Les démons de midi," *Revue de l'histoire des religions,* CXV (1937), 142–73; CXVI (1937), 54–83, 143–86. For the passage from Thomas of Strassburg, see above p. 195, n. 46.
34. Tr. Charles Glenn Wallis (Indianapolis, 1965), pp. 7, 8.

The most important differences are that Pico says nothing about the doctrine of poverty and bodily austerities but stresses the role of the human will in what appears to be a Pelagianism that would have been unacceptable to our heretics. In these respects Free Spirits were more traditionally Christian than he. But Pico was not so specific about the possibilities of deification on earth as the radical Free Spirits. The most important agreements are that both were unusually optimistic about man's potential for union with God and both saw this as man's ultimate end without thinking in terms of material betterment.

5. ULTIMATE FAILURE

There is no evidence that Pico della Mirandola, familiar as he was with scholastic writings, knew anything about the northern European Free Spirits. Nor did anyone suspect him of this: the papal condemnation of his theses refers only to Pico's revival of pagan and Jewish errors without any mention of the errors in *Ad nostrum*.[35] None of this is surprising, since by the end of the fifteenth century the doctrines of the Free Spirit were known only to encyclopedists and antiquarians. The heresy is of interest primarily as a moment in the history of European thought, not as a link in a chain of progressive Enlightenment. The heretics of the Free Spirit were not enlightened and had no direct influence on subsequent intellectual or social developments other than in their role as minor heralds of the lay spirit.

The movement was ultimately unsuccessful, paradoxically, because it was not radical enough for some groups and too radical for others. It had no lasting appeal for lower classes because of its lack of social content. We have seen that Free Spirits taught the abandonment of worldly goods rather than their acquisition and were rarely millenarians: in contradistinction to a Fra Dolcino very few said anything about an imminent destruction of the established order and none appealed to force. Therefore, it is not surprising that there were no known Free Spirits in late medieval Pastoureaux uprisings, Jacqueries, or even urban revolts. Only when heretics were ready to say that they were sent to sweep out all evil including material injustices and that they would proceed against the enemies of God with fire and sword could there be a really forceful union between heretical thought and

35. Giovanni di Napoli, *Giovanni Pico della Mirandola e la problematica dottrinale del suo tempo* (Rome, 1965), p. 102.

social discontent. In Germany this stage was only fully reached in the time of Thomas Münzer.

Of course, even the Münzerites blazed out like meteors in the historical skies. In European history new modes of thought and action had to be accepted by at least a weighty part of the influential orders of society in order to have staying power. For this the Free-Spirit heresy was ultimately too radical in its theology and hostility to the Church. Indeed, it is surprising that the heresy was as successful as it was among the upper classes, but this transitory success must be attributed to the adversities of the fourteenth century. In an age of incessant war, famine, and plague, as well as sharp economic insecurity, extremist systems become attractive. The Free-Spirit heresy was essentially an escape: a turning toward God by denying the world and even the Church. But unlike traditional monasticism the Free-Spirit program could become destructively antisocial and respectible people could hardly associate themselves with it for long. Reprisals were bound to come and even in the Middle Ages not many members of the established orders had a real taste for martyrdom; indeed, even without persecution the life of a *Schwester Katrei* or beguine of Schweidnitz was martyrdom enough to dissuade all but the hardiest from pursuing it. As the Inquisition became more active in the second half of the fourteenth century it found very few Free Spirits and most that it did find were isolated eccentrics. By the fifteenth century, when the Church was no longer entirely on the defensive and times were getting better, the heresy gradually disappeared. Enthusiasm grows best in stormy seasons and cannot be bottled and stored like old wine.

LIST OF MANUSCRIPTS

The publication of Herbert Grundmann's *Bibliographie zur Ketzergeschichte des Mittelalters (1900–1966)* (Rome, 1967) makes a listing of published works on heresy superfluous. I list here instead the unpublished manuscripts used for my study in the hope that some may prove useful to others.

BASEL. Öffentliche Bibliothek der Universität.

A. IX. 21, fol. 91r–109v. Rudolf Buchsmann, *Positio pro defensione beginarum*; John Mulberg, *Materia contra beghardos, beginas, lolhardos et swestriones.*

CAMBRIDGE. Peterhouse.

1. 3. 9. Philip the Chancellor, *Sermones super evangelia.*

GÖTTINGEN. Universitätsbibliothek.

Lüneburg 38. Jordan of Quedlinburg, *Opus Jor.*

KARLSRUHE. Badische Landesbibliothek.

Reichenau (Augiensia), CXLVII. Johannes Spenlin, *Speculum religiosorum.*

Reichenau (Augiensia), 116, fol. 356r–357r. "Es ist ain frag ob der beghârt und der beginen stât vor der hailigen gottes kilchen verworfen und verbotten sig." (Ruling of canon lawyers of Strassburg on status of beguines, 1404.)

KLOSTERNEUBURG. Stiftsbibliothek.

352, fol. 175r–207r. Hermann of Schildesche, *Tractatus de vitiis capitalibus duplex.*

LINZ. Studienbibliothek.
177 (old 69). Anon. (Peter Zwicker?), "Primus gradus perfeccionis beghardice dicitur. ..."

LONDON. British Museum.
Royal 9 C. VII. John Baconthorp, *Questiones in sententiarum.*

MILAN. Ambrosiana.
S. 58, SUP, fol. 87r–96v. Gerard of Siena, *Tractatus super octo erroribus begardorum beghinarum in clementinis constitutionibus condemnatis.*

MUNICH. Bayerische Staatsbibliothek.
Cgm 2026. *Modus Procedendi wann Malifiz Recht gehalten wird In Malefiz Sachen.*
Clm 3740. Philip the Chancellor, *Sermones super evangelia.*
Clm 6603, fol. 277r–290r. Anon., *De beghardis sive lollardis* (=Felix Hemmerlin, *Contra validos mendicantes*).
Clm 14216, fol. 175r–180r. Annotated legislation against beguines (derived from Mulberg's *Materia?*).
Clm 14959, fol. 230v–232r. "Hec est sentencia lata contra Martinum hereticum. ..." (Cologne, 1393.) "Isti articuli et errores inventi sunt in inquisitione facta per D. Johannem Argentinensem. ..." (Strassburg, 1317.)
Clm 15177, fol. 275r–282r. Anon., *Reprobacio secte peghardorum et Beginarum regni Alimanie et errorum eorundem* (=John Andreae, extract from *Apparatus in Clementinas*).
Clm 17541, fol. 32r–52r. *Excerpta undecunque, scilicet historica. . . de haereticis.*

OLOMOUC (OLMÜTZ). Cathedral Chapter.
385, fol. 17r–24v. Gerard of Siena, *Tractatus super octo erroribus begardorum beghinarum in clementinis constitutionibus condemnatis.*

PARIS. Bibliothèque nationale.
Fonds latins 3280. Philip the Chancellor, *Sermones festivales.*
Fonds latins 3281. Philip the Chancellor, *Sermones super evangelia.*
Fonds latins 12422. William Perrault (Peyraut), *Sermones.*
Fonds latins 14594. Philip the Chancellor, *Summa super psalterium.*
Fonds latins 15958. Lucas de Bitonto, *Sermones.*
Fonds latins, nouv. acquisition 410. Lucas de Bitonto, *Sermones.*
Fonds néerl. 40, fol. 31r–32v. "Von den 10 Punkten."

POMMERSFELDEN. Schlossbibliothek.

141 (2743), fol. 1r–1v. "Isti sunt errores in quibus quedam Begine circa sacramentum penitencie erraverunt." (Mühlhausen, 1368.)

ROME. Vatican Library.

Vat. lat. 4265, fol. 101r. Anon. (Peter Zwicker?), "Primus gradus perfeccionis beghardice dicitur. . . ."

Vat. lat. 13119. Original protocol of examination of *"moniales caputiatae"* at Schweidnitz (1332) and report of the assassination of John Schwenkenfeld.

Vat. Pal. lat. 600, fol. 212r–223v, 226r–227r, 228r–235v, 245r–246r. Controversy between John Wenck and an unknown master of Heidelberg (1441) and assembled literature concerning beguines with Wenck's marginalia.

WOLFENBÜTTEL. Herzog-August-Bibliothek.

Cod. Guelf 122 Helmstedt, fol. 385r–392v. "Errores baghardorum cum reprobacionibus eorundem. . . ." (=extract from Alvarus Pelagius, *De planctu ecclesiae*).

Cod. Guelf 279 Helmstedt, fol. 264r–269v. Notarial act concerning the trial of William of Hildernissen at Cambrai (1411).

Cod. Guelf 279 Helmstedt, fol. 282r–284v. Protocol of the examination of Hermann Kuchener at Würzburg (1342).

Cod. Guelf 311 Helmstedt, fol. 42v–43r. "Sententia diffinitiva lata contra Metzen de Westhoven." (Strassburg, 1366.)

Cod. Guelf 311 Helmstedt, fol. 103r–112r. Documents pertaining to episcopal campaigns of the fourteenth century against beguines and beghards of Strassburg.

Cod. Guelf 315 Helmstedt, fol. 199r–217r. Papal and imperial documents pertaining to beguines and beghards and documents pertaining to the late fourteenth-century controversy about the orthodoxy of the Brethren of the Common Life.

Cod. Guelf 876 Helmstedt, fol. 73v–94v. Conrad of Megenberg, *Lacrima ecclesiae*.

WÜRZBURG. Staatsarchiv.

6, fol. 27v–28v. Protocol of the examination of Hermann Kuchener at Würzburg (1342). (Other copies of this protocol are in Würzburg, Staatsarchiv, Standbuch #2, pp. 461–466 and Würzburg, Universitätsbibliothek, M. ch. f. 51 and M. ch. q. 96.)

INDEX